Lone Mothers in Ireland
A Local Study

A. McCashin

Oak Tree Press
Dublin
in association with
Combat Poverty Agency

Oak Tree Press
Merrion Building
Lower Merrion Street
Dublin 2, Ireland

A catalogue record of this book is
available from the British Library.

ISBN 1-86076-024-4

Combat Poverty Agency Research Report Series No. 21

The views expressed in this report are the author's own
and not necessarily those of the Combat Poverty Agency.

Printed in Ireland by Colour Books Ltd.

Contents

List of Tables

List of Figures

Preface

Introduction

This study was initiated by the Parents Alone Resource Centre (PARC), which provides a range of activities and services to women who are parenting alone in the Coolock area in north Dublin. The research was undertaken by Tony McCashin of Trinity College Dublin, who has considerable experience in policy research. The study was funded by the Combat Poverty Agency and builds on the Agency's earlier work in this area by documenting the social and economic circumstances of a group of lone mothers. The study makes a significant contribution to our understanding of lone motherhood in Ireland and should be of interest to a wide audience.

Before examining some of the findings of the research and their implications for policy development, we must first ask to what extent small-scale local surveys can inform policy at a national level. The report of this study demonstrates that by defining the boundaries of the research clearly, guarding against over-interpretation of a necessarily selective sample, and by carefully grafting the results of the local study onto national demographic trends and the findings of previous research and current policy, local studies such as this one can inform the development of future policy. Tony McCashin has displayed the skill and attention to detail required to achieve this difficult goal. The value of this research lies first in its ability to capture the day-to-day experiences and circumstances of this group of lone mothers and then to offer an analysis of the findings of the study within the context of the wider social and economic structures of Irish society.

Research Findings

The use of qualitative methods in the study to interview in depth a small number of lone mothers from varying backgrounds has resulted in a report with interesting findings on the diversity of human experience. The research is particularly successful at conveying the experiences of those interviewed: their routes into lone parenthood, their range of support networks, their financial circumstances and their aspirations for the future.

A central finding to come from the research was the positive aspiration many of the lone mothers had to work or to return to work when their children are older. The indicators are that this trend is shared by many mothers in two-parent families as well. The lack of affordable, reliable child care and access to (re)training were found to be barriers to lone parents finding employment. The provision of more accessible, high-quality and affordable child-care facilities must be a priority. Such a policy would also help to create more employment in its own right. In addition, the Agency believes that the development of good-quality pre-school facilities for disadvantaged children would help to tackle educational disadvantage.

Employment, however, is not possible for all lone parents: some may choose not to enter the labour market in the interests of their children or they may lack the necessary level of education and training needed to compete for the available jobs. Such women may be dependent on social welfare payments for a long period of time and are particularly vulnerable to experiencing poverty and deprivation. This study provides further evidence on the need to increase the adequacy of social welfare payments to families with children dependent on social welfare.

The study also highlights the central role that Child Benefit plays as a stable and direct payment to mothers. In keeping with the results of the Agency's earlier study on *The Cost of a Child*, the present study has found that women with adolescent children find it particularly difficult to cope financially because of the budgetary costs of older children. It is now time to re-examine the case for making Child Benefit age-related to reflect this age-related need.

Finally, the study noted also the importance to some of the women in the study of Supplementary Welfare Allowance, particularly during crisis periods in their lives. It also unfortunately reiterated, through example, some of the problems of the scheme previously highlighted by the Agency in its publication, *A Scheme of Last Resort?* The scheme must now be amended and updated as a matter of urgency.

Further Research

A secondary objective of the research was to pilot the feasibility of undertaking a similar study at a national level. The results of this study are encouraging that such a larger study would be both possible and very useful. Furthermore, providing a forum through research for locally-based community groups to feed back their experiences of policy at the grassroots level would be a useful exercise for local communities, service providers and policy makers. This could be done through, for example, the establishment of locally-based research observatories — this is something that the Agency hopes to investigate further in light of the findings of this research and the positive and productive reaction by community and voluntary groups to the recent call for submissions to the National Anti-Poverty Strategy.

This study has also highlighted the value of a longitudinal study which would be able to identify, for example, when lone parents were most at risk of experiencing poverty and why; movements in and out of poverty; and the long-term impact on children of living in a lone-parent family that is experiencing poverty. Such a study would also benefit from including other family types such as two-parent families and lone fathers.

Conclusion

In conclusion, three main lessons can be drawn from this study:

- The need to improve the provision of adequate and reliable child care

- The need to improve social welfare payments to families with children dependent on social welfare

- The need to undertake further national and longitudinal research into the causes, needs and consequences of lone parenthood.

Combat Poverty Agency
June 1996

Foreword

Popular mythology around lone parent families has been an issue for Parents Alone since it was founded in 1986. Lone parents involved in the Parents Alone Resource Centre (PARC) did not recognise themselves or their children in the media images of helplessness, inadequacy, misery and dysfunction. Having recovered from the trauma of marital breakdown or unplanned pregnancy, the vast majority of lone parents using the Centre are rearing their children in exactly the same way as married parents within the constraints of their economic and social circumstances.

The founding aims of the Centre reflect these concerns and are just as relevant 10 years on. They are:

- To bring together lone parents in the catchment area of the Centre and to support them in jointly identifying and tackling their problems

- To undertake policy research to highlight the needs and issues of one-parent families and to seek to educate state agencies and the local community about the rights and needs of lone parents

- To promote a co-ordinated and integrated approach to services and facilities for lone parents and their children; and to develop an independent resourced group of lone parents who will have the skills to manage the resource centre and to engage in analysis and debate about the needs of the changing family and the issues of concern to it.

One of the operating principles arising from these aims is the participation of lone parents in all levels of the decision-making process in the Centre. Using creative writing, drama, inputs to conferences and participation in evaluation reports, numerous lone parents involved in the Centre have revealed details of their personal lives and circumstances to journalists, students studying social science, policy makers and politicians, in an effort to change public attitudes to lone parenthood.

While the importance of research has always been accepted by PARC, it required time, resources and skills not often readily available. The publication of this research study is timely. Family life forms are changing in the Ireland of today and the voices of lone-parent families must be heard in the inevitable debates.

The publication of the research is warmly welcomed by PARC. On behalf of the lone parents who participated in the study, I thank Tony McCashin of Trinity College, Dublin for his respectful and supportive approach to his work and the Combat Poverty Agency for funding the project.

Noreen Byrne, Director
Parents Alone Resource Centre

Acknowledgements

This study was instigated by Noreen Byrne, Chairperson of the Parents Alone Resource Centre, in Coolock, Dublin. Her commitment to improving the circumstances of women in Irish society extends to an understanding of the role of research in that process. I am very grateful to her for her commitment to the study and to the Combat Poverty Agency which provided the funding. Professor Jane Millar of the University of Bath gave useful advice and encouragement in the early stages of the research, for which I am very grateful.

When the fieldwork on the study commenced, the workers and participants in PARC's centre smoothed the way and facilitated the project in practical ways. In particular, Amanda McLoughlin, Carmel Clarke, and Maura Keating helped in identifying potential respondents and in organising the fieldwork. Also, some members of PARC's management committee — themselves lone mothers — agreed to be included in the study. Their interest and willingness is gratefully acknowledged.

A wide range of people commented on the first draft of the study report. They include anonymous referees and members of the Combat Poverty Agency's Research Sub-Committee. Their contribution to improving the report was valuable and necessary. They are: Patricia O'Hara, Chairperson, Deirdre Carroll, Sean Byrne, Finola Richardson, Ann Lavan, Chris Curtin, Tim Callan, Barbara Murray, Walter Lorenz, Gerry O'Hanlon. Tim Callan provided particularly helpful comments on Chapters 5 and 7. Helen Johnson produced a composite report of all the comments and this greatly eased my task in writing a final report. David Silke and Joan O'Flynn processed the final report for publication.

I owe a great deal to Amy Murray who patiently undertook the word-processing work on the drafts of the study report, and to Anne O'Neill, Jackie O'Connor and Tracy Curran who produced typed interview transcripts from tape recordings of interviews.

I am indebted also to Noreen Kearney, Head of Department of Social Studies, Trinity College, and Anthony Coughlan, Senior Lecturer, who allowed me the time away from Departmental duties to undertake the fieldwork.

The Economic and Social Research Institute gave me permission to reproduce some tables of data from ESRI publications, for which I am very grateful.

Finally, I wish to thank the women who were interviewed in the study. They willingly spoke about their lives and their families and this may have been painful for some of them. I hope that they will feel that the study genuinely reflects their stories and addresses their concerns.

I alone am responsible for any errors, omissions or misinterpretations.

Anthony McCashin
June 1996

Executive Summary

Background, Objectives and Methodology

The number of lone parents in Ireland has been increasing rapidly in recent decades. Lone parents are overwhelmingly women. In Ireland, a series of contentious and divisive political debates has accompanied the emergence of lone-parent families — these debates have centred largely on the legal and constitutional regulation of family life. However, the socioeconomic aspects of lone parenthood have received relatively little attention in public debate, policy analysis and social research. This absence of policy research was identified in studies published in 1992 and 1993 by the Combat Poverty Agency and the Economic and Social Research Institute respectively (Millar et al., 1992; McCashin, 1993).

In this study, which was initiated by the Parents Alone Resource Centre in Coolock, an attempt was made to document the social and economic circumstances of lone mothers. The study was undertaken in the Coolock area of Dublin and consists of extended interviews with 53 women — some single, some separated or deserted, and a few of them widows. All of the women had at least one dependent child. The women were invited to give general accounts of their lives but a particular focus of the interviews was the social and economic aspect of their lives as lone mothers: their incomes, their financial problems, sources of support from family and community, and their access to, and experience of, social welfare and related services. The study is local, small scale and qualitative. It does not include two-parent families. Therefore, caution must be exercised in interpreting the material from the study.

How the Women Came to be Lone Mothers

Among single women there was considerable diversity in the personal circumstances that led to their becoming pregnant. In some cases, they had been in long-term relationships and their pregnancy was actually welcomed; in other cases, the reaction was one of shock and surprise.

The sample was self-selected in that women who became lone mothers were not compared the with those who did not, but it is striking that the women recalled the decision to keep the baby as clear and definite. Support from the women's mothers was a universal aspect of the decision. The women had remarkably little contact with health or social services during the pregnancy.

While some women were abandoned by their partners during their pregnancy — and in some cases because of the pregnancy — this by no means applied to all of the women in the sample. Some have continued their relationships, and their boyfriends or partners are involved in their lives and the lives of their child(ren).

Separated and deserted women likewise reveal considerable diversity in their personal circumstances, but three patterns of marriage and marriage breakdown were evident:

(1) There was a group of distinctly younger women who discovered patterns of unacceptable behaviour in their partner and who quickly resolved to end the relationship. These women had relatively high standards of education.

(2) There were some women who were married for extended periods and who endured neglect, irresponsibility, and even violence, for a long period of time.

(3) There was a category of women who were happily married for a long time but whose marriages deteriorated, leading eventually to separation or desertion. In common with the single women, the formerly married women did not, on the whole, avail of social services for advice or support.

Poverty and Financial Circumstances

The study afforded an opportunity to describe in some detail the sources of income, and the adequacy of the incomes and living standards of low-income, social-welfare dependent lone mothers. To place the incomes of this category of lone mother in context, the study arrived at an estimate of average income in the economy as a whole: 47 per cent of the women in the sample fell below 60 per cent of this threshold and one third fell below a half of this (estimated) average. The study sample was therefore found to have incomes that are low by the standards of Irish society at large.

Furthermore, the actual living standards and life styles of many women in the sample were very meagre. This emerged from the measures of deprivation applied in the study and, very graphically, in the women's accounts of their daily lives and their financial struggles.

Three sets of circumstances shaped the way in which the women's low incomes affected their living standards:

(1) Many women share their parents' homes and, consequently, their standard of living reflects that of the wider household.

(2) Among women of any marital status a range of additional, "in kind" supports may add to their resources — these supports include direct borrowing and gifts from family members, generous

support with purchases of clothes for children, free child care and baby-sitting to allow women some freedom to work or to have some relaxation.

(3) Many women — mostly separated women — have added costs or needs such as large debts left by husbands and partners, or heavy mortgage repayments or rent payments to be met out of very low incomes.

The responsibility of managing the family's finances was a daily struggle, and a source of great worry for almost all of the women. Some women, however, were pleased to be in control of their family's money and preferred this to the earlier experience of trying to manage while hindered by an irresponsible, wasteful, or neglectful partner.

Employment and Paid Work

A striking feature of the aspirations and views women expressed was their positive orientation to paid work. Some were in paid employment; most of them were not. Women with young children in particular were inclined consciously to choose parenting as their only or primary role. Such women, however, also tended to have a longer-term aspiration to return to paid work in the future.

One distinct set of experiences was that reported by women who felt excluded from work because they perceived the net benefits from work as minimal or negative. They felt that child-care costs, travel-to-work costs, income tax and PRSI deductions from wages would cumulatively erode the financial gains from work. This set of experiences contrasts with the actual calculations that might apply in their situations. Notably, the modifications in the social welfare means test introduced in 1994 have undoubtedly increased the financial return from paid employment for lone mothers receiving social welfare who take up work at relatively modest wages.

The women's orientations to paid work were bound up with their wider personal situations. Their escape from difficult relationships, their growing confidence of being able to manage alone and their need to establish themselves independently of parents and family were all factors that enforced the women's strengthened desire to work or their interest in taking up training.

Some women — not surprisingly since the study was undertaken in an area of high unemployment — were unemployed and actively looking for a job, and described themselves as unemployed. This finding is a reminder that many of the women have social and economic

characteristics that are shared by the wider population of the unemployed: they have relatively low levels of education and training,
and employment experience in the low-skill, low-paid segment of
the labour market. Some women explicitly mentioned training and
clearly saw it as a route of advancement for themselves in the
future.

The Experience of Being a Lone Mother

The women interviewed in this study were virtually unanimous in
their view that poverty and deprivation were the worst aspects of
being a lone mother. However, they placed their difficult financial
circumstances in the context of their lives as a whole. Lone motherhood also brought with it the experience of greater independence.
Separated women placed great emphasis on the freedom and independence they enjoyed. For some, living on a low income was counter-
balanced by their financial and personal independence. This sense of
enjoying their independence was strongest among women who had
endured a particularly difficult marriage.

Single women also experience a distinct sense of independence,
but that experience is based on a different frame of reference. Their
views of marriage tend to be negative and they see their single status
as something to be appreciated and not to be given up lightly. However, they also acknowledge that while they are free of the potential
difficulties of marriage they are not as free as bachelors: they cannot
simply enjoy the social or personal freedom that single women without children enjoy. In this sense their social context is somewhat
ambivalent.

For separated women the feeling that may accompany the enjoy-
ment of independence is one of occasional loneliness. Some women
referred to the absence of a companion — someone to talk to, quite
simply. Loneliness and independence were often spoken of together, as
if they were complimentary aspects of the one experience.

The separated women expressed few concerns about the impact
their marriage breakdown had on their children. Most tended to point
to the absence of conflict and of the destructive effects that the marital situation had been having on their children. Single mothers for
the most part had very young children. Their accounts of their involvement with their children showed that the children were accepted
into a loving, welcoming context, that they were extensively involved
in caring for the children, and that they saw this as an important and
enjoyable task. They also acknowledged the physical and emotional
demands that their children made on them.

Future Research and Policy

Child care — especially, but not only, for working mothers — was the first social policy issue to emerge in the study. Women saw it as essential that they have access to affordable reliable child care to allow them to work now or at some point in the future. The study does not specify one particular set of detailed policies that should be pursued. Rather, for one area and one group of women with particular needs, it highlights the potential benefits of a more explicit, concerted programme of child-care services for families in general.

Social welfare issues also loomed large in women's accounts of their problems and their suggestions for policy improvements. All women on social welfare insisted that the standard of living afforded by their social welfare payment was simply not adequate. This clearly highlights the need to improve social welfare payments for families with children dependent on social welfare.

Lone mothers' strategies of financial management hinge to some degree on Child Benefit, and this raises two broad policy issues:

(1) The study offers further evidence in support of a significant improvement in Child Benefit.

(2) Child Benefit is important not just because of the financial contribution it makes but also because it is secure, and non-means-tested, and does not vary according to women's circumstances.

The policy changes affecting Child Benefit, particularly in the 1995 Budget, but also in the 1996 Budget, are therefore strongly endorsed — the payment was significantly increased and the role of Child Benefit relative to Child Dependent Additions was enhanced. Policy should move further in that direction.

The study also lends support to the direction recent policy has taken in relation to the means-testing of the Lone Parent Allowance. Lone mothers are generally positive about paid employment: the moderation in the means-test introduced in the 1994 Budget is therefore to be welcomed. It will improve the financial return on paid work for lone mothers in low-paid employment, and lone mothers receiving social welfare who take up paid employment.

Supplementary Welfare Allowances also played a role in the finances of the women in the study. Policy in the future should focus on reducing the time involved for women in obtaining their social welfare entitlements. This would mean a reduction in the transition period during which women must rely on supplementary welfare. A more localised and integrated system of administering the social welfare system in general could achieve this. The social welfare system offers public sources of income to lone mothers. Private sources are also relevant. In this regard, the women's experiences revealed the difficulties they had in obtaining access to family maintenance payments and earnings — the two most important potential sources of private income. The study offers no specific solutions to these problems. However, it is clear that a whole range of policies, in social welfare, child care and training must be directed at improving the opportunities for training and employment for low-income lone mothers, and that policies focused on judicial solutions to family maintenance problems will have limited success.

On the whole their housing circumstances did not feature among the concerns raised by women in the study. Two issues arise for consideration, however:

(1) Young single women living at home with their parents do not generally prefer this as a permanent arrangement. Housing policy and provision should not be based on the assumption that single mothers in these situations do not require independent housing.

(2) The Health Board Rent Allowance system which subsidises families' mortgages and rents can still leave families with very low incomes after housing costs have been paid. For lone-mother families, or for other types of households, it is not clear that this allowance is an adequate response to the housing needs of those on low incomes.

In conclusion, the study points to the need for a wide range of further research. Future primary research on the circumstances of all types of families should be carried out on a wider scale, and should be longitudinal and representative. Strategic policy analyses which do not require primary research should also be undertaken in a number of areas. Priorities here include:

• A review of policies and services directed at single mothers

• An analysis of systems of family maintenance payments in different countries

• The unit of taxation and benefit most appropriate to the evolving labour market and family system.

1: Background, Objectives and Context of Study

1.1   Introduction

This report presents the findings of a study commissioned by PARC (Parents Alone Resource Centre, Coolock, Dublin) and funded by PARC with a grant from the Combat Poverty Agency. The research on which the report is based was undertaken in the Spring and Summer of 1993 — the specific objectives and terms of reference of the study will be outlined later.

First, the term "lone mother" requires definition. Interpreted literally, the term would encompass a wide range of family circumstances — for example an elderly widow living in her own home with her adult son or daughter, a young, teenage mother caring for her small child, or a separated woman with custody of her children. These are very different families in respect of the stage of the life cycle, their likely access to resources of different types, and the forms and sources of "loneness" that they experience.

Given this diversity then, what should be the primary focus of a study such as this, the central aspect of which is the socioeconomic and social policy dimensions of lone motherhood? This study follows the formulation of O'Higgins:

> In terms of the primary public policy concerns about lone parent families, a useful definition would require that the parent be non cohabiting, while the children be below a conventional age of labour market and financial independence (e.g. 16 or 18) with other children included if they were still in full-time education, were financially dependent and had their home residence in the family home (O'Higgins, 1987).

In short, the focus of this study is on lone mothers with young and dependent children.

The research and policy literature contains varied terms to describe this kind of family: "one-parent family", "fatherless family", "single-parent family", for example. Clearly, the adjective "single" is unsuitable in the context of this study as it can be taken to mean "single" marital status. The terms "one-parent family" and "fatherless family" ignore the fact that all children have *two* parents — whatever the actual relationships between the parents and between the parents and their children. "Lone" is neutral with respect to marital status and it invites a contrast with the more usual two-parent family. Furthermore, it may accurately invoke the parenting experience of the mothers who are the subject of this study — they have the sole, or prime responsibility for their children for very extended periods of time, in the continued absence of a husband, or partner.

In using the term "lone", however, no presumption is made at the outset that this description applies to their *general* social situation. For while the mothers in this study are "lone" in the sense in which the term has been defined, they may not be alone, or feel alone, in daily social and family life. Some lone mothers, for instance, may live in extended family situations offering extensive practical and emotional help. They may also have networks of acquaintances in the community, in the workplace or the neighbourhood. In other words, the association, if any, between their "lone mother" status and the extent of their more general social participation and integration is a matter for research.

With the above qualifications in mind, the term "lone" is used throughout. However, as the study includes women of various marital statuses, the context will occasionally require the use of other terms such as "single", "separated" and so on.[1]

1.2 Context — The Growth of Lone Parenthood in Ireland

Recent research has documented a significant increase in the presence of lone-mother families in Ireland (McCashin, 1993). Table 1.1 shows the growth in lone-parent family units over the intercensal

Table 1.1: Families with at least One Child Under 15, by Family Type (in Private Households), 1981, 1986 and 1991

Family Type		Number			% of Families			% Change	
		1981	1986	1991	1981	1986	1991	1981–86	1986–91
1	Couples	383,409	386,963	367,813	92.8	91.4	89.3	0.9	-5.0
2	Lone Mothers	23,684	30,568,	38,235	5.7	7.2	9.3	29.1	25.1
3	Lone Fathers	5,974	5,785	5,836	1.4	1.4	1.4	-3.2	0.9
4	Lone Parents (2+3)	29,658	36,353	44,071	7.1	8.6	10.7	22.6	21.2
Total		413,067	423,316	411,884	100.0	100.0	100.0	2.5	-2.7

Source: Census of Population 1981, Vol. 3; Census of Population 1986, Vol. 3; Census of Population 1991, Vol. 3.

---

[1] This introductory section draws heavily on the introductory chapter in a recent publication (McCashin, 1993: 11–14).

periods, 1981–86 and 1986–91. The number of lone-parent families with at least one child under 15 had risen to over 44,000 by 1991, a total increase of 21.2 per cent during the previous five years, following an increase of 22.6 per cent in the period 1981–86. By 1991, these families comprised 10.7 per cent of all family units. Lone-mother families are increasing in number, lone-father families remaining static, and family units based on couples are declining in number.

Table 1.2 is based on numbers of children, and generally reflects the trends revealed in Table 1.1. During both recent intercensal periods the numbers of children under 15 in lone-mother families increased by over 30 per cent. By contrast, in the last intercensal period the number of children in couple-based family units declined markedly. Children in lone-parent units, therefore, account for a rising share of the total child population (Central Statistics Office, 1994A).

Table 1.2:   Children Aged Under 15 in Private Households, by Type of Family in which They Live, 1981, 1986 and 1991

	Family Type	*1981*		*1986*		*1991*		*% Change*	
		No.	*%*	*No.*	*%*	*No.*	*%*	*1981–86*	*1989–91*
1	Couples with Children (of any age)	804,450	78.0	810,184	79.7	732,037	78.4	0.7	-9.6
2	Couples with Children (and others)	132,767	12.9	114,360	11.3	101,181	10.8	-13.9	-11.5
3	Couples 1+2	937,217	90.9	924,544	91.0	833,218	89.2	-1.4	-9.9
4	Lone Fathers	11,651	1.1	11,003	1.1	11,500	1.2	-5.6	4.5
5	Lone Mothers	42,213	4.1	56,016	5.5	73,783	7.9	32.7	31.7
6	Lone Parents 4+5	53,864	5.2	67,019	6.6	85,283	9.1	24.4	27.3
7	Others	39,970	3.9	24,492	2.4	15,329	1.6	-38.7	-37.4
	All Family Types	1,031,051	100.0	1,016,055	100.0	933,830	100.0	-1.5	-8.1
	Total Private Households	910,700		976,304		1,029,084			

Note: The "other" category includes multiple-family households and non-family households and a small number of one-person households of one individual under 15; the lone mothers and fathers categories include lone-parent families with children and other persons.

Source: Census of Population 1981, Vol. 3; Census of Population 1986, Vol. 3; Census of Population, 1991, Vol. 3.

The proximate sources of this growth in lone-parent families are well documented in the Irish and international research, (McCashin, 1993; Gilliand, 1989). First, there has been a dramatic rise in Ireland, and in many other countries, in births outside marriage. This has combined with a fall in the number of adoptions, giving rise to a rapid increase in the number of unmarried women with children. Table 1.3 records this trend for the three decades 1961–1991.

Table 1.3:   Non-Marital Births and Adoptions, 1961–93

Year	Births	Adoptions	Adoptions as % of Births
1961	975	547	56.1
1962	1,111	699	62.9
1963	1,157	840	72.6
1964	1,292	1,003	77.6
1965	1,403	1,049	74.8
1966	1,436	1,178	82.0
1967	1,540	1,493	96.9
1968	1,558	1,343	86.2
1969	1,642	1,225	74.6
1970	1,709	1,414	82.7
1971	1,842	1,305	70.8
1972	2,005	1,291	64.4
1973	2,167	1,402	64.7
1974	2,309	1,415	61.3
1975	2,515	1,443	57.3
1976	2,545	1,104	43.4
1977	2,879	1,127	39.1
1978	3,003	1,223	40.7
1979	3,331	998	29.7
1980	3,723	1,115	29.9
1981	3,914	1,191	30.4
1982	4,358	1,191	27.3
1983	4,552	1,184	26.0
1984	5,116	1,195	23.4
1985	5,282	882	16.7
1986	5,877	800	13.6
1987	6,381	715	11.2
1988	6,336	649	10.2
1989	6,522	615	9.4
1990	7,660	648	8.5
1991	8,766	590	6.7
1992	9,303	523	5.6
1993	9,664	N.A	N.A.

Notes: N.A. is Not Available.
Source: Annual Reports of an Bord Uchtála (Adoption Board), Reports of Vital Statistics.

Second, the last decade in particular has witnessed a marked rise in marital breakdown. The official data, which are subject to some qualifications, are given in Table 1.4. The data show a *three-fold* increase in the total stock of separated persons, with the number of separated persons per 1,000 married persons increasing from 11.5 in 1981 to 41.4 in 1991. Both of these demographic developments — non-marital births and rising marital breakdown — would together contribute to a substantial rise in the *inflow* to lone parenthood. It should also be noted that these trends have continued in the 1990s.

**Table 1.4:   Marital Breakdown in Ireland 1979–93:
Number of Persons "Separated" (including
"Divorced", "'Annulled", etc.)**

Year	Males (000)	Females (000)	All (000)	Per 1,000 Married Persons
1979	2.4	5.2	7.6	6.1
1981	5.1	9.0	14.1	11.5
1983	8.3	12.8	21.1	16.2
1984	8.5	15.9	24.4	18.3
1985	8.0	17.2	25.2	19.0
1986	14.6	22.6	37.2	28.6
1987	11.2	20.6	31.9	23.7
1988	11.9	24.6	36.5	26.9
1989	12.8	25.0	37.8	28.1
1990	14.2	25.5	39.7	29.7
1991	21.3	33.8	55.1	41.4
1992	20.1	34.2	54.3	39.7
1993	20.4	37.7	58.0	42.2

Notes: 1979, 1986 and 1991 are Census data; other years Labour Force
Survey Data. The LFS data are rounded.

Source: Census of Population 1979, 1986, 1991, Vol. 2: Ages and Marital
Status. Labour Surveys 1983, 1984, 1985, 1988, 1990, 1992 and 1993

However, the influence of a countervailing factor should also be noted — the decline in widowhood among young and middle-aged adults. As Table 1.5 shows, the number of widows per 1,000 married persons has declined over an extended period: the figure fell from 163 in 1971 to 139 in 1986. This reflects the secular increase in life expectancy and is associated with an ageing of the widowed population. By 1991, the absolute number of widows in the younger and middle-aged categories had become very small — for example there were only four widows per 1,000 married persons aged under 35 years in that year.

The number of *elderly* widows, by contrast, has risen significantly. Over the decade 1981–1991 the number of widows aged over 65 rose by 17 per cent, and the share of widows of this age among all widows reached 75 per cent. The increase in non-marital births and marital breakdown must be viewed in the light of these trends. Not only has there been an increase in the *extent* of lone parenthood, but also a shift in the *nature* of lone parenthood: away from adult mortality as the traditional source of lone parenting and towards these "new" forms arising from non-marital births and marital breakdown.

Table 1.5: **Widows per 1,000 Married Persons in Different Age Groups, Selected Years**

Age Groups	1971	1981	1986	1991
15–24	11	2	2	0
25–34	4	3	3	4
35–44	18	12	11	10
45–54	69	58	49	46
55–64	200	197	188	166
65–69	432	419	425	402
70–74	782	694	697	669
75–79	1,174	1,194	1,170	1,110
80–84	1,864	2,111	2,140	1,882
85+	3,365	3,762	4,351	3,884
All Ages	163	139	139	145

Sources: Census of Population 1971,1981 and 1991.

1.3 Lone Parents — The Research and Policy Response

What has been the response in Ireland in terms of the research and policy aspects of lone parenthood? Perhaps the most notable feature of the Irish context has been the dominance of moral, legal, and constitutional issues in public and political debate. For example, in 1983 and 1986 respectively contentious referenda were held on the issues of abortion and divorce. In 1992, the White Paper, *Marital Breakdown: A Review and Proposed Changes,* was published (White Paper, 1992). This document contained remarkably little analysis of the social and economic aspects of lone parenthood.

In 1993, with the formation of the Fianna Fáil–Labour Party Part-nership Government, a commitment to hold a further referendum on divorce was included in the Programme for Government. More recently, the Government of Renewal also gave a commitment that a referen-dum would be held. This referendum took place in November 1995, and was passed by a narrow margin.[2]

Despite the growing number of lone-parent families and the con-tinuing debates on moral, legal, and constitutional issues, there has been no coherent, overall analysis of the social-policy implications of lone parenthood. In contrast, two decades ago in the United Kingdom, the Government published an authoritative, two-volume study, the *Finer Report*, containing detailed analysis of a whole range of public-policy issues affecting lone parents: social security, taxation, housing, family law, child-care services and so on (Finer, 1974). No such official review has been undertaken or even proposed in Ireland.

The absence of coherent official analyses, and of comprehensive data, has not prevented occasional public and political debate on some social policy aspects of lone-parent families. A number of themes re-cur in the public debate meeting:

- Accompanying the significant shift in demographic patterns there has also been an increase in the number of lone-parent families receiving social welfare, leading to a growth in public expenditure in this area.

- The reliance of many lone mothers on social welfare payments has raised concerns about their susceptibility to poverty and inade-quate living standards.

- The proliferation of social welfare schemes for lone parents in Ire-land has occurred in the absence of a broader income maintenance policy for *all* families, and this has given rise to concerns about the relative treatment of lone-parent and two-parent families.[3]

In many other countries also, the growth of the lone-parent population has spawned a controversial academic and public debate on the social

---

[2]   A challenge to the result of the referendum was underway at the time this report was going to press.

[3]   An excellent illustration of these themes is given in an *Irish Times* article on 18 June 1993, "Welfare Rules Attack Family". This reported the previ-ous day's meeting of the Dáil Committee on Public Accounts where somewhat extreme comments about these issues were made.

and economic status of lone mothers, and on the social security "costs" of lone motherhood.

However, Ireland differs from the UK and other countries in that exceedingly little social research or policy commentary has been undertaken in Ireland to date. At this point, a formal review and assessment of the available research will not be attempted. In our analysis the existing literature will be drawn on in the context of the findings of this study — to compare results, to assist in interpretation, and to provide a context.

The research material available to date can, however, be briefly noted. Published commentary on the social implications of the growing number of lone mothers can be first identified in the 1972 report, *The Unmarried Mother in the Irish Community* (Kilkenny Social Services, 1972). This document published the proceedings of a conference addressing, for the first time, the social needs of unmarried mothers and how legal, social, medical and other services should respond. However, the first primary piece of data collection resulting in published work was undertaken by O'Higgins, in relation to marital desertion in Dublin (O'Higgins, 1974). This study reported the results of some in-depth interviews of women "deserted" by their partners, examined the background to their marriages, and explored the factors associated with the breakdown of the women's marriages.

In 1974, Vivienne Darling published a pioneering study of adoptive parents and adoptive services — an issue intimately connected with births outside marriage (Darling, 1974), and some years later Kirke provided an overview of unmarried mothers in Ireland (Kirke, 1979). The first research study of non-marital births based on primary data collection, was reported in 1984: Darling's study, *And Baby Makes Two*, recorded the actual experience of young single women in coping with their lives as lone mothers (Darling, 1984). Finance, housing accommodation, and child day-care were the main deprivations recorded in the study. Also in 1984, an overview of adoption trends was published, showing, most notably, the diverging trends in relation to non-marital births and adoptions. A long-run decline in the level of adoptions was evident in the emerging context of a rapid increase in the number of non-marital births (Abrahamson, 1984).

In the mid 1980s and more recently, two research projects used hospital locations to obtain profiles of unmarried women having children. The Federation of Services for Unmarried Parents and their Children (FSUPC) in 1987 published the results of a census of women who had non-marital births in all the Irish maternity hospitals and units in 1983 (O'Hare et al., 1987). This study was largely descriptive and contained data on the socioeconomic background of the mothers as well as their access to, and utilisation of, health and welfare services. One finding in this study, relevant to this exercise, was the marked concentration of women from the lower socioeconomic groups and the stronger tendency of these women to keep their babies rather than relinquish them through adoption. A team of researchers based at the National Maternity Hospital in Dublin has also conducted successive hospital-based studies; these studies have obtained demographic, social, and social service utilisation data on a sequence of annual cohorts of unmarried women giving birth in the hospital. Some specialist papers have been published, based on these studies, as well as individual reports covering annual "waves" of the project (Richardson and Winston, 1989; Richardson, 1991; Flanagan and Richardson, 1992).

Finally, recent work from the Combat Poverty Agency and the Economic and Social Research Institute has focused largely on the financial and economic aspects of lone parents. Ward analysed Department of Social Welfare and Court Maintenance data and documented the weakness of the system of judicial maintenance in procuring adequate maintenance for deserted women and their children (Ward, 1990). An overview of demographic changes and a critical analysis of the efficiency and equity of the social security system affecting lone parents was given in McCashin's study. This study suggested a high risk of poverty among lone mothers living in independent households and a high level of dependence on State benefits and services (McCashin, 1993). In their overview of the public policy issues about lone parents in Ireland, Millar and her colleagues also reported the demographic background and documented the growing numbers of lone mothers in receipt of State payments (Millar et al., 1992).

1.4   Lone Parents — The Rationale and Objectives of This Study

The chronology of research published to date reveals its limited and unsatisfactory state. It is either partial — examining only one *form* of lone parenthood, (unmarried mothers, for example) or limited to only *one* aspect of policy (judicial maintenance, for example). Furthermore, most studies (Darling, 1984; O'Higgins, 1974) are on a very small scale.

In their recommendations for future research Millar and colleagues identified the following gaps in information relevant to policy:

- Basic demographic data

- Sources and levels of income

- Employment and training barriers
- Social welfare support
- Costs of lone parenthood.

Ideally, a study of these issues should be on a large scale; it should be statistically representative and longitudinal, and should include two-parent families. Such a study would allow the experience over time of lone parents to be studied and would also facilitate comparisons between families of different types. The resources to undertake such a study were not available. PARC and the Combat Poverty Agency therefore devised this study, the terms of reference of which are guided both by the research needs outlined by Millar and the policy interests of both PARC and the Combat Poverty Agency.

The aims and objectives of this study are therefore as follows:

(1) To outline the process whereby women become lone mothers

(2) To document the incomes and standards of living of lone mothers

(3) To describe how lone mothers manage their incomes and resources and the impact low levels of resources have on their families

(4) To ascertain the role that their children's fathers and their extended families play in the social and economic support of their family

(5) To explore lone mothers' views on what public policies should be reformed, and in what way, to address the problems of lone motherhood

(6) To describe lone mothers' experiences of social and community life and their aspirations for the future.

The study was undertaken in one area of Dublin, with an intended sample of somewhere between 60 and 80 women — this size being the range dictated by the time and resources available for the study. In the next chapter, a full account of the methodology of the study will be given. At this stage some comments about the overall design of the study are warranted. First, the study was located in one area — Coolock and environs — where PARC is based. This allowed us to draw on PARC's membership lists and other contacts as a way of contacting lone mothers and securing their participation in the study.

Second, the study is small-scale. As we will see later, the final number of respondents included in the study was 53. The approach to the research was based on maximising the potential inherent in a small-scale, local study. A qualitative methodology was applied, using a semi-structured interview guide, allowing the respondents to express their experiences and opinions freely and in their own words. In this approach the methodological recommendations of Millar and her colleagues in their plea for future research are being explicitly acknowledged. They point to the essential role of qualitative material in the overall research agenda on lone parents which they propose.

> We would argue that such a survey should combine the quantitative with the qualitative, and include in-depth interviews and case studies of the different types of lone parents. Good ethnographic data, describing the quality of life of lone parents and highlighting the dilemmas and difficulties that they face, does not substitute for the overall figures, but it does bring home to decision-makers the lack of opportunities, the frustration and human suffering which lies behind the statistics and which their policy provisions must be designed effectively to address. (Millar et al., 1992: 98)

Third, in addition to the substantive objectives of the study, there is a further, methodological objective, namely, to treat the study as a pilot for a larger, more representative national survey. In particular, the scope to use locally-based projects as a mechanism for identifying respondents was to be explored. This is an important issue for future research: previous work (McCashin, 1993; Millar et al., 1992) has noted the difficulty of obtaining a representative sampling frame for survey purposes.[4] Given the emergence in a number of locations of community-based lone mothers' organisations, the potential to use these as "sites" for more general and more large-scale research was to be examined. In a more general sense, the study is also a "pilot". It attempts to identify the substantive issues and questions that might be addressed in a national survey.

Finally, this is a study of lone *mothers*. Research in this area, as Millar has observed, is typically concerned with women who are the *custodial* parents — we therefore discover little about the background, characteristics or perceptions of the fathers and (ex) partners of the women (Millar, 1989).

---

[4]   Thus, general surveys, such as the Household Budget Survey, contain only very small numbers of lone parents. Administrative lists — social welfare, tax records, court orders, etc. — refer only to subsets of lone parents. In short, there is no existing mechanism that allows a proper sample of lone parents to be selected.

2: Methodology:
The Location, the Respondents and the Collection and Analysis of Data

2.1   Introduction

In this chapter the methodology of the study is outlined — where it took place, how it was conducted, and who was included in the study. The study, in summary, is small-scale and *qualitative* in nature. At the end of this chapter, therefore, the research and policy issues entailed in the use of a study such as this are considered.

2.2   The Context and Location of the Study

The study was undertaken in Coolock, a large, densely-populated cluster of urban housing, four miles north of Dublin city centre. Specifically, most of the fieldwork was undertaken in the community surrounding the Parents Alone Resource Centre in Coolock. This part of Coolock consists of some local authority housing — both flats and houses — some local authority housing now owner-occupied, and private owner-occupied housing.

The area is one of relatively high social need. In the past decade it has been seriously affected by a range of inter-related social problems:

(1) It has been sharply affected by rising unemployment with a high proportion of unskilled and semi-skilled employees and early school leavers. The national employment crisis is disproportionately reflected in the area.

(2) Large parts of the area have been physically developed and housed since the mid-1970s. The area is therefore inhabited largely by families in the early to middle stages of the family cycle — placing a heavy demographic burden on social services and amenities in the area. This combination of demographic pressure and high unemployment has given rise to widespread social deprivation in the area.

(3) These underlying demographic and economic pressures have been reinforced by the impact of housing policy and the operation of the housing system. Some parts of the area comprise only local authority tenancies, with many households dependent on social welfare, and families "filtered" into these neighbourhoods by the system of local authority housing allocations. The area then has "pockets" of particularly high social need.

Some summary data for nine District Electoral Divisions (DEDs) in Coolock, drawn from the Combat Poverty Agency's social indicators study (Combat Poverty Agency, 1993), are given in Table 2.1 below. Most of the project fieldwork was undertaken in this area; the data reveal the relative social deprivation of the area when compared with Dublin as a whole, with the region and, finally, with national data. The nine DEDs had a population of just over 26,000 in 1991, a decline of 8 per cent on the figure for 1986. Clearly, on social, demographic and economic criteria the area is relatively deprived. The demographic burden of young dependants (0–14) is significantly higher than that for Dublin as a whole and higher also than for the national and regional figures — likewise the data on lone parents. The Coolock figure of 15.5 per cent is one and a half times that for Dublin and close to *twice* the national figure.

Table 2.1:   **Socioeconomic Indicators for Nine DEDs in Coolock, Dublin, Eastern Region and Nationally, 1986–91**

	Coolock	*Dublin*	*Regional*	*National*
Indicators	%	%	%	%
Population Change (1986–91)	- 8.8	- 4.9	1	- 0.4
Population Aged 0–14	30.6	19.8	25.8	26.7
Households Lone Parents	15.5	10.2	9.3	8.8
Leaving School < 16	34.7	31.2	23.6	23.6
Unemployed	33.3	21.7	18.2	17.9
Unskilled	15.3	11.3	9.7	10.2

Notes: See Combat Poverty Agency (1993) for definitions; all data are for 1986 except where otherwise stated.

Source: Combat Poverty Agency, 1993.

Turning to socioeconomic data, it can be seen that a similar pattern exists. The area is characterised by markedly higher levels of unemployment — almost twice the national rate — higher proportions of early school leavers and of persons in the unskilled, working-class occupations.

The Parents Alone Resource Centre is located in this area and provides a range of activities and services to women in the Coolock area (and more widely) who are parenting alone. PARC was the original instigator of this study and the Combat Poverty Agency (CPA) its financial sponsor. For practical and for methodological reasons the study was located in the Coolock area. In the first instance, the CPA and

PARC were *primarily* interested in issues affecting low-income, poor, lone mothers as distinct from the general population of lone mothers. Undertaking the study in one area — Coolock — would be a means of concentrating on that specific subset of the lone-mother population. Furthermore, PARC, because of its location and its involvement with lone mothers in the community, had direct access to many lone mothers, and this access was to be the means of contacting mothers to be included in the sample.

A final point about this aspect of the study concerns the general methodological obstacles in the way of a larger, more representative study. There are no ready-made "lists" or "registers" of lone mothers, locally or nationally, from which a sample could be drawn. The *only* way of constructing a sample was to draw on the resources and contacts of an organisation, such as PARC, with continued involvement in a practical way with lone mothers. There is also an "experimental" aspect to this methodology. The study was to explore the potential role of locally-based lone mothers' groups (of which there are now a number in different parts of Ireland) in facilitating access to lone mothers for purposes of social research. More generally, the small-scale nature of the study was intended to give it a pilot character: the findings could be tested in further, more representative research at some later date, resources permitting. What all of the foregoing implies for the validity and representativeness of the study is discussed below in Section 2.4.

2.3   Data Collection

PARC was the conduit of communication with prospective respondents for the study. At the outset, it was intended to include between 60 and 80 women in the study and to identify these by using the names and addresses of women who had contacted the PARC centre, used its services, or participated in its activities.

Specifically, five regular attendees at PARC agreed at the request of the PARC co-ordinator and the researcher to participate in a pilot interview. These "test" interviews were sufficiently successful to be included in the final study. They demonstrated that the PARC centre was an appropriate venue for interviews and that a joint approach to women by PARC and the researcher would elicit a good response from women invited to be interviewed.

Subsequent to this "test" phase (which took place in February 1993), PARC identified from its records 90 women living (most of them) in the Coolock area. These women were invited by letter from PARC to participate in the study and were given a choice as to the arrangements for the interview. PARC's records in most (but not all) cases contained some information about the circumstances of those being invited to interview, and this information was used to structure the sample. The study design specified that:

(1) The unit of study was to be the lone mother family — that is, that the women be parenting alone and have one or more dependent children

(2) Women in a variety of marital circumstances — single, separated/deserted — were to be included

(3) Some diversity in housing tenures (local authority rental, private rental, owner-occupiers) and household circumstances (whether living as independent families or subsumed in an extended family household) was to be reflected in the final sample.

The initial block of fieldwork in March/April 1993 produced over 20 interviews with separated/deserted mothers and only four with unmarried women. In a subsequent phase of fieldwork from April to June 1993, considerable effort was made to identify and interview single mothers: PARC's records in some cases contained information on housing/family circumstances and it was possible to identify single mothers according to their household circumstances — whether living independently or in their parents' homes. Overall, it proved more difficult to engage the unmarried mothers in the research: they were more likely to refuse to participate and to fail to keep appointments for interview. The voluntary organisation, CHERISH, based in Dublin City assisted in the final phase of the fieldwork by facilitating interviews with two young women who were in private rental accommodation — the Coolock-based fieldwork had generated only two respondents in this tenure.

It was discovered during three interviews that the women did not come within the definition of the unit of study, as they did not have a dependent child. These were *not* included in the final analysis.

In all, 56 interviews were completed, three were excluded, leaving a total of 53 for analysis. The balance of respondents approached fell into three categories: those who returned the invitation-to-interview reply card agreeing to be interviewed and then failed successively to keep the appointment; those who returned the card with a refusal; and a small number who had moved out of the area or were no longer lone mothers. The total number of interviews available for analysis, 53, falls a little short of the original intended target. However, the number is adequate for *qualitative* analysis. Furthermore, it was clear *before* this number of respondents had been interviewed that the essential experiences of lone mothers had been recorded, and that the *key differences* between categories of women in the study had been identified.

Tables 2.2, 2.3, and 2.4 provide descriptive information on the 53 interviewees included in the analysis. As Table 2.2 shows, the respondents are evenly divided between single women and formerly married women (23 and 28 respectively, with two widows), and span the family cycle, as indicated by the data on the age of the youngest child. In terms of age, the respondents themselves range across the age categories from under 19 to 50–59, 20–29 being the modal category. Most respondents had one dependent child at the time of interview.

Table 2.2:   Demographic Characteristics of Lone Mothers

	Number	*%*
Marital Status		
Separated/Deserted	28	53
Single	23	43
Widowed	2	4
Age of Youngest Child		
0–4	25	47
5–9	14	26
10–14	12	23
15 or over	2	4
Household Circumstances		
Separate Household	37	70
With Parents	14	26
Other	2	4
Age		
Up to 19	4	8
20–29	20	38
30–39	15	28
40–49	10	19
50 — 59	4	8
Number of Dependent Children		
One	30	57
Two	11	21
Three	6	11
Four or more	6	11

Note: N = 53; percentages may not add up to 100 per cent because of rounding.

It can be seen from Table 2.3 that the attempt to obtain a mix of respondents in terms of household circumstances and housing tenure was successful. Although most (37) of those interviewed were in their own independent households, 14 were living in extended family households; all but one of these 14 were young single women living in their family of origin with their parent(s). The modal housing tenure was local authority rental; however, it was not the majority tenure, as some respondents were owner-occupiers and a small number were tenants in privately rented accommodation.

Table 2.3: Housing and Household Characteristics of Lone Mothers

	Number	%
Housing Tenure		
Local Authority Rental	22	42
Owner-occupied (Private Mortgage)	11	21
Owner-occupied (Public Mortgage)	12	23
Private Rental	5	9
Other/Not Known	3	6
Type of Dwelling		
House	44	83
Flat or Apartment	9	17
Number of Bedrooms		
One	5	9
Two	6	11
Three	34	64
Four	8	15
Type of Household		
Lone-Mother Family Only	37	70
Lone-Mother Family with Original Family	14	26
Other	2	4
Number in Household		
Two	13	25
Three	10	19
Four	7	13
Five	7	13
Six	6	11
Seven or more	10	19

Note: N = 53; percentages may not add to 100 per cent because of rounding.

Table 2.4 provides summary socioeconomic information. Given the self-selected nature of the sample, these data are not particular revealing. For the most part, respondents had left school at 15 or 16, the majority are out of the labour market, and for two-thirds of the women social welfare is their main source of income.

Table 2.4:   Socioeconomic Characteristics of Lone Mothers

	Number	*%*
Age Left School		
Twelve or under	1	2
Thirteen	7	13
Fourteen	6	11
Fifteen	12	23
Sixteen	12	23
Seventeen	11	21
Eighteen or more	4	8
Higher-Education Qualification		
None	13	25
Primary Certificate	11	21
Intermediate/Group Certificate	15	28
Leaving Certificate	12	23
Higher	2	4
Main Income Source		
Social Welfare	35	66
Earnings	8	15
Training Allowance (SESs, etc.)	5	9
Maintenance	3	6
Other/Supplementary Welfare/Not Know	2	4
Employment Status		
Full-time Mother	30	57
Full-time Employee	7	13
Part-time Employee	7	13
Training	4	8
Unemployed	1	2
Other	2	4
No Answer	2	4

Note: N = 53; percentages may not add to 100 per cent because of rounding.

The material collected in the interviews — which took place either in respondents' homes or in one of two local centres — reflected the broad terms of reference of the study. Information was collected on the women's family background, their marriage history, details of their original family and their own children, their incomes, work experience, housing conditions and their take up of social services. Their experiences of coping with lone motherhood and the impact this had on their own and their children's lives were central issues in the interviews. Women's views on public policy affecting lone mothers were also sought.

The data-collection procedure was that of the in-depth *semi-structured interview*. A pre-defined list of topics (see above) was covered in each interview, with a limited number of standardised questions being asked to ascertain *factual* information such as age, marital status, etc. However, the interviews were semi-structured in that the exact order of topics and the relative importance of topics in the interview were determined in part by the respondents themselves. The interview strategy both *required* and *facilitated* the women to express their views and experiences in their own words, to switch from topic to topic and to inter-relate topics as their own lives and experiences deemed appropriate. The research technique for this study, therefore, conforms closely to Walker's textbook definition of the in-depth interview method as a:

> conversation in which the researcher encourages the respondent to relate, in their own terms, experiences and attitudes that are relevant to the research problem (Walker, 1988: 4).

In the interviews the women were invited to talk about *specific* events and incidents and not just their general impressions and opinions. As far as possible, the interviews attempted in this way to record women's concrete experiences. For example, many women stated that it had been "impossible" or "very hard" to get maintenance payments from their partners. They were then asked to tell *exactly what happened* — whether they had sought maintenance, and how, and what the particular sequence of events had been. Likewise, when women made a general complaint about the Supplementary Welfare Allowance scheme they were encouraged to recall in detail the last time that they had applied for SWA and to link their current impression of SWA to particular aspects of it — how the Community Welfare Officer spoke to them, the environment in the local health centre, the urgency of their need as they saw it at the time, and so on.

This interview strategy had the general advantage of encouraging the more reticent respondents to talk. It also helped to avoid the danger that women might merely report as their own perceptions generally "taken-for-granted" assumptions and opinions, and ensured that their perceptions were linked in part to their concrete daily experiences.

It is important to note that most of the interviews were tape-recorded. Of the 53 interviews used in the analysis, 38 were tape-recorded (in only three cases did women actually *refuse* out of shyness or suspicion; the balance of the non-recordings can be ascribed to poor recording conditions — no suitable power outlet — background noise, etc.). The data consist of full transcripts for 38 interviews and detailed handwritten notes for the 15. In addition, a questionnaire covering factual material was completed in *all* cases. With such transcript material, it is possible to convey fully the complexity and diversity of people's experiences and perceptions and to compare respondents systematically across various categories.

The research technique and research instruments employed (in-depth, semi-structured interviews facilitated by a semi-structured questionnaire) are especially appropriate in this context. First, as outlined earlier, the study has a "pilot" dimension in that the topics covered in the study and the methods of data access, collection and analysis may shape future studies on this general issue.

Second, some of the topics addressed in the study are, in the terms invoked by Julia Brannen, "sensitive subjects" (Brannen, 1988). Some of the material provided by respondents is highly personal and intimate. As a result, respondents might be more easily identified than in statistical survey analysis because of the unique nature of the data and, furthermore, identification brings with it the risk of stigma. In addition, some of the study topics — how respondents' marriages broke down, or what circumstances led to pregnancy among single women, for example, may be difficult and stressful for respondents to confront and to talk about. Direct, "straight", categorical questions would be highly inappropriate in these circumstances. On the contrary, respondents will be more informative and candid if allowed to share control of the interview process and to control the way in which — and the point in the interview at which — they talk about such topics.

Third, the research has a policy dimension. It is attempting to convey to policy-makers, and to a wider audience, the day-to-day experience of lone motherhood — "what it feels like", in brief. This is best achieved by avoiding statistical description, and reporting, in respondents' own words, their lives, experiences and aspirations. To quote Walker:

The researcher may wish to gain first hand experience of the situation or problem. The research could be oriented towards action and reflect a concern to bring about change, in which case considerable emphasis is likely to be placed on dialogue and feedback. (Walker, 1988: 22).

2.4   Analysis of Interview Material

By definition, the data obtained are for the most part qualitative, although specific, descriptive information such as age, marital status, etc. was obtained for all respondents. In analysing the material the conventional method of presenting tables of "results" is avoided for the most part. The small numbers in the sample do *not* permit meaningful classification and the sample, moreover, is not statistically representative. Spurious quantification is not attempted, although numbers in particular categories are reported, sometimes in tabular form, to provide a context for qualitative analysis.

The approach to analysing this type of data of necessity relies on continual reading and re-reading of transcripts and interview notes. In this process the researcher searches for respondents' own definitions of their situations and for how these change over time and vary between respondents. This study in particular focuses on *key choices* made by the women (to keep their baby; to separate from their spouse; to take up paid work, for example), on how women identified their choices, and on the range of situational factors which affected their choices and behaviour. The objective in this form of analysis is to identify themes and to construct typologies that distil the women's perceptions and experiences.

The material analysed and presented consists mostly of openended, free-flowing responses by the interviewees to questions. Often this data is presented in the form of quotations, sometimes quite extended quotations. This allows the responses to be conveyed to the reader as the respondent conveyed them — with apparent contradictions, emphases, qualifications and so on. It is possible to use this approach successfully where — as in this study — much of the material has been tape-recorded.

As the study is small-scale, local, and qualitative, considerable care is required in assessing the generalisability and policy relevance of the material. First, as emphasised above, no claims of *statistical* representativeness can be made. In particular, it is important to recall that the sample is *self-selected* with respect to socioeconomic factors. All of the women are, by national standards, on low incomes, and any patterns obtained in relation to income, family maintenance payments, work experience and a whole range of other variables are therefore distinctly *unrepresentative*. The extent to which the income and other socioeconomic circumstances of the women in this study approximate those of *all* lone mothers can only be ascertained by a large-scale, statistically representative survey.

Second, while the self-selected nature and the size of the sample make it *statistically* unrepresentative, they simultaneously enhance its role as a study that is *illustrative* of the circumstances of an important subset of lone mothers. The *context* and location of the study are representative in one important sense. Coolock undoubtedly typifies many urban housing estates in Ireland: it is characterised by high levels of unemployment, a disproportionate share of local authority tenancies, and individuals and families in lower socioeconomic groups, as well as a higher than average incidence of lone-parent families in the population.

This *structural* representativeness must be considered alongside the *national and invariant* character of many of the factors examined in the study. Social welfare legislation, for example, does not vary from one area to another, nor does judicial maintenance legislation, nor, arguably do the labour-market conditions facing low-income, social-welfare dependent lone mothers. The lone mothers in the study sample, therefore, live in an area that is in some respects typical of other areas in which many lone mothers live and they face the *same* administrative, welfare, legal and other institutional arrangements that impinge on the generality of lone mothers. Therefore, the experiences and circumstances of the women in this study illustrate the *range* and *type* of responses and perceptions of women living in many other similar areas, and relating to the same national structures and institutions.

Third, to assist in the interpretation of the study material, it is placed in a broader context, where possible, by citing other studies, by presenting aggregate national data, or by outlining the legislative and policy scenario in Ireland as a whole. For example, the information on the level of women's incomes in the study can be juxtaposed with official data on average earnings and disposable incomes, so that the study data can be set in context. In the case of the women's comments on their "poverty", their experiences can be evaluated in the light of more representative Irish data on poverty and deprivation and of international studies on women and poverty.

Therefore, while we must avoid claims of statistical representatives, generalisation can be attempted where:

(1) Women's experiences arise from some readily identifiable fea-
     tures of social or economic structure that are universal or very
     common across a wide area of society, or

(2) Women's accounts are strongly mutually consistent, or

(3) National statistics or independent studies support and reflect
     particular findings.

2.5 Presentation of Interview Material

In reporting the interview material, the women's responses are drawn
on fully. Often the device of an extended, verbatim record of what a
woman said is used in the text. In these instances the text is italicised
and indented. Other phrases or quotations from women's responses are
given in double quotation marks. The intention is, as far as possible, to
convey the nuances and complexity of the women's situations, as they
reported them. Names are assigned to respondents where their circumstances are being cited in detail, or where they are being quoted
at length. However, these names, and *all* names mentioned in the responses, are fictional, so that the identities of the women and their
families are protected.

3: Becoming a Lone Mother: Single Women

3.1   Introduction

In this and the next chapter the processes and decisions that lead to the women becoming lone mothers are described. Clearly, the nature of the choices faced, on the one hand, by unmarried pregnant women and, on the other, by married women in unsuccessful marriages, is very different. The material is therefore divided into two chapters. Chapter 3 deals with unmarried women and Chapter 4 with separated and deserted women.

At the margins these categories can be inappropriate to the complexity of women's lives. For instance, one respondent is classified in terms of marital status as "single". However, her circumstances, experiences and needs are more akin to those of a widow. She is in her thirties, her partner with whom she had cohabited, but never married, had died one year before the interview, leaving her with two children. In her own words "my sisters now, they tease me about being a widow — 'there she is, the widow', they say'". This woman had had a child in an abusive relationship ("I was sexually abused, to be honest") at the age of 15. Some years later, she became the cohabiting partner of the man who had recently died; she had a stable relationship — for a long period of time (and had a child). She is therefore experiencing a second "bout" of lone motherhood.

A second woman, now in her early forties, had first married at the age of 16. She remained married to this partner for about six years and they had six children. The marriage was annulled (by Church annulment) and afterwards she embarked on a second relationship. In this relationship she had further children, and the relationship lasted almost 20 years. One year (approximately) before the interview this second partner had, in her terms, "simply disappeared — he never came home one day. All I know is he's in London, because he rang, but I don't know why he left, and I've no address". This woman too is experiencing a second bout of lone parenthood, and like the case cited above her unusual life history cannot be neatly captured by a simple married–single–separated classification.

Further examples of the complex relationship between women's lives and their formal marital status will arise in the analysis. However, at this point the conventional classification is adhered to as a useful tool to subdivide the material.

3.2   Age, Residence, and Employment at Time of Pregnancy, and Number of Children

Table 3.1 summarises the data in respect of the age at which these unmarried women (first) became pregnant, their residence and employment status at the time they became pregnant and the number of children they have. All of the women were young when they became pregnant, 15–19 being the modal age category; three were still in full-time second-level education. Most of these women were living in their parental home at the time of conception, and at the time of interview almost all of them had *one* child.

Table 3.1:   Single Mothers — Age at First Pregnancy, Residence, and Employment Status at Time of Conception, and Number of Children at Time of Interview

	No. of Children
Age at First Pregnancy	
15–19	11
20–24	10
25–29	1
30 or over	1
Residence at Time of Conception	
At Home with Parents	16
Living Independently	7
Employment Status at Time of Conception	
Employed	17
Unemployed	3
At School	3
Number of Children at Time of Interview	
One	19
Two	2
Three	2

Notes: N = 23; the seven classified as living independently include two who were in non-parental family households (one with a brother; one a sister). Mean (S.D.) for Age of First Pregnancy is 19.8 (3.7).

Interestingly, only three of the 23 women were unemployed at the time they became pregnant. If these are aggregated with the 17 who were employed, to give a figure of 20 in the labour force in total, then it implies an unemployment *rate* of 15 per cent. This is not unduly high either by local or national standards. This figure should be treated with caution. It is significantly lower than the figures obtained in other Irish studies. Richardson and Winston (1989) recorded "unemployed" as the status of 52 per cent of the unmarried women in their study of births in the National Maternity Hospital. Likewise, O'Grady's study of recipients of the Unmarried Mother's Allowance revealed a high level of unemployment among this segment of lone mothers (O'Grady, 1991). If, however, the unemployment rate found in this study were found to be representative, it would raise questions about explanations of non-marital pregnancy among young women that emphasise their lack of employment opportunities (Moss and Lav, 1985). In this study young women's employment opportunities — defined in terms of their unemployment rate at the time of conception — were *not* associated with pregnancy.

It should also be noted that the unemployment rate among *men* may be the important factor here. For example, Richardson and Winston found an unemployment rate of 33 per cent among the fathers of the women in their study (1989: 33). Some recent international literature, notably that relating to the US, has pointed to the role of male unemployment in the long-run increase in lone motherhood (Wilson and Neckerman, 1986). This study does not contain information on the employment history of the fathers of the women's children.

There are further possible explanations for the unemployment findings in this study. It may be that paid employment — and the personal and financial autonomy it brings — increases the likelihood of involvement with men compared with being unemployed or remaining in education. A further interpretation might be that pregnancy is related to more general labour-market prospects. It could be argued that women employees — such as those in this study — who are in low-paid, low-status employment are more likely than other women to become pregnant. Finally, it is of course possible that the unemployment finding is particular to the *local* labour market in which the study took place.

3.3   Pregnancy — The Context

What was the context in which these women became pregnant? The almost universal pattern is that the women were in relationships — *none* said that they had conceived as a result of a very short-term or casual relationship. The shortest period of time a relationship had existed up to the time of pregnancy was four months and the longest was three years. The relative stability of the relationships at the time pregnancy commenced can be gleaned from these summary facts:

eight of the women had either made definite plans to marry or had discussed this with their partners, or effectively thought of themselves as married — some of these had been cohabiting with their partners; a further 10 women who did not mention that they had been planning or discussing marriage had been living with their partners; two women pointed out that they had known their boyfriends, who lived locally, for a long time.

To illustrate these three types of situations, the relationships of three women are outlined. First, an example of a girl who perceived herself as getting married. Tanya, aged 23 when interviewed, has a 2-year-old baby and lives with her parents. She became pregnant when aged 20 and living with her boyfriend. When asked in the interview about the background to her pregnancy and the relationship she explained:

> I was going out with him for nine months when I got pregnant.... We were actually living in his brother's house at the time. He had actually given us the house, but it was still in his brother's name. And all our ideas of staying together, living together and getting married eventually just went out the door.

The category of relationship includes one woman from outside Dublin, who moved to Dublin with her three children, to escape an abusive relationship — she too had lived with her partner on-and-off over a period of years and she remarked: "I just always thought of myself as married". It also includes the woman referred to at the outset of this chapter whose partner had died and who jokes about "being a widow, really" despite not having formally married her late partner.

Secondly, there is the category of relationships that entailed living together at the time of conception, but which was not described by the women as equivalent to marriage, or as preliminary to marriage. For example, Leanne, aged 28 at the time of the interview, with a 6-year-old daughter, had left school with a Leaving Certificate at 17 and got "a good job". She became pregnant at 22 when living with her boyfriend with whom she was "in love, totally blind in love". But she knew that the relationship would not last:

> I was tied to a guy that I sort of knew I wasn't going to be spending the rest of my life with, but I was too afraid to leave — do you know that way?

She left her boyfriend, who was a drug addict, after her daughter was born.

This category includes a number of other women who were in difficult relationships — their partners being abusive or tending to drunkenness. One women, Kay, who was born in Canada, had returned there at the age of 18 or 19, met a boyfriend and, when living with him, had become pregnant. "He was an alcoholic," she claimed; after the baby was born she returned to Ireland.

The third type of relationship typically involves a long-term pattern of "going out together", "going steady", and invariably with a boyfriend from the local area. Evanne, for example, is 19, has a 3-year-old daughter and lives with her parents. She became pregnant when at school, aged 15, and had the baby when 16 years old. Her boyfriend, with whom she is still involved, is the same age. She explained that her boyfriend was the brother of a close friend living locally.

> *You know Jenny that was just here? It's her brother. We kind of always knew each other since primary. It wasn't just a one-night thing or anything like that. I knew him very well from primary (school) up to fourth year. We had been going out with each other.*

3.4   Pregnancy — Motives and Intentions

If these women were for the most part involved, as they perceived it at the time, in stable relationships, what were their intentions, if any, regarding pregnancy? In addressing this question it is important to note that specific questions were not put to all of the women about contraception and where this fitted in with their pregnancy. Many of the women interviewed were young and gave the impression that specific questions on this topic might be embarrassing or difficult for them. To conserve good rapport overall, this explicit topic was avoided. However, some women mentioned the topic; and other women, when asked about their response to their pregnancy, talked about contraception. Still other women again were quite confident in the interview, and in these cases a direct question about their use of contraception was tried.

Before presenting interview material on these topics it is important to make some preliminary points. Much discussion of unmarried mothers' pregnancies is couched in negative terms: "unwanted", "crisis" or "unplanned" pregnancies are widely-used terms. Perversely, some popular argument criticises the welfare system for facilitating or "encouraging" pregnancies. According to this view, unmarried pregnancies are "planned" or "deliberate" — to obtain a local authority house or welfare payment, for instance. In other words, the images of non-marital pregnancy which shape public and professional debate are somewhat contradictory: these pregnancies are simultaneously presented as caused by ignorance or passivity *and* by rational, deliberate behaviour. Academic analyses of pregnancy, however, point to the complexity of motivations, as Oakley's definitive work suggests:

> People do not have clear motives so far as having children is concerned; few organise their lives according to some overall plan. The subject of having children provokes ambivalent feelings, so that "planning" is a euphemism for allowing one particular feeling or pressure to gain an upper hand.... Despite its complexity, the question "did you want/ plan a baby?" may be easier to answer than the parallel question "why did you want a baby?" This taps a vast minefield of unexplored or half-explored motives and reasons. Some women have never asked themselves this question, or when they do the answer is framed in terms of "always" having wanted a baby; others describe a long process of critical self-examination (Oakley, 1979, quoted in Phoenix, 1991: 60).

What is attempted here is a presentation of a rough classification of the women's general orientations to pregnancy at the time they conceived. This classification is based on what the women said about their relationships, about their attitude at the time to becoming pregnant and about their use and knowledge of contraception. This classification can be constructed for 20 of the 23 unmarried mothers.

First, there is a very small number (two) who both *wanted and planned* to conceive. One of those women was aged 19 when she conceived, in a stable relationship for over three years with a boy who lived locally. Her perception was clear. When asked had she used contraception she stated about her boyfriend and herself that:

> *We wanted to get pregnant. I was with him since I was 16. We thought we wanted a baby. I was delighted, overjoyed when I found out I was pregnant.*

In that instance, and in the next one that cited below, *both* partners wanted a baby and deliberately conceived. This second woman conceived when 21 and in a stable relationship. In discussing her feelings about the conception and about her knowledge of contraception, Joan stated:

> *We had wanted to have a child. My boyfriend was delighted — because he thought he had me then — to keep me.*

Second, there are those women (three) who said that they "wanted" to have a baby in this sense: they were *pleased* when they discovered that they were pregnant, but they did not state that they and their partners had consciously chosen or decided to have a baby. Leanne illustrates this scenario well.

Leanne, for example, had left school at 17, with a Leaving Certificate and is now in her late twenties with a 6-year-old daughter. At 21, she became pregnant when living with her boyfriend. When asked to cast her mind back to her pregnancy she recalled:

> *I was living in Ballymun at the time and just went in and had the test. Positive. I was with a bloke that my parents despised and hated. And I was on a sort of love buzz at the time. I was delighted with myself. He was delighted.*

When then asked about contraception, she replied:

> *I came to your man so tight I didn't care whether I got pregnant or not. That was my excuse for it. I was madly in love, totally blind.*

Third, there were women (six of the 20) who were definitely attempting to avoid pregnancy. These women mentioned that they had been using contraception — it was clear from their accounts that they had either mistakenly used the method or had failed to use it on one or more occasion. These women were shocked and surprised to discover that they were pregnant. For example, Hannah, who is 21 now has a baby boy of one. She had been going out with her boyfriend for two years and she described her reaction to her pregnancy in terms of shock and surprise:

> *First thing was I just cried, you know? And I couldn't believe it at first. It was tough to get used to it.*

When asked had she had any experience of contraception or of trying not to get pregnant at the time, she replied:

> *Oh yeah, that's what happened. I wasn't on the pill but we were using condoms. But, you know — just I don't know. Like we were using them. But something must have gone wrong for us.*

The other women in this category had similar experiences: one was also using condoms — but "it just happened"; one was using the pill but stopped using it because of the side effects and found the coil too expensive, so she "took a risk"; one "made a mistake once" when using condoms; and another forgot "just once" to use a condom.

A fourth group of women professed *ignorance about contraception* at the time they conceived. This took the form of being embarrassed about inquiring, or not connecting their sexual relationship with the possibility of pregnancy, or being very badly informed about contraceptive methods. Evanne's case illustrates this pattern rather well. She is aged 19 and has a 3-year-old child, having conceived as a schoolgirl of 15. This is her account of her use of contraception:

> *No. Me Ma once turned round and said she didn't believe in the pill, or something like this. I'll never forget one night Mike [her boyfriend] said to me, "Would you not go on it?" And I said, "I don't believe in it", just saying what me Ma said. I thought it was this little tablet that you take before you have sex and that's all. I never knew you had to take it every day. I never knew that. And even to have a baby, when I went into Holles Street, I went to the ante-natal classes and they told me you had to go ten inches. I though that you just got all these mad pains and the baby comes. I never knew you had to go into labour. Even in the school, we were never taught about these things. You learned the best part of it on the street. You definitely should be taught.*

This category also includes: a woman who mentioned that she was "too embarrassed" to find out about contraception; a young girl, pregnant at 18, who simply "never thought"; a girl who said that she thought contraception was "for older people", and became pregnant when 17; and a girl who conceived when 15 who said about the pregnancy: "It's something I never even thought of happening".

A final observation to make about this material on contraception concerns the two women in the study who had three children. They both attempted, after the first child, to avoid further pregnancies by using the contraceptive pill. Both mentioned difficulties with this — one described the difficulties she experienced because she was "very fertile":

> *You might find this very strange to believe, but I always used contraception. I can't take it, though. I've known that for a long time. I'm just one of these women. I had very severe migraines and clots and stuff, and I wanted to have a coil fitted after Michael was born and nowhere would fit a coil, as I was only nineteen. The only other alternative was condoms and the cap. The cap is — it's not nice, people .... condoms didn't work. I want to be sterilised now, again. I'm hoping to go in about six months' time. I have an appointment with them. A six-month appointment to be assessed and a year's appointment. It's a long time.*

In another case a woman reported that she had been on the wrong dose of contraceptive pill.

The material analysed here on contraception refers to a mere 20 cases. Therefore, the *numbers* in each of the categories should not command any significance. However, it is important to note that other research would support the kind of categorisation given here (Phoenix, 1991). In interpreting the categorisation, a number of points should be borne in mind. In the first place, the analysis has merely classified either the response of the women to one general question, or their remarks in the context of a general retrospective account of their pregnancy. This is not an adequate description or analysis of their intentions or motives at the time they conceived. In particular, the categorisation of some women as having limited knowledge of contraception leaves a further question unanswered. Were these women actually indifferent about conceiving, or perhaps unconsciously positive about the possibility? They were, after all, sexually active in an on-going relationship.

Clearly, a further understanding of the choices and circumstances and behaviours culminating in a conception would require more detailed and focused questioning. Notably, the material here suggests the need to distinguish between *general* facilitating factors that provide a context in which a pregnancy is desired or legitimised, on the one hand, and more immediate or *precipitating* factors on the other. Into the first category would come factors such as a strong relationship with a partner, the existence of other single mothers in the family or social network, or encouragement or insistence from a partner. The latter category could refer to situational factors such as becoming engaged, "moving in" with a partner, losing a job — all of which might alter the context in which the women behave. Such situations might relax the pressures against pregnancy or refocus a woman's and her partner's perceptions of the consequences of a pregnancy.

In addition, further analysis would need to examine the role that personality and psychological factors play in women's pregnancies. It is notable that among the 20 single women on whom there is sufficient information *six* mentioned problems in their childhood or parental family. For example:

- One woman is from a family of 17 children headed by an alcoholic father who died at a young age leaving her to be reared by her other sister — this young woman's first pregnancy arose out of "sexual abuse".

- One young girl is the daughter (now aged 19) of a lone mother who is separated from her husband.

- One girl became pregnant at 15 and went to a school, as she described it, "for troubled children".

In view of the numbers involved, too much significance should not be attached to these six cases. Nevertheless, it would be important in future, more representative research, to investigate whether aspects of young women's childhood and family experiences are related to their "risk" of experiencing early and non-marital pregnancy.

Finally, the general warning about the limitations of the study bear repetition here. To gain a full perspective on these single mothers, a proper comparison with *married* mothers and single mothers from a range of social backgrounds is necessary. For example, it might be the case that young *married* women with children display the same mix of attitudes, motives and intentions regarding pregnancy and contraception.

3.5   From Pregnancy to Motherhood — The Role of Partners

In the interviews, the women were invited to recall how their feelings about the pregnancy evolved over time, and how other significant people in their lives responded. It will be clear that the pregnancy was very much a time of transition; a time during which key decisions had to be made. To distil the nature of this transition, firstly how the "significant others" responded to the women's pregnancies is analysed, and then how the women came to arrive at their decisions is recorded.

Starting with the women's *boyfriends* and partners, it is possible to discern four distinct patterns.[1] One pattern reflects the widely-held stereotype of the father abandoning the mother during the pregnancy, and *because* of the pregnancy. This was the case with seven women. Their partners' departure was precipitated by the pregnancy. In one case the woman, now in her early thirties with a young daughter, had become pregnant for a *second* time in her relationship with her partner who was himself separated from his wife and children. She had terminated the first pregnancy and her partner, according to her, made it clear that he did not want her to continue with this pregnancy either. Cathy's remarks when asked about whether she had been in a relationship were as follows:

> *Q. So, tell me, were you involved in a relationship at the time or...?*

---

[1]   Twenty-one of the 23 women could be categorised in this way.

A. No, previously I was living with Geraldine's father up until I was six months pregnant. Now, he was a married man and separated, not legally — he just, they didn't get on; he had separated from his wife and we were living together. And as soon as I found out I was pregnant I knew then and there.... There was no word said, but there didn't have to be, and then it proved it when I was six months pregnant: that was the last time I seen him.

Q. He just left, did he?

A. Yes, he just left.

In the context of explaining how she responded to this situation she gave the background to her earlier, terminated pregnancy.

Well I suppose I had been pregnant beforehand and I had an abortion when I was a lot younger, when I was twenty-two. So, and actually it was the same fella, and it was due to all these kind of feelings that I was getting that ... he had suggested that it would not be a good idea, that things would be financially tight if we did, because he was kind of supporting his wife, and we would have to live on my income; and then having a child and all that, so I did have an abortion when I was twenty-two.... On the second one I think I thought "no, I am not going through with this. I am not" — regardless of what, I was going to do my best for this child and I was not giving it up, and I was not having another abortion.

Q. In other words, you wanted to have this child?

A. I wanted this child, now — when I found out I was pregnant I didn't want to have it. When I found out I was pregnant I was deeply shocked and I was really kind of upset but as soon as kind of, I think saying it to so many people actually made me realise "you were pregnant" and that I was actually saying "right, this is it, I am having it". And I think probably earlier on in the relationship it was when I decided I was having the child that there was kind of problems. There was a different feeling there. He didn't have to say it and even when he did kind of say anything it was not a negative thing. He was saying things — like, he would say like kind of "How do you feel?" and things like that — they were kind of things like I thought that probably he does care; and then other times he would be saying things like "How are we going to support this child?" No, sorry, it wasn't "how are we?" — "How are you going to support?", you know. And I think that it was kind of little things that was putting up kind of warning signs to me was, you know, this is your baby, my baby, not his baby, what are you going to do about it, not what are we going to do about it, how are you going to support the baby'. So, kind of I reckoned very early on that I realised that it was only going to be my baby and he didn't want to have anything to do with it, and he did not [emphasis in original].

Other examples of this pattern include the following experiences:

- A girl who became pregnant at 20, but was living with her boyfriend: "I was going out with him for nine months when I got pregnant. I was with him for three months after I got pregnant, and then he went off with somebody else"

- A girl who got pregnant also at the age of 20, but was living with her parents and involved with a boy who at the time lived nearby. When she discovered that she was pregnant she told her partner first and, "the next thing I knew, he was going to Manchester". She did not hear from him again until three months after the birth of the child

- A woman whose partner was (unknown to her) married, and who did not see her from some time shortly before the birth. Their final exchange she recorded as: "'Well, you're after leaving me with this, and you have a wife and whatever'. So, he said, 'there is nothing I can do'. Like, it was all my own fault, the way he put it. But I haven't seen him since"

- A young woman who was a schoolgirl of 15 when she became pregnant by her boyfriend who lived very near her. He was 19 and had already moved to England to study there before they knew of the pregnancy: "So he was nineteen. I was sixteen and he'd gone to start his training and when he was there I realised I was pregnant. He didn't take it well, either." Her partner remained in England and their relationship ended.

The pattern of abandonment by some of the men is found in research studies — for instance, in Darling's study (Darling, 1984: 56). However, it is equally significant that some women experience a *second*, very different type of response — one that is both positive and supportive. In this study this applies to about a quarter (six) of the 21 relevant cases. Rita's circumstances illustrate this pattern rather well. She became pregnant at 18; she was "shocked"; her boyfriend of 21 was also "shocked", but when the baby girl arrived was "pleased". In her case her partner suggested, "'if you want to get engaged or anything', and I said 'no I don't'". This girl's baby is now six months old and the baby's father comes and brings the baby to his own family home. The couple are still continuing their relationship and he offers financial support for the child.

Other examples of this situation include the experience of Dana, who has two small children. She first became pregnant when she was 15 and living at home with her parents. She has continued her relationship with her boyfriend by whom she had the second child. When the second child was born she obtained her own accommodation. Her relationship continues but is not close, and is focused around his regular visits to the children. When asked if she was still seeing her boyfriend, she claimed:

> *Mainly on a Saturday; mostly he takes them out for a while — about an hour and a half — mostly to his mother's.... He's never taken them for the weekend. He's taken them overnight, once, when I went down to my sister's.*

Further examples include one girl aged 19 with a child of three who has remained involved with her boyfriend. She lives with her parents, and he stays with her one night a week and is involved with their child. In her description, she is engaged, intending to be married at some point in the future, and is saving in the Credit Union to this end. According to her, her partner does "have the interest" in their child but is constrained from further involvement because he lives with his own family:

> *Every Sunday he used to take her for a few hours but that's only one day of the week. I used to be going mad, saying "It's not fair!" And with so many people living in his house he couldn't take her over. She'd be crying and they'd all be complaining and being woke up and having to get up for work and that.*

Her partner is now unemployed and in her view does, and ought to, spend more time with the baby:

> *He can take her more now, to give me a break. That's only lately. Before that I had her all the time.... I'll have to be more pushy and start getting him to come over and take his part.*

A *third* pattern concerning relationships with boyfriends is somewhere between the first category of those who "left" and the second of those who "stayed". This pattern is exemplified by the couple having an "on–off" relationship, or a relationship that was in difficulty before the pregnancy, but which they tried unsuccessfully to stabilise once the pregnancy occurred. Typically, the couple would mutually recognise that their relationship was uncertain, then live together during some or all of the pregnancy because of the impending birth, and finally go their separate ways having found that they were unhappy together.

This scenario applies to four of the women and is well illustrated in the case of Áine. She is 24 years of age, having conceived at 20; her child is now three years of age, and she lives in her parents' home.

In her case, she had been "going out" with a boyfriend from when they were both 13 — he lived two doors away from her. When they were both 18 they went together to England and were living together and engaged. Then, in her words:

> We were due to get married and before I found out I was pregnant we decided to cancel the wedding because things weren't going well. So I had to come home to cancel the wedding and I was staying over here for a couple of weeks and that's when I found out I was pregnant....

She had the baby in England while continuing to live with her boyfriend.

> He was pleased, he was over the moon about it. We left the wedding because I wasn't getting married just because I was pregnant.... We were living together in England and I had Paul and I came back and we lived for a while in a flat with two rooms, a shower and bedroom, and we split up after about four weeks there. We split up for a year and we got back together last year for probably, yes, I think we were back together for a year and we split up in October just gone.

Here the couple's relationship has ended. However, her partner is involved, somewhat uneasily, in a limited way with their child, in a situation where they have now both resumed living with their respective parents who are two doors apart. She gave this reply when asked how frequently he was with the child.

> It is twice a week. He works nights so he doesn't get out of bed till about three or four o'clock, so he takes Paul on Tuesdays and Thursdays every week from four till seven, and every second Sunday.

However, when asked about whether the child's father wanted more time with the child, she gave a long account of their negotiation from which this excerpt is taken:

When we split up, he asked me, he wanted to arrange times to see Paul and all that so I said "What about Mondays?" and he said "Oh no Mondays is out" because he goes golfing on Monday, so I said "Fair enough", and I said "Tuesdays", and he said "Tuesdays four till seven", and he said "Another evening then during the week", and I said, "Thursday" and he said "All right", and I said "Well what about any Saturday?" and he says: "Oh no, leave Saturdays free", and then Sundays — "Well every second Sunday, just those times." I asked him one Saturday: I was going I think it was to a twenty-first or something — and I hadn't got a baby-sitter for Saturday night, and "Would it be all right if you took him Saturday night seeing as you will be having him on Sunday morning anyway?" and he said "No I am not going to be your baby-sitter, I'm not going to." So, I said "Right forget about it", and I never bothered after that. He is very like that — he wouldn't take him to suit me, he only takes him to suit himself.

This pattern of attempted stabilisation of relationships is illustrated by these further cases:

Helen got pregnant at 21; she was ending the relationship at that stage and when she told her boyfriend of the pregnancy they met and "he suggested getting back together and making a new go of it". They took a house in the suburbs and lived together for a month, after which she moved back to her parents. Here also the boyfriend has maintained contact with the child. Helen perceives that this contact is unsatisfactory, however:

He was out for Alan's birthday but that was only for show as far as I am concerned.... But it is now and again when he does these things. You know, he hears his conscience getting to him, because he is living with another girl now.

Sheila had lived with her boyfriend in England for a few months and when they came back their relationship ended. They remained good friends, however. She became pregnant at 20:

It was really weird because I had just broken up with the boyfriend ... so we were really good friends. We went out for a meal one night and of course I stayed there and I got pregnant this night. The boyfriend was not really into kids and ... well, at first he was saying "Oh God, would you not think of abortion or adoption...?" So I said to him "If you want to go, you can go, I don't mind, I'll cope by myself". But he said "No, I don't want to go." We stayed together for a while.

The boyfriend now lives "across the road" and sees the baby "every day". He is extensively and willingly involved with the baby, she says: "he would look after her for the day, or the weekend, or whatever. He would have no problems doing anything for her."

The *fourth* and last category in relation to boyfriends refers to those women who very decisively ended their relationships after they became pregnant or had their child, because the relationship had been, or had become, destructive or abusive. Dolores, for instance, had left home at 15 because there she had been the centre of "loads of hassle". She met an older man, took a flat in the city centre and lived with him. In her recollection (she is now 20, her child over two), she "lost contact" with her family, and her boyfriend was the "only person I could count on". When she became pregnant:

> *He just changed, although I could see it in him all along, but it was too late. I thought that I could change him. So he started turning into a right bastard. He started hitting me, so basically that was it then. I thought, this is it, but it wasn't like.... It took a long time to get away from him because he always found out where I was.*

One other instance of somewhat extreme conditions is of a woman whose boyfriend was a drug addict. She left him after their child was born even though in her words she had been "totally in love" with him and had been "delighted" when she learned of her pregnancy. In her case she was in her early twenties when the child was born but calculated that she could not stay with this man "the rest of my life", because "it would never have lasted".

This category typically has a pattern of partners not taking responsibility and not adapting their lives to the pregnancy and the coming baby — this occurred even in some cases where the partner was initially pleased about the pregnancy. Joan's story illustrates this situation well. She is now 25 and living alone with her daughter of four. She had left school at 18, having obtained her Leaving Cert, and she worked in secretarial work for three years. When unemployed she went to live with her brother and at this point met her partner. She lived with him for about 18 months from when she was four months pregnant. Both were pleased with the pregnancy. However, as time passed, he became less involved with her and, later, with the baby:

> *He wasn't around at all. There was never any money coming in. He was never there. I asked him to baby-sit twice — each time I came home, she was screaming.*

She left him, moved to live with her sister, and then later got her own accommodation. In her view, her boyfriend had only expressed pleasure at the pregnancy because he saw the child as a device to hold on to her: "He thought he had me then, to keep me".

3.6   From Pregnancy to Motherhood — Parents' Responses

After the women's partners and boyfriends, the next category to be considered is their parents. This material is readily summarised as there is a definite uniformity in the parents' responses to their daughters' predicament. Of the 23 women, 19 could be classified as having experienced support from their parents. The family circumstances of the remaining four were exceptional: in one instance both parents were deceased; in another they were both elderly and very ill — one with Multiple Sclerosis; and in the remaining two cases, the parents were not fully supportive. In the latter instance, in one of the families, the girl's father was instantly and totally supportive, while her mother was withdrawn — this unusual scenario will be discussed again in the next section.

The other "non-supportive" case concerns a girl whose mother was deceased, whose father refused to accept the pregnancy and has continued up to the present to remain aloof from her and the child, now three: "He wouldn't talk to me.... He's never really come around". During the pregnancy and since, her sister and one of her three brothers have been her main family support.

If most of the parents' responses can be classified as "supportive", it still remains to specify how that support was offered. A three-fold categorisation is useful here. *First*, the single most common pattern to be found (13 cases) is where the girl's mother is — to some degree at least — accepting, while her father is angry and rejecting at first but eventually changes. The change of response on the father's part takes place over a period of time — in some cases he does not relent until after the child is born. The net outcome in these situations was that when the baby was born, it arrived into a fully accepting, positive and welcoming family context.

Dana's case is a clear illustration of this process. When she became pregnant she was 15 and living at home with her parents. She recalls her parents' response to learning of the pregnancy as follows:

> *I didn't tell my mother that I was; she realised it herself. She just asked me. And she kept saying "How could you?" .... I thought my dad would kill me, 'cause he was real old-fashioned,*

> *but when he found out then he kind of changed, but I wouldn't sit in the same room as him .... but when I had him [the baby] then — he loves him now, you know? He just kind of changed.*

Similarly, in the case of Ann:

> *I went home and told them. My mother said she had had a feeling that I was pregnant and my father wasn't talking to me.... My mum kind of knew so she wasn't very hard on me, but my Dad wouldn't even talk to me. But when they got used to the idea, well that was it and I got on great with them. They were up with me from morning to night and they were there for me all the way through the pregnancy.*

There is some variation within this pattern of initial mother acceptance/father rejection. In some cases, the mothers were shocked and annoyed, while quickly reverting to a mood of acceptance and support. Likewise in the case of some fathers. Some of them showed very strong hostility which did not abate until well after the birth of the child. Evanne, referred to earlier, anticipated her father's anger and went to stay in her sister's house nearby. Her father summoned her from there one day:

> *I used to stay in my sister's up the road, and he found out and I was told to come up to the house — he wanted to see me. So I sat down at the table and my Ma was there and she was trying to keep the conversation going about anything. Then she got up and walked out, and I said, "Here it comes now, he's going to say...." But he didn't He just sat there, looking at me, looking me up and down. In other words, "You slut". You know, all these looks. About half an hour I was sitting there and I said, "F*** that." He didn't say anything so I said, "It's over", so I went back up to my sister's then.*

She described her father's continuing hostility after the baby was born:

> *So she was born then and I came home from hospital, I was sitting there with her in my arms, and my Dad just came in and looked at her and walked out. So I started crying.*

Now, three years later, when asked in the interview if her father's feelings had changed at all, she described her father as "completely different. He loves her now".

The second category of parent supportiveness, which applies to four cases, concerns cases where *both* parents were fully in support of their daughter. Sheila's situation is a case in point here. She got pregnant at 20 when living with her parents: she and her only brother are adopted, and in her view this may have conditioned her parents' response:

They became more positive as time went on. I suppose really the feelings for them was, they never had any children of their own — do you know what I mean? I don't know if that had anything to do with it or not, but they're very good. They gave me great support all the way through, from day one. Like, when I told them, they were crying, the usual, but as soon as that was over, my father was saying, "Oh, you'll be grand, you'll be grand. Wait till you're going to the hospital." When we walked in the door on the way home from the hospital, my mother said, "Yes, she had a scan. It's alive." So, from then on it was, "Mind yourself", "Don't do this", "Don't do that", so they were good, real, real good. They were very good.

Third, a category of situations was encountered which loosely be designated here "the emergency stop". This refers to those women, (three out of the 23) who had left home, having rebelled against their parents and become involved with partners of whom their parents disapproved, only to be encouraged to come home and welcomed home when the crisis of the pregnancy struck. In these cases, the girls returned to live with their parents for a time either before or immediately after their baby was born. Dolores's circumstances illustrate this pattern. She had become pregnant when 17 and living in a flat in the city having left home:

Oh there was loads of hassle and I kept running away from home. I left school after my Inter and I got a job and a flat and I was only sixteen at the time.

A year later, she became pregnant and, as it transpired, her boyfriend changed and became abusive — she then needed to escape from him. She contacted her mother:

I just felt really guilty because I knew that for my Mam I was the only one and I knew that it would really kill her. I rang her and told her on the phone because I couldn't tell her to her face, and I was still crying. "Don't worry about it," she said. "It's OK", and she just said she would ring me back.... When she rang next time, she just kind of yanked it all out and she said "Well you'd better not bring him [boyfriend] *up 'cause your Dad will kill him."*

She moved back home when seven and a half months pregnant. Once there, her mother's chief concern was to protect her physically during the pregnancy and to ensure that she finally broke off her connection with her boyfriend who had become difficult and abusive:

My mother was great. She was just on about pregnancy and health — and she would never really mention him, you know. If I went down [to him], *she was giving me loads of grief and hassle. "Oh, where are you going? Where are you going? You'd better not go to there" and "You'd better not go to him", "If you go near him, he will kill you and that baby will die" and, and you know, or "You'll have a miscarriage", and I was always going behind her back and going to see him, all of this. Like, he was never allowed to ring or call up or anything, so my two young brothers were ashamed and called me a slut and all that, and my Dad didn't talk to me at all, he was finished with me.*

One month after the baby was born, she moved out of home, but moved back shortly afterwards. The other cases in this "emergency-stop" category are very similar. Both involve situations of girls returning home, having earlier been in conflict with parents, and been in disapproved-of relationships, and then moving again to independent accommodation at a later point.

In the analysis above of parents' responses, the common thread is some level of support and acceptance by parents. Notably, in all cases their mothers were supportive, and in some cases had even *anticipated* their daughter's revelation. One other common — indeed universal — thread in all these cases was that parents did *not* attempt to pressurise their daughters into marriage. Some parents mentioned the option of adoption, and one or two actually suggested "living with him" rather than marriage. In Darling's study, based on fieldwork done in the late 1970s, 61 per cent of the girls' parents had tried to influence them in some way regarding the future, whether it was marriage, abortion, adoption or some other course of action (Darling, 1984). It may be an indication of changes since that time that almost all the parents in this sample were by-and-large supportive without insisting on any one course of action. The sample in this study is, of course, small and unrepresentative and would not of itself sustain a general conclusion about trends over time in parents' reactions to daughters' pregnancies.

Finally in this section, it may be of interest to note the limited material in the interviews about the point in their pregnancy at which the women sought antenatal care. The pregnancy was already some time in the past at the point at which the women were interviewed, and therefore no information was sought here. Nevertheless, it emerges in the interviews that at least five (of the 23) women deferred any further medical appointment after their pregnancy test. In these cases, the follow-up antenatal visits were linked psychologically to telling their parents of the pregnancy. The first antenatal visits in these cases were very delayed; "I put it off for a while"; "I didn't go near anyone for seven months"; "It was five months before I told anyone". These quotations are symptomatic of the worrying findings in a national study conducted by the Federation of Services for Unmarried Parents and their Children (FSUPC), which showed that almost 50 per cent of unmarried women receive their first antenatal check at 20 weeks or later (O'Hare et al., 1987).

Before preceding to an analysis of the women's decision-making in relation to the pregnancy, it is useful to note that the *specific circumstances* in a family to some degree shape the response that parents make. With the very small numbers involved it is impossible to categorise these circumstances. They can be *illustrated*, however, by reference to individual cases. One girl, for example, perceived, that her parents' first reaction to her pregnancy was conditioned by the fact that the baby was to be their first grandchild; in another case, the girl and her only sibling (brother) were both adopted, and she adverted to her parents' pleasure at the prospect of a "real" baby in the family. In other instances, it is likely, *a priori,* that parents' supportiveness is conditioned by family size — quite literally the existing number of persons in the household — although this was explicitly mentioned by only *one* person in this study. In short, any comprehensive analysis of the factors affecting parents' responses would require an analysis of the diversity in family size, structure, stage of the life cycle, and family history.

3.7   The Decision to Keep the Baby

The previous two subsections have shown how the women's partners and parents responded to their pregnancy. In the former case, considerable diversity emerged — some partners absconding and, at the other extreme, others remaining involved in the relationship and becoming involved with the child. In the latter, the response was, in general, one of support, marked in most cases by initial hostility from the girls' fathers.

Against this background then, it is interesting to observe a virtual unanimity in the women's approach to the decision to keep their child. They were almost all emphatic and unrelenting in their decision to keep their child and not even to *consider* the alternatives of adoption or abortion — nor was there any rush to marriage. The sample is, naturally, self-selected: *by definition*, it consists of those women who chose to "keep the baby". Nevertheless, it is striking that the women in the study were so strong and unwavering in their decision — a decision that in almost all cases was made early in the pregnancy.

To illustrate the nature and the context of the women's decisions, a four-cell table can be constructed, based on two key aspects of the women's pregnancies — whether they had wanted to conceive, firstly; and secondly, what happened to their relationship with their boyfriends. In the material below, four cases are presented.

Figure 3.1: Nature and Context of Women's Decisions

Boyfriend's Role	*Woman Wanted to Conceive?*	
	Yes	*No*
Positive and Supportive	1	2
Negative	3	4

Note: The numbers in the cells refer to the case numbers used in the text below.

The first case is where the woman had been very positive about becoming pregnant and where the boyfriend was helpful and supportive throughout. The fourth, and exactly opposite, situation — Case 4 — is where the woman had been definite about not becoming pregnant and where the boyfriend either left or impelled her to leave because of his behaviour. These two scenarios, when combined with the intermediate situations — Cases 2 and 3 — offer a diversity of contexts in which the girls made their decision. This diversity in context is *not* matched by a diversity in decisions, as the case material illustrates.

Taking Cell 1 first, this is a context which would be, on the whole, somewhat supportive of a decision to retain the child. Lisa met her partner in the mid-1980s when she was aged 30 and living in Dublin with her parents. She left her job, a white-collar job, and went to live in England with her boyfriend. In her account, she went "for a change" and recalls, "I was 30, I thought I knew enough". In the UK, she discovered that her partner was "a real stay-at-home" and experienced her relationship with him as "disappointing". Three years later, she moved back to Dublin with her partner and one child. Although she had now decided not to marry him, their relationship continued and they had a second child.

At the time of the interview, they were no longer a couple, but they remain on friendly terms — he sees her and the children regularly, and pays regular maintenance payments. He works a lot outside Dublin (in Ireland and abroad) and leaves his car with her for her use. When he is in Dublin, she explained:

> *He brings the kids out. We might all go out together as a family. He stays in the house sometimes and I go out for myself.*

In Lisa's case, the only decision she had to make, as she sees it, was about *marriage*. As the relationship evolved and she became pregnant, and then pregnant again, she and her partner discussed marriage. When pregnant first, "I was going to marry but only for my mother"; later, during the second pregnancy, he raised it again as an issue — she sensed that he, who had been married before, did not really want to get married, and as she summarised it in the interview:

> *If I had got married it would have been for all the wrong reasons — not to be* <u>unmarried</u> [emphasis in original].

A contrast in circumstances is offered by Case 4, representing the lower right-hand corner of Figure 3.1. Teresa had been using contraceptives to avoid pregnancy but became pregnant at the age of 20 when living with her boyfriend. Her reaction was one of "shock" and she returned to live with her parents. At this point, her boyfriend left and became involved with someone else — her predicament was worsened by the fact that he denied paternity. Her ex-boyfriend has not seen her (the baby is now two) since that time nor has he seen the child. She and her mother discussed her future:

> *My mother's reaction was, "I suppose it's better than getting cancer!" That was her way of looking at it. She's not one of those people that come down heavy. Then she went through the options that were available for me.*

When asked what options her mother outlined and what sort of things she weighed up in her mind, she replied:

> *I didn't actually weigh up many options. I just thought, "I'm going to have this child and that's it...." She mentioned adoption, let her raise the child, abortion, sending me off down the*

country, down to relatives to have the child. So, I stuck to my guns, I said I was going to have the child and rear it myself.

She was pressed on the consideration she gave to the various options:

Q. Did you actually consider — did you really think about any of the other options at all?

A. No, but I have since! [Laughing] *I decided to stick to my guns and face it. I got myself into it. I'll go through with it, do the best I can.*

This scenario is one where a determination to rear the child is not diluted by difficult circumstances — a boyfriend denying paternity and an unintended and unwanted conception. Moreover, in this case, the girl was at home with her parents and five other children and was conscious, as she said, that her parents "had to make room for me and somebody else" and that this "created tensions" even before the baby was born.

Case 3 in Figure 3.1 refers to one of the situations with a "Yes" and "No" dimension in the typology: a positive desire for a child in the context of a relatively enduring relationship, combined with a negative or neglectful response by the woman's partner. Róisín's case is a neat illustration. Now aged 24 and living in a local authority house with her daughter, she became pregnant at 19 by her long-standing boyfriend who lived locally. In her recollection, they both assumed that they would marry, and in her case she was "delighted" to be pregnant. However, during the pregnancy, and for some time after the baby was born, she lived with her boyfriend who "changed". In her words, he was "childish" and "not preparing for the baby" and was "drinking and abusive". Despite the deteriorating situation she remained definite about her course of action:

I did not consider adoption. I knew from the moment I was pregnant. I did everything to have a stress-free pregnancy — being pregnant was <u>my job</u> [emphasis in original].

Róisín was definite that her original preference — and her assumption all along — was for a conventional marriage-and-child situation. Although she anticipated that her mother would "push me into a shotgun wedding", in fact her parents did not pressurise her into marriage but suggested that she "live with him". His parents, however, *did* try to pressurise them both into marriage, which made her definite about *not* getting married: "I was now determined not to get married." When

her child was six months old and she was still living with her boyfriend she became pregnant again and had an abortion, about which
she feels guilty and upset:

> *There again, my father said: "Whatever chance you have with
> one child, you've no chance with two." I just went out and got it
> done — nobody knew. Still, I don't agree with abortion. I didn't
> use the word "baby" about the abortion.*

Finally, Case 2 is an instance where the woman definitely was trying
to avoid pregnancy but, once pregnant, her boyfriend remained positive and supportive. Deirdre had conceived at 15 and had her baby at
16. In her case, she had definitely not wanted to become pregnant but
was ill-informed about contraception. Her relationship with her boyfriend has continued. She and he lived for a time in their respective
parents' homes which are in the same area, and since her pregnancy
at 15 she has had a second child by her boyfriend. At present, she
lives separately in a local authority rented house. She recalls her discussions with her parents at the time of her pregnancy:

> *They talked about adoption and things like that, but I wanted to
> keep him. They said that whatever I'd choose they'd stick by me.*

When asked to spell out the discussions she had with her parents, she
recalled the following:

> *Well, my Dad brought the two of us into the house and said we
> had options either to adopt or whatever. He said there were
> families that would look after the baby. And I just said "No!" I
> didn't want to listen to adoption. I just said No, I wanted to keep
> him, and he said "OK, fair enough then."*

Asked whether she discussed the situation with anyone outside the
family, she said, "Nobody really". When pressed whether she had come
to her decision having weighed everything up, her reply was:

> *I just didn't want to give him up. I never considered it. I just
> said I never would 'cause when you get old and you end up hav-
> ing a baby then you're thinking about what the other one would
> have been like or ... I wouldn't do it.*

One *exceptional* case may help to cast light on the strength and unanimity of the women's decisions. This case concerns Ellen, now aged 25
with a 5-year-old child, and living at home with her parents, two

brothers and a sister. She became pregnant at 20 and her boyfriend effectively abandoned her. For five months she put off disclosure of her pregnancy to anyone, parents included, and during that time she did not visit a GP or any other antenatal clinic. She told her father first who was initially angry and upset. However, her mother was *more* upset when she told her some days later: as she had anticipated, her mother's reaction was more severe and less understanding than her father's. During the pregnancy, she was quite ill and regularly attending the doctor. Her mother helped her with this but, as she recollects, her mother seemed to put boundaries on the nature of her support:

> *She was supportive of me, but I got it into my head that I think the best thing to do, to keep my Mammy happy, would be to have the baby adopted, so I seen the social worker and I was going to have the baby adopted.*

She had been discussing her plans with her parents, and as events unfolded it transpired that her father was against adoption and her mother against keeping the child.

> *My Mammy was all for it* [adoption]. *"Yes that would be the best thing to do. You can get on with your life afterwards!" My Daddy was totally opposite. He didn't even know we were talking about this. He said "Right, when the baby comes, everything will work out — you'll see, everything will be grand — you have your room upstairs — there will be room — we will make room. What is one more mouth to feed? We will get by."*

After a difficult birth, when her parents were shown the baby by the nurses, her father, she now recalls, overhead a nurse saying that the child had to go to the nursery immediately; that she (Ellen) was not to be given the baby, as the baby was "for adoption". Ellen had said to the hospital staff, before the birth, that she was having the child adopted. What followed then was a difficult five or six days. In hospital she did not have her child and held it only once. On leaving to go home, she went to see the baby, dressed him and, with the social worker's permission, had a photograph taken of her holding the baby. She came home without her child who was fostered out.

However, her own father was in continual contact with the foster mother and telephoned every few hours to check on the baby's feeding and sleeping. This is her protracted account of how she came to reclaim the baby:

So I came home without Barry on Tuesday and he went to a foster home, a woman in Rush. Now, my Daddy had made it clear in the hospital that he wasn't going anywhere until he knew where he was going. I didn't know this, I thought he was going and that was it and I just happened to say to my Daddy, I said "I wonder", I think on the Wednesday like I was afraid to talk about him and like on Wednesday I said to my Daddy "I wonder if he is all right, is he eating food or you know, taking his bottle or anything." Anyway my Daddy says "Ah, he is." I said "How do you know?" He said "Because I have been ringing the woman that has him." He got the phone number of the woman that had him and he would ring her after every feed, like every time Barry was to be fed, like every four hours, my Daddy was ringing her, "How much did he take?" Now the woman used to just answer the phone and say "Hello John. He has had so many ounces; he is fine; he is going to the toilet; he is passing this and he's doing that." By Friday I wanted him and I knew I wanted him but I couldn't have him. The social worker I had from Coolock Clinic was going away for a long weekend. She had taken Friday off, so we had no way of contacting her. So I had to wait till she came back on the Monday and she was due to come up to see me but I didn't wait till she came down — I went up to the clinic on Monday morning and I said "I want to go and get Barry." "Oh well," she says, "it is not as easy as that." I said "It has to be as easy as that." I said "He is my child — I want him." She said "Well there is formalities and things that have to happen." I said "Well I never signed any forms." I said "You gave me loads of forms," I said, "I never signed any of them." I didn't ever sign the form for the woman that was minding him in case of an emergency to bring him to a doctor in case it was a different way of putting it that I couldn't have him back. I knew in the back of my mind I wanted him all the time, but I was terrified. So she said "Oh well, it would have to be late this afternoon before I could possibly see whether you could have him or not." So I said "Fine."

Later that day, accompanied by her father, she and the social worker collected the baby from the temporary foster mother and brought him home. According to Ellen, when she went into hospital she was "totally confused", and when asked in the interview whether it was her mother's view that made her feel uncertain she replied "Yes, definitely".

The significance of this exceptional case lies in what it may reveal about the central role of the responses of mothers in affecting their daughters' decisions. Here is found the only example in the study of a lone mother who came close to having her baby adopted. She herself ascribes this situation to the preference her mother expressed for adoption. Clearly, the fact that she was able to retrieve the situation can be attributed, in part, to the equally unusual situation of a father who was strongly in favour of her keeping the child and who would go to considerable lengths to facilitate this.

Finally, were the women's decisions affected in any way by their access to, or utilisation of state services and supports? First, it seems clear that any general argument that the decisions pregnant girls make are strongly conditioned by the availability and amount of social welfare support is *not* supported in this study. Not one woman even adverted to social welfare issues in recalling the decision that they had made — two referred to how "hard" it was going to be, but none of the interviews contain references to social welfare which suggest that it was a positive factor or inducement to keep the child.

A further variant on the welfare inducement argument might be that the lone mothers' decisions not to *marry* were affected by their social welfare entitlement. Here too there is no supportive evidence. Some women had intended to marry, or presumed that their relationship would lead to marriage, but found themselves abandoned; others left their relationships because they were abusive or difficult for themselves and their partners — none of them were impelled or encouraged by their parents to marry. In short, their rejection of the marriage option by the women seemed to be dictated by personal considerations and circumstance rather than awareness on their part of any financial advantages or supports. However, in a later chapter there will be an analysis of how their attitudes to family and marriage evolved over time, and it will emerge that their social welfare support does condition the way that women begin to perceive their choices in the long term. At this point, where we are concerned with the *initial* decisions emanating from a non-marital pregnancy, social welfare support seems to be irrelevant to the choices women make.

If the State's social welfare support did not exert an influence on the women studied here, did the voluntary and statutory social work services play a role in women's decisions? The answer here also seems to be decisively "No". It should be noted that all the women were asked who, if anybody, they consulted during the pregnancy, and were asked if they had consulted social workers, GPs, clergy, counsellors or voluntary social services. With two exceptions, the women usually said that they consulted no services or professionals. Typically they responded "Nobody, really", or, "No one". Some of the women stated bluntly that they did not want to, or need to, get any help at the time. As most maternity hospitals in Dublin offer a social work service for single mothers, the women's comments on these services may be worth noting. They spoke in a very casual way of the contact with the social workers: "She just asked me if I was keeping the baby and I said 'Yes'", or "She said it was her job to mention adoption to me" — these recollections typify the women's record of their contact. This is not a critical reflection on these social work services: it is a reflection of the clarity and decisiveness of the choices women had made by the time that they entered hospital or encountered social work services.

In concluding this chapter it is important to recall the restrictions that must apply to the interpretations put on the data in this study. The sample is small, local, statistically unrepresentative and, in particular, it is *self-selected*. This therefore means that women in this study who chose to become lone (unmarried) mothers cannot be *compared* with women who terminated their pregnancies, or had the child adopted, or who married. It is only by comparing women who exercised *different choices* that the factors that influence women to "choose" lone motherhood can decisively be identified. The next chapter deals with those women who arrived at the destination "lone motherhood" from the starting point of marriage, by the route of marital breakdown.

4: Becoming a Lone Mother: Separated Women

4.1   Introduction

This chapter is concerned with marital breakdown — the other main route[1] through which the women in the study became lone mothers. As in the introduction to the material on unmarried lone mothers in Chapter 3, it is useful at the outset to recall the difficulties in devising unambiguous labels that accurately reflect the complexity of the women's lives and relationships.

For one woman in the sample who describes herself as "separated", this label does not properly summarise the background to her present circumstances. She had become pregnant almost 20 years ago as a schoolgirl. At about this time her father had died and her mother was unable to cope. Consequently, she entered a "mother-and-baby home" prior to the birth of her child, and through this experience she was, she said, "put off adoption". Although she recalls that her family "did not pressurise" her, she got married to the father of the child as it was "a way out". She was 16 and he 18. Moreover, he wanted to get married and, as she now sees it, "In those days it was different." Her marriage lasted six years and she had one further child. However, her first child who is now in her late teens was largely reared by her husband's extended family.

She is now living as a lone mother with her second child, now aged 14. Her husband has since entered a new relationship and has another family. This woman, now in her late thirties, has therefore confronted the dilemmas, choices and problems of both the young, unmarried pregnant girl and the adult married woman whose marriage breaks up.

A further example of the limitations of standard terms such as "separated" is that of the woman, now in her early fifties, who struggled in the interview to find a word to fit her circumstances. She lives with her daughter of 13, her other three children having grown up and left home. In a financial, sexual, social, and emotional sense, her marriage has long since ceased to exist. Her husband is an alcoholic, having failed on more than one occasion to recover from his addiction — they have over the years availed of counselling and psychiatric and other services, but this did not rescue the marriage from unhappiness and violence. Despite being legally "barred" from the house a number of years ago, he persists in using the "family home" as his address. He comes to the house most nights, sleeps in an upstairs room and in the morning leaves again — he does not speak to anyone in the house or

---

[1]   This chapter is based on material from women who are separated/ deserted/divorced — material in relation to the three widows in the sample is not included.

morning leaves again — he does not speak to anyone in the house or communicate in any way. Furthermore, he is involved in a relationship with another woman:

> *He comes into his own bedroom at night, and he leaves in the morning. He doesn't talk to the kids — he is involved in another relationship. But he just walks in the door, and up the stairs and out again in the morning. He doesn't eat with us — he has no involvement.*

In this instance, the woman considers that she no longer has a marriage and, in fact, is an active member of some groups in the Parents Alone Resource Centre. However, her husband's insistence on maintaining an address and a physical presence in the house conveys an outward impression of a marriage. More important still is that she cannot claim a social welfare payment such as Lone Parent's Allowance or Deserted Wife's Benefit; nor could she claim a Lone Parent's Tax Allowance against any income she might earn.

These two cases are included in the study and classified as "separated". All of the women in this category used the term "separated" in the interview when asked what their marital status was. None of them used the word "deserted" even though many of them were in receipt of "Deserted Wife's" payments from the Department of Social Welfare.

4.2   Selected Characteristics of Separated Women in the Sample

Table 4.1 gives summary data on the separated women in the sample. They are for the most part in their thirties and forties and, as a comparison with Table 3.1 shows, they are older than the unmarried women in the sample. (Average age for the separated women was 38.9.) Most of the separated women had married young — 63 per cent of them in the 20–24 years of age category; average age at marriage was 21.9. If the distribution of age at marriage is viewed cumulatively, it highlights their relative youth at marriage: 82 per cent had married by the age of 24.

The data on numbers of children and duration of marriage should be viewed together. In these respects the sample is quite diverse. There are small numbers of women in the sample in each category of duration of marriage, reflecting in part the diversity in the ages of the women. The modal duration of marriage category was 5–9 years but the sample includes some women married only very briefly and some married for over 15 or 20 years. (Mean and Standard Deviation for duration of marriage are 10.9 and 6.8 respectively.)

Table 4.1:   Separated Mothers — Age, Age at Marriage, Number of Children, Duration of Marriage

	No. of Children	*%*
Age Category		
20–29	3	11
30–39	12	44
40–49	8	30
50–59	4	15
Age at Marriage		
15–19	5	19
20–24	17	63
25–29	4	15
30–34	1	4
Number of Children (Total)		
1 or 2	13	48
3 or 4	6	22
5	5	19
6 or more	3	11
Duration of Marriage (Years)		
0–4	4	15
5–9	10	37
10–14	7	26
15–19	4	15
20 or more	2	7

Notes: N = 27.
Percentages may not add up to 100 per cent because of rounding.
Mean (S.D.) for Age, Age at Marriage, Number of Children and Duration of Marriage respectively are: 38.9 (8.0); 21.9 (3.5); 3.5 (2.5); and 10.9 (6.8).

The data in Table 4.1 on number of children refers to the *total* numbers of children the women have had, as distinct from the number of *dependent* children. As will be seen later, for some women in the older age groups these two categories are different. Just under half of the separated women have had one or two children, a further fifth have had three or four, a fifth have five and a small number have had six of more. In general, the demographic differences between the separated women and the unmarried women are what would be expected: the former are older on average, have a higher number of children, and are at more diverse stages in the family life cycle.

4.3   Factors Associated with Marriage Breakdown

In the study no attempt was made to analyse the "causes" of marriage breakdown. A cursory glance at the extensive bibliographies on the subject would be sufficient to highlight its complexity. Before proceeding to analyse the marital histories available in this study, however, it is necessary to distinguish in this vast repertoire of studies different *levels* of research on marital breakdown.

First, there is a significant body of research in economics, social history, sociology, law and demography on the *macro* aspects of marital breakdown — in particular, on overall levels of marital breakdown across countries and on trends over time. This type of research is essentially aimed at understanding the relationship between structural factors such as employment trends, secularisation, the welfare state or legal arrangements on the one hand, and differences across countries or changes over time in *overall rates* of marital breakdown on the other. (For bibliographies see James and Wilson, 1986, Hart, 1976.) Among the issues addressed in this type of research are:

- The possible link between income maintenance provisions for lone-parent families and a growth in the number of such families

- The role of increased incomes and employment opportunities for women and the rising level of marital breakdown

- The relationship between historical changes in values and culture — for example, the decline in religious commitment — and increased rates of divorce and marital breakdown in many countries.

In this study no attempt is made to explain the recent rise experienced in Ireland in levels of marital breakdown — rather it is taken as given on the basis of recent research (Ward, 1990; McCashin, 1993) that such a trend is now well underway. The women in this study are therefore a very small and specific subset of this rapidly increasing segment of the population.

Second, a *psychological or case-work* theme in research can be identified (see Dominian, 1968; James and Wilson, 1986; Clulow and

Mattison, 1989). The concern of this type of research is to understand the psychological and interpersonal aspects of marriage and in particular to uncover the characteristics of individuals and individuals' marriages that lead to *particular* marriages breaking down. Associated with this is the concern to evaluate various forms of intervention in marital crisis and to develop therapies. Research work in this vein would typically focus on issues such as these:

- The role of psychological disorders arising in childhood in contributing to marital problems

- The relative effectiveness of individual counselling, group therapy and other forms of intervention in resolving marital conflict

- The impact of specific personality or behavioural disorders such as alcoholism, violence or drug addiction in contributing to marital breakdown

- The strain experienced by particular families in coping with specific difficulties such as financial problems, stresses of parenthood, enforced absence caused by emigration, hospitalisation, etc.

Material on these topics arose in the interviews as a natural by-product of the interviewees' accounts of their lives and marriages. However, as the main focus of the study is on the social and economic aspects of lone motherhood, the women were not questioned in *detail* about their marriages, nor was any attempt made to examine the psychological and interpersonal aspects of their marriages.

Third, some research is concerned largely with lone motherhood as a *social and economic experience*. Such studies focus on the impact of lone motherhood on living standards, and on the role of state income maintenance and other policies in mediating the link between lone parenthood and poverty (for example, Marsden, 1973; Millar, 1991; Graham, 1987). The study reported here is primarily in this vein, attempting as it does to record and analyse the social and economic experience of the women. To understand this experience it is necessary to obtain contextual information about the women's experiences as married women, because these affect their lives as lone mothers in many respects. For example, if women were neglected financially by their former partners, they will assess their *current* economic situation partly by reference to this past experience. More generally, if the women had very negative or destructive experiences in marriage, this may strongly condition their evaluation of their lives as lone mothers.

To ensure that this link is made between the women's former

marriages and their current experience, information was collected on the following topics:

- The age at which the woman married

- The duration of their marriages

- The evolution of their marriages in terms of the number and spacing of children

- The "problem" aspects of their marriages and how these changed over time

- The "decision" to end the marriage and become lone mothers.

So, what factors were there in these women's marriages that might be associated with their eventual breakdown? Table 4.2 compiles summary information from the study, and, to set it in wider context, compares it with the evidence of O'Higgins' study of deserted women published in 1974 (O'Higgins, 1974: Table 15). These data require some explanation — they simply list the number of cases in this study, and in the O'Higgins study, in which certain patterns and behaviours were reported by the women (now separated/deserted) as having been present in their marriages. It is important to note that the categories overlap, that they are based on the wives' retrospective descriptions, and that the designations "alcoholic", "disturbed", etc. are based on the labels and categories used by the women themselves. For example, the 19 cases in this study in the category "alcoholic abuse" include all those cases in which the woman variously referred to alcoholic drink as a problem: "He was an alcoholic; "Drink was the problem"; "He drank too much".

In this study an attempt was made to record the respondents' *experiences*. They were not invited to give a considered assessment of their marriage or ascribe, as they saw it, relative degrees of importance to the various negative factors they experienced. However, some women offered, in passing, summary statements of what they perceived with hindsight to have been "the real problem".

Before reporting in detail on the material, it may be useful to consider the categories reported in Table 4.2, commencing with alcohol. This category of behaviour was the one most commonly cited — it arose in 70 per cent of the cases. Likewise in O'Higgins' study, this was the most commonly cited spousal behaviour reported by the women. Associated with this is the high level of reported violence in this study and in O'Higgins' work. As will be seen later, the violence was in some cases horrific and followed a pattern of worsening over time — a pattern noted in other Irish (Ruddle and O'Connor, 1992) as well as international studies of domestic violence.

Table 4.2:   Number and Percentage of Cases in which Certain "Negative" Factors in Marriage were Reported: Present Study and Desertion Study, 1974

	A: Present Study		B: Desertion Study	
Negative Factors	N	%	N	%
Alcohol Abuse	19	70	21	52
Violence	10	37	21	52
Pre-marital Pregnancy	8	30	13	33
Infidelity/Adultery	3	11	13	33
Disturbed Background — Husband	4	15	14	35
Disturbed Background — Wife	6	22	3	8
Irresponsibility	7	26	7	18
Average Age at Marriage	21. 9		22.7	

Notes: N (Base) study A = 27; N (Base) study B = 40.
Data for panel B from O'Higgins (1974), Table 15 and Table 10; the figures in panels A and B refer to the number of cases to which *each* factor applied and they add to more than the total N. The differences between the two studies should be noted in interpreting the table: they are two decades apart; the 1974 study was a sample of *women*, while the present study was of lone *mothers*, the 1974 study was of *deserted* women only; the methodologies of the studies differ — the 1974 study used a structured questionnaire, while the current study was qualitative in approach.

The third item — pre-marital pregnancy — is also commonly cited in both studies and again reflects findings in international research. About a third of the women in the present study offered the observation that they had conceived before marriage. As the women were not explicitly *asked* about this in this study, it is distinctly possible that the actual figure may be higher. Clearly, as the case material below will reveal, pre-marital pregnancy is associated with youthful marriage. Only three women in this study mentioned infidelity or adultery on their husband's part, while greater numbers mentioned that either their own or their husband's childhood background had been disturbed in some way, or that their husband was an addictive gambler or financially irresponsible.

In a separate row in Table 4.2, the average age at marriage is given: 21.9 in the present study and 22.7 in that of O'Higgins. The distribution of age at marriage in the study of domestic violence in Limerick (Ruddle, Lyons et al., 1992) also revealed a concentration in the younger age groups. Ninety per cent of Limerick women using the ADAPT refuge had married at or before the age of 24, compared with a figure of 82 per cent in this study (see Table 4.1 above) and 70 per cent in O'Higgins' analysis (O'Higgins, 1974: Table 10).

4.4 From Marriage to Marriage Breakdown

To convey the process of marital breakdown as experienced by the women in the study, it is necessary to move beyond the simple categorisation in Table 4.2 and to illustrate the way in which the women's marriages actually evolved. A three-fold typology[2] of the cases is used to divide them into broadly similar types of marital experiences.

First, there is a category of women whose marriages were relatively *brief*, seven years or less, who are themselves relatively young and whose educational qualifications (Leaving Certificate) mark them out as significantly more educated than the sample of cases as a whole. In these cases the women made decisions rather quickly and definitely when faced with difficult relationships, or readily accepted that the marriage was effectively over. Other women in the sample either accepted or endured similar circumstances, or only became aware of problems, or experienced problems, after a long period of time. The former category can conveniently be labelled "short marriages". It includes 10 cases (over one-third of the sample), all of whose marriages lasted only seven years or less — considerably below the mean duration of marriage for the sample as a whole (10.9 years).

Betty's marriage illustrates this category of circumstances rather well. She is now 27, has two children, aged six and four, and lives with her children in her parents' home, with her parents and one of her sisters, aged 24. Betty has lived in the area from the time she was a small child, went to school there and stayed on in school till 17, when she took her Leaving Certificate. At this point she took a job in a restaurant and became a trainee cook. After about two years she met her husband, and they became engaged after six months. In 1986, when she was 20, she became pregnant, and she got married in the Spring of 1987 after her first child was born.

---

[2] This typology successfully reflects the mix of cases: there are only three cases which do not unambiguously fit into a category.

In Betty's account, she did not marry because of the pregnancy: "It was something I was going to do anyway. " After marriage, she moved to an outer, newly developing suburb and conceived again after a few months. However, when she was three months pregnant her partner effectively deserted her. She said, when asked about the background to the marriage breakdown:

> *He just went to a stag party and didn't come home. And a couple of days later he said this was it! Basically he wanted to leave.*

She stated that she had had no foreboding: "I had no inkling at all." She returned to live with her parents and made one unsuccessful effort to obtain maintenance. He "just disappeared" when he was summoned to appear in court about maintenance obligations. The net outcome for Betty was that at 22 she was pregnant, had one child of about one and was separated after less than one year of marriage. Her family was supportive and helpful: "I have a great family."

Many of the elements of this case are reflected in the case of Maura. She is 24 and has a boy of about two. Like Betty, she had lived in the area all of her life and went to school there. She stayed at school till 17, and left with the Leaving Certificate. After school she took a secretarial course, finished this at 18, and went to work in an office for a year. At 19 she went to live in London and there met her partner. She got married at 21; her husband whom she had known for about two months was 28. In her own words: "I knew him about two months, but at the time it was one of these whirlwind romances, you know. I felt I was madly in love".

Two months after their marriage, they moved address to an outer suburb of London, at which point she experienced the beginning of the end of the relationship.

> *Well we got married in December and we were living in a place, Oxted, at the time. We moved from Oxted to Kent, Bromley in Kent, in about February and things weren't going too well — we were getting bored. I was working away as a training surveyor and he was a bar manager, so as far as the financial end of things go, we were fine. But we came home in April for a weekend to see my Mam and Dad because they hadn't met him before. So that went off pretty well and then we went away to Tenerife. It was great. But about two weeks after, that was May, about two weeks after we came back, he started to get violent towards me and he really knocked me about quite a bit, so I left him for about two or three weeks and I went to stay with my brother.*

Maura then attempted to reconstruct the marriage. They went to live in another city and "he was quite good for a couple of months". However, after five months, the violence resumed and she was now pregnant. At this juncture she was quite definite, as were her parents, that she should leave her husband: "I decided there was no way I wanted my child to grow up in that kind of environment." She took the opportunity to leave and return to Dublin with her parents on a weekend when they were visiting her brother who was then living elsewhere in England. That weekend her husband became very angry and violent at the prospect of her seeing her parents when they came to visit them, and this situation precipitated her leaving him:

> *Basically he did not want me seeing my family. So he knocked me about quite a bit because I wouldn't tell my father not to come and see me. So he got me in trouble one day with meeting my family. So the next morning he did not go into work and I was due to go into town. So, I went into town and got my giro that I was due to get and basically left straight away with some calls like his sister and came home then with my family that weekend.*

As this situation unfolded it was clear that her parents would not only accept the situation if she left her husband, but that they would actively help her to do so. She recalls her father's role that weekend:

> *They wanted me out of the situation straight away. Before I left I rang and I said, "I'm going to come over to you." And he said "He's been hitting you, hasn't he?" And I said "Well, Yes." So he said "Well, just get the next train and come over to me straight away."*

She returned to Dublin that weekend with her family and commenced living with them. At the time of interview she was still living with her parents who have been supportive of her and her small child all of the time since.

These two cases between them illustrate most of the elements that characterise the type of marriage experienced in these "short" marriages:

- Marriage at a very young age

- Pre-marital pregnancy

- Short relationship prior to marriage

- Decisive end to the marriage and unwillingness to tolerate the situation

- Support from parental family.

Typically, these women are younger, better educated and more likely to be employed (full-time or part-time) at the time of interview. Another case in this category is that of Finola. In her case, she left school at 18 with the Leaving Certificate. She wanted to train further in some field but because of the financial pressures of a large family at home she could not afford to. At the age of 20, she married after a short relationship, and had a baby girl when she was 22. However, she was married for only three years. Her husband had a "good job" but was "selfish with money". He had, she recalls, "a basic disinterest in paying bills — it was money for himself for drink and so on". She succinctly stated that: "I decided to call it a day." Currently she lives with her daughter, now six, and is supported by a secure maintenance agreement with her husband. Her family agreed with her decision: "They said 'You did the right thing.'"

Other examples of this type include:

- One woman now in her early thirties who married when pregnant one year after she left school with her Leaving Certificate and who remained married for six years to a husband who was "irresponsible with money"

- A woman in her late thirties, with a son of three, living with her parents again, who had married a man — who transpired to be a heavy drinking, addictive gambler — when she became pregnant after a "holiday romance" with him

- A young mother of two children, who obtained a good clerical job after she obtained her Leaving Certificate, and married when 22 a man who was "irresponsible with money" and had a personality problem from childhood because of "a domineering mother".

On the whole, the lives of these separated women are akin to those of the (mostly) young unmarried women described in Chapter 3. Their similarities — youth, stage of the family cycle, brevity of relationship with partners, role of parental support — are a reminder of the continuities between the circumstances of unmarried and separated women and of the need for caution in using the "married–unmarried" classification. At this point, we turn to a second and very different category of marital breakdown.

This second category comprises *older women who were married for a long time* and whose marriages were difficult from a very early stage. In their cases the marriage was a gradual process of discovery and change, rather than a definite, clear decision, as was the case with the first group of women. There are nine cases in this category — a third of the sample, with ages ranging from 38 (youngest) to 57 (eldest); in six of these nine cases drunkenness and violence on the husband's part affected the marriage from the outset.

Maeve, aged 51 and the mother of four children, experienced a marriage virtually identical to the "ideal type" summarised above. She had grown up in a rural area, left school after obtaining her Leaving Certificate and come to Dublin to work in an office job after she had completed a secretarial course in her home town. Until she got married at the age of 25, she shared a flat with her sisters — on marriage, she and her husband acquired a new house in the area where she has lived every since. They had four children — the eldest is now a young adult living independently and the remaining three are aged 22, 20 and 14. During their marriage, her husband was continuously employed in a semi-skilled occupation and supported her and the children: "He looked after us all — he handed me his cheque every week."

As Maeve recalls it, her partner — to whom she was married for 19 years — could be "quite violent" and could be "in and out of drink". Over time, Maeve said, she was: "changing, and beginning to answer back". However, it was her husband's violence towards her daughters that made the situation intolerable for her. When her eldest daughter was 17, a particularly nasty incident occurred:

> *She came in late at one in the morning. Next day, he confronted her and smashed a cup in the kitchen; he dragged her and kicked her and threw her out the front door — she wasn't ever, ever to come back again. There had been incidents like this before. Another time I rescued Cliona* [second daughter] *— he came after her with a stick with nails in it.*

These particular incidents were occurring in the sixteenth year of the marriage. A period of two years then ensued in which her husband came and went, and during which she obtained a barring order. He breached this, was jailed for contempt, and eventually relented by leaving and moving out of Dublin. As recounted by Maeve, the situation was worsening over time and her husband's obsessive behaviour and the threat to her daughters' safety impelled her to change her situation. Her immediate family, including her mother and brother, sympathised with her decision, having also been assaulted and abused by her husband. She did not resort to counselling, marriage guidance or social work services of any kind in ending the marriage — she did, however, avail of voluntary legal aid services in relation to the barring order.

Elements of this story can be found also in the case of Christine who is now aged 38 and has four children. She married at 21, and after living first with relatives, and then in a flat, she moved to live in the area. When she moved to the house in the area, they already had one baby and she was pregnant again. At this point, she was a full-time housewife — she had worked in the Civil Service until marriage. She recalls that from the time their first child was born the situation began to deteriorate, prompting her to move house into the area, and to move again after that.

> *At that stage things started to go badly wrong with the marriage. I was putting it down to the fact that we were cooped up with one another and we moved to Coolock. Things went from bad to worse and, more or less jumping from the frying pan into the fire, to a transfer to Darndale, and I suppose from the time I lived there I would have preferred to live alone — he was never there.... He became very violent, gambled, drank, and left us with no money — he was like that.*

Christine's story is akin to that of Maeve in these respects: the violence worsened over time; violence against the children finally impelled a change; and her own independence enraged her husband even further — she was extensively involved in community activities.

> *And the rows got more violent. He actually tried to wreck the home. He threatened the kids with a carving knife so I said "That's it I can't take any more."*

It was the threat to the children that ended the marriage: some time before this he had beaten her up badly when she was very pregnant: "He battered me and I ended up having an emergency section on her." But her final decision awaited the actual threat to the *children*. Christine recalled that her husband was an alcoholic. She had consulted with a psychiatrist about his behaviour and this led her to an analysis of her marriage.

> *I got involved in Darndale from more or less the time we moved in. I thought to myself: "If I have to live here, I am not going to stay in the house all day...." But I firmly believe now that it was a jealousy situation — that he wanted me at home all the time....*

And one of the biggest hang-ups he had was why did I have to be a perfect wife and mother, that I could cope with the kids, I could cope with all he was doing and still find time for outside interests — and that wasn't in his vocabulary at all, he just couldn't handle that.

In all, she was married 14 years. She finally barred her alcoholic husband from the home after being beaten when pregnant with their last child and after his threats to the other children. Her account of the long endurance of the situation ended with the statement: "I mean, I took my marriage vows very seriously."

These patterns can be seen also in the other cases of these "long-suffering" marriages. For example:

- One woman, now aged 45, with three children at home, had married at 20 when pregnant, having been "pressurised", and over a period of 18 years endured violence and drunkenness made tolerable by occasional retreats to her mother's house — she eventually sought help from a social worker, having become depressed and attempted suicide, joined Al-Anon[3] which "gave me choices" and which helped to decide on a barring order and a separation after 18 years of marriage

- A woman who is now 41, with two children, was married 11 years to a man who was "always a heavy drinker"; two years after being married, he became violent when she was pregnant, and at this early stage: "I was pregnant — the relationship was over — he had hit me"; she stayed a further nine years and finally separated when his violence against her and the children was intolerable — for the last two years of their marriage she and the children locked themselves in an upstairs bedroom every night at 9 o'clock.

Finally, in this selection of cases of marital breakdown we turn to a category of marriages which — like those just illustrated above — were of long duration. The distinction between this category and the third category of this study is that in the latter the marriages were uneventful and — to the women at least — normal and happy for a lengthy period. In these marriages it was only after a considerable period that the relationship changed and deteriorated drastically, to the point where separation, (or desertion) took place. The term *disimproved* marriages can be used as a convenient caption for these experiences.

---

[3] An abbreviation of the name of the organisation for the spouses and partners of alcoholics.

The most striking illustration of this pattern concerns Laura, (mentioned at the outset of Chapter 3), who married when pregnant at the age of 16, and separated some six years later from her husband who was the same age as her. She then became involved with a second partner and between both relationships she has had 10 children. Laura described the second "marriage" — the subject of the commentary here — as "very happy". Her second partner was involved as a father and cared for their new family of four children as well as the six children from her first relationship. Her second marriage lasted 17 years, at which point the family home contained seven of the children as well as her partner and herself. The breakdown of the marriage, in her account, took the form of desertion, and she was bewildered by it.

During this relationship, her partner was employed for a long time as a long-distance lorry driver and supported her and the children.

> *He did long-distance lorry driving, and sometimes he would say he would like to have a job at home all the time because the kids would miss him terribly and he loved being with them, you know, like he was definitely a home person ... he would fix everything, you know? He would make things out of little or nothing, he was great, you know, great with the children, great with me.*

Some years before the desertion, her partner had lost his job and was employed only occasionally. Over time, he developed ulcers and required hospitalisation and medication. In Laura's recollection, this led to some arguments between them — he refused to give up smoking, for example and on one occasion discharged himself from hospital. It was during one such argument three years prior to the interview that the stage was set for his departure. He left the house to go to the doctor but never returned.

> *Every time I'd see him rolling a cigarette, I'd just go, "Oh God, you know, he is killing himself" and as a result, like, he couldn't stop smoking ... we were arguing and fighting all the time and this day he decided to go over to the doctor — he went out, we were fighting like mad. I said "Go on, get out", you know, like this, so I was really worried, you know, and he never came back — he never went to his doctor, you know. He arrived in England, sent me a card, told me not to be worrying, you know, I was in shock, I really was in shock, you know, and he told me he sent word to the kids and everything because like they were in bits, you know, "Where's Daddy?" and all this, and he was telling them all he was going to do this, that and the other. Alan, as I said, fell off the horse and he phoned up — I don't know if I was*

in the hospital or not, and Alan was unconscious and when he came around he was saying "Daddy's in the waiting room", you know, and I was saying "yes", you know. The others were going mad, you know, and he phoned up and he didn't know this had happened and Sorcha just screamed at him, screamed, and she told him never to phone again, not to bother writing, nobody wanted to know about him. What she was trying to say was "Come home" — we needed him badly here — and she said to me afterwards he was sobbing, he was really crying and we never heard a word, not a thing after that....

The second instance of this type concerns Leona, now in her early fifties, who has five children ranging in age from 19 to 7. She was born into a large family on the Northside of Dublin, left school at 13 without any qualifications and worked in a variety of jobs in shops until 21. At that point, she married a man about the same age as herself and they began their married life living in a flat in the city centre. After five years, they moved out of the inner city and bought a private house in the suburbs, with a mortgage from Dublin Corporation.

As she now recalls it, their marriage was happy for the first 10 years. He had a "good job" with "good wages" and their relationship was close: he would phone her "two or three times a day" from work. Then his regular phone calls diminished and ceased entirely and she discovered that he was in a relationship with someone else. Leona explained that he had wanted more children — they had three — and she did not. In this crisis she agreed to another pregnancy "to see would it work", but when this new baby was six months old they separated: "I asked him to go." However, with her agreement, he returned six months later and she conceived again. Meanwhile, it appeared that her husband's affair was continuing and a violent confrontation took place when she tracked her husband and his girlfriend to a city-centre pub one evening. There she was assaulted by the other woman and left with bruises, a broken rib, and burst blood vessels: at this time, unknown to her husband or his girlfriend, she was pregnant.

This marriage, then, ended somewhat abruptly and in deep crisis. Partly as a result of the assault, she was ill and required hospitalisation twice thereafter — her children had to go into care during these periods of hospitalisation. In all, Leona spent five months in hospital, and when she returned home after the end of the second spell she commenced her role as a lone parent.

Other examples of this scenario of long marriages which go into decline include the following:

- A woman aged 53, who has 10 children and who was married for 18 years, the first 10 of which were uneventful — then "He started to drink and gamble and it got worse and worse" until they separated some eight years later

- A mother of four children, all still in school, who was married for 21 years until a year and a half prior to the interview — for 10 years she noticed "nothing wrong", but then realised that her self-employed partner "drank a lot" and neglected money matters. She was unsuccessful in her attempts to get him to attend counselling or mediation.

4.5   Marital Breakdown — An Overview

In the section above, the aim has been to convey the experience of marriage breakdown as reported by the women in the interviews. The classification of types of marital breakdown was devised essentially on the basis of the duration of the marriages. It is important to note that while the classification is a useful means of summarising broadly similar types of marital careers, it is also directly relevant to the *social* and *economic* aspects of lone parenthood. As will be seen later, women who have been married a long time are at a later stage of the family cycle and face a different mix of needs (for example, more children to maintain) and resources (housing, consumer durables, children with incomes) than their much younger counterparts, married only very briefly.

Bearing in mind that the material here is confined to the women's accounts of their marriages, the question can be asked whether there are any underlying common dimensions to the variety of experiences recorded here. When the specific histories and circumstances of the marriages are set to one side, it is possible to observe a general tension, if not a struggle, for *control*, in many, although not all, cases. This tension took the form, invariably, of the husband's attempts to retain control of financial resources or of his wife's life and activities. A common element in many of the cases was the husband's retention of income as "his own" for gambling or drinking. However, equally common was the husband's effort to keep his wife "at home — with the kids", by insisting on another child, or by ignoring or belittling her attempts to be involved in activities outside the home (adult education, community involvement, etc.). Differences among the women in the sample can therefore be seen as differences in the type of response women offered to their experience of being "controlled".

Future research could test this line of interpretation more fully. In particular, it would be important to establish whether the individual responses were shaped, and in what way, by wider social and cultural changes. The women in this study married, had families and separated during a period of rapid social change and of intense and widespread debate about the nature of the family, gender relations and a whole array of issues affecting relationships between men and women in society. None of the women expressed their experiences in these terms, nor were they invited to. But any satisfactory analysis of the rise in marital breakdown in Ireland must link broad social influences to the contexts in which individuals act and to the frames of reference they adopt.

As with the experience of young, unmarried women, it is remarkable the degree to which women did *not* avail of state services or support. About six of them at some point availed of a social worker, counsellor or marriage guidance or mediation counsellor, and many of them approached the Gardaí and Courts when faced with a crisis. It is difficult to assess with the limited material here what *effect* these services had on women's decisions. One recurring theme in the women's remarks was that they experienced that they had "options" — this kind of comment was offered in relation to Al-Anon, Health Board Social Workers, Resource Centres and private counselling. In short, women whose situations are very difficult may feel a sense of choice if given *any form* of support and encouragement.

Finally, not one woman mentioned her financial situation or her potential social welfare entitlement as one of the ameliorating aspects of her decision to separate. As will be seen later, the search for income support in the form of maintenance, earnings and social welfare was one that appeared to arise as a *consequence* of the marriage breakdown. It is not clear from the evidence of these cases how the social security system can be seen as directly implicated in the process of marital breakdown.

5: Poverty and the Lone Mother

5.1   Introduction

In the previous chapters the processes that led to the women becoming
lone mothers were described. The focus now turns to one of the central aspects of the women's lives as lone mothers — their incomes and
financial circumstances. Inescapably, this leads into issues of poverty
and deprivation, as most of the women in the study have incomes that
are low relative to the incomes of the generality of families.

The chapter is structured as follows. Section 5.2 below gives basic
descriptive information about the amounts and sources of the respondents' incomes. In Section 5.3, this study's approach to "poverty" and
"deprivation" are set out explicitly and then the income data from the
respondents are analysed to assess the *adequacy* of their incomes —
whether they are poor. Section 5.4 extends the discussion of poverty
beyond incomes and income adequacy to examine social deprivation
— the respondents' actual standard of living.

5.2   Sources and Amounts of Income

In the interviews, respondents were asked about the amounts of their
income from all sources. For most, this income comprised a weekly
social welfare payment, an additional fuel voucher where the respondent was a household head, and a monthly child benefit payment. In
very few cases were respondents receiving regular maintenance payments from the father of their children, or earning income from part-
time or full-time work. To set the income information in context, it
should be recalled that the interviews were undertaken in the Spring
of 1993. The social welfare payment rates then in force were those
announced in the Budget of 1992 and implemented in July 1992.
Those interviewees receiving social welfare payments were, at the
time of interview, in receipt of the rates enforced since July 1992.

The single most common income profile in the study would be
that of a woman receiving a weekly social welfare payment, the
monthly child benefit and (in the majority of cases) the fuel
voucher payment for the winter months. For a woman with one
child, this income at the time of interview would consist of:

	£
Lone Parent's Allowance	71.80
Child Benefit (Weekly equivalent)	3.95
Fuel Voucher	8.00
Total[1]	83.75

---

[1]   The Child Benefit payment is calculated by dividing the monthly rate
by four and the fuel voucher figure includes the additional smokeless

Therefore, a woman with one child would have an income of about £84 per week, and £75 during the non-winter months when the fuel voucher was not in payment.

There is some variation in the sample on this illustrative pattern. Some respondents received rent allowances from the Health Board; a very few women had regular maintenance payments from spouses; some women were temporarily "employed" on training schemes and receiving an additional income. On the whole, however, the women's financial circumstances were shaped by the social welfare system.

Tables 5.1 and 5.2 below summarise the key data on income sources and income levels for all of the women in the study. In Table 5.1, it can be seen that most of the women rely on social welfare (or SWA administered by the Health Board) for their main[2] source of income. This reliance on State social welfare payments reflects the fact that the majority of the women (59 per cent) are full-time mothers. The top panel of Table 5.1 shows a figure of 37 per cent for economically active; in fact, less than half the women in this category are actually employed *full-time* and the remainder are unemployed, on training schemes, or working part-time. Further information on social welfare payments is given in the middle panel of Table 5.1: this refers to the type of social welfare payment being received (whether or not it was the woman's main source of income). The Lone Parent's Allowance and Deserted Wife's Benefit — in that order — were the two most common social welfare payments.

Data on the role of maintenance are given in the lower panels of Table 5.1; these data are not relevant to the two widows in the sample. Three-quarters of the women *never* receive maintenance payments. Specifically in relation to the week before the interview, 84 per cent had not received any maintenance payment from the father of their children. Clearly, maintenance has a very limited role in the finances of these women.

The consistency of the data in Table 5.1 with other relevant findings should be noted. Work by Millar (1989) and McCashin (1993) for the UK and Ireland respectively showed a high level of dependence among lone-mother families on State transfer payments and a low level of labour market participation. Likewise, the analyses by Ward (1990) for Ireland and Bradshaw and Millar for the UK (1991) revealed low levels of maintenance support and infrequent maintenance payments

---

fuel allowance which applied in certain areas of Dublin, including the study area.

[2] "Main" source of income refers to the source of income which provides the largest regular amount of income.

from fathers. The small local sample for this study may therefore be somewhat typical, in respect of their income levels and sources, of that subset of lone mothers who have low incomes and who are out of the labour market and largely dependent on State social security payments.

Table 5.1:   Economic Status and Income Sources of Lone Mothers

	N	%
Economic Status		
Full-time Mother	30	59
Economically Active	19	37
Other	2	4
All	51	100
Main Income Source		
Social Welfare (incl. SWA)	36	69
Earnings/Training Allowances	13	25
Maintenance	3	6
All	52	100
Type of Social Welfare		
Lone Parent's Allowance	21	40
Deserted Wife's Benefit	15	28
Widow's Pension	2	4
SWA	2	4
None	13	25
All	53	101
Maintenance Received Last Week?		
Yes	8	16
No	43	84
All	51	100
Frequency of Maintenance		
Never	38	75
Sometimes	5	10
Regularly	8	16
All	51	101

Notes: The numbers on which the percentages are based vary from one panel of the table to another: the maintenance information does not apply to the two widows, for example. "Economically active" includes those working full-time or part-time and those who are on "training schemes" or unemployed.

Some percentages do not add to 100 because of rounding.

Table 5.2 summarises the information on weekly income levels. As there are families of different sizes in the sample, it is necessary to standardise the weekly income figures in order to compare the incomes of families of different sizes. This is done in the conventional way by applying per capita *equivalence scales* to the income figures. In this instance, the scales used in the official Household Budget Survey and also in the recent work on poverty and household incomes by researchers at the ESRI (Callan, Nolan et al., 1989) were applied. The scales are as follows:

Head of Household	1.0
Each Additional Adult	0.66
Each Child	0.33

The CSO/ESRI practice of weighting all 0–14 year olds as children, and others in the family (apart from the lone mother) as 0.66 is followed. It should be noted that these weightings were implicit in the structure of income maintenance payments in Ireland in 1987, the year to which the income data in these representative studies refer.

In applying the scales, the actual income figure is simply divided by the number of "adult equivalents" in the family to obtain a per capita equivalent income figure. For example, a lone mother with an income of £100 per week, rearing two children, one aged 15 and one aged 10, would have a per capita equivalent weekly income of £50.25 (£100 / (1.0 + 0.66 + 0.33)).

One important point to note about the income information is that it refers to the lone-parent *family* unit comprising the mother and her *dependent* children, and not to the *household* unit. In other words, if a lone mother and her child(ren) were part of a wider household (for example, living with her parents) no attempt was made to collect data on incomes of other household members, or to calculate the per capita equivalent income on the basis of the full household.[3] Almost all of the children of the women in the study were financially dependent. In the very small number of cases of older or adolescent children who *had* incomes, these were not aggregated with the mothers' incomes, nor

---

[3]   This is a significant limitation on the income information, but a necessary one. Pilot interviews revealed that where women were sharing homes — in almost all of these cases they were in their parents' homes — they were very vague about the incomes of other household members. Any attempt to obtain accurate information would have been fruitless and would have hampered the conduct of the interview overall.

were these secondary "earners" included in the count of adult equivalents. This procedure allows the consistent adherence to the lone-mother family (of mother and economically dependent children) as the unit for analysis of family incomes.

Table 5.2:   **Summary of Income Information for Lone-Mother Family Units (Category of Weekly per capita Equivalent Income, £)**

1. Weekly Income	*N*	*%*	*Cumulative %*
20–39	1	2	2
40–59	20	38	40
60–79	14	26	66
80–99	13	25	91
100+	5	9	100
Total	53	100	
2. Weekly Income plus Fuel Voucher	*N*	*%*	
20–39	1	2	2
40–59	17	32	34
60–79	17	32	66
80–99	13	25	91
100+	5	9	100
Total	53	100	
3. Weekly Income plus Fuel Voucher and Child Benefit	*N*	*%*	
20–39	0	0	0
40–59	15	28	28
60–79	11	21	49
80–99	18	34	83
100 +	9	17	100
Total	53	100	
4. Weekly Income and Child Benefit	*N*	*%*	
20–39	0	0	0
40–59	18	34	34
60–79	9	17	51
80–99	18	34	85
100+	8	15	100
Total	53	100	

All of the panels in Table 5.2 present income information standard-ised on a per capita equivalent basis. The top panel refers simply to the weekly income received by the women in the form of social wel-fare payments or other income. To these figures are added the weekly fuel voucher (£8.00 per week for the winter months for respondents who were heads of households and receiving social welfare) for some respondents; these figures are given in the second panel. The third panel adds Child Benefit payments to the income figures in panel 2, while the fourth panel is based on the weekly income figure plus Child Benefit (with the fuel vouchers excluded).

Each set of figures is based on a specific measure of resources. The weekly income figure refers, literally, to the amount of income received per week. The fuel voucher is *not* income in the sense that, although it adds to the family's *resources*, it is assigned to fuel consumption and is received for only part of the year. Child Benefit unambiguously forms part of regular income and can logically be added to weekly income to arrive at a measure of the *regular income* at the family's disposal. Table 5.2 attempts to convey a profile of the incomes of the families according to the various combinations of incomes and resources.

The first point to observe about the data is that the vast majority of the families have a (per capita equivalent) weekly income in the range under £100 — whichever measure is adopted. If the regular" income concept of weekly income and Child Benefit is taken, then 85 per cent have an income of £99 or less, and about half have £79 or less. One-third (34 per cent) have an income below the very stringent threshold of £59. Second, the frequency distribution of incomes does not vary significantly from one income measure to another. This can be attributed to the limited arithmetical effect of the inclu-sion/exclusion of fuel vouchers/Child Benefit on per capita adjusted incomes. Few families are re-classified from one income category to another, as the income categories are wide relative to the amount of families' incomes.[4]

To illustrate the pattern of incomes, the very common instance in the sample of women in receipt of the Lone Parent's Allowance as their sole weekly income can be noted. Such a woman with one child would have a per capita weekly disposable income of £53.98; if the "child" were aged 14 or over it would be weighted in per capita terms as 0.66 (rather than 0.33) and the income (per capita equivalent)

---

[4]   For example, adding a monthly Child Benefit figure for one child to weekly income increases the latter figure by a mere £2.96 (£15.80 divided by four to convert to a weekly figure, divided by 1.33 to adjust to a per capita equivalent amount).

would, correspondingly, be calculated as £43.25. Cases such as these in the sample would be classified in panels 1 and 4 of Table 5.2 in the £40–£59 income range. Another common pattern was that of the separated women in receipt of Deserted Wife's Benefit (which is not means tested) and supplementing this benefit with part-time employment or a training allowance. For example, one woman had a weekly income of £248 from a combination of Deserted Wife's Benefit and net earnings from a full-time job (the latter amounting to £112). When the per capita adjustment is made to her income to allow for her five dependent children (one older, four younger), her per capita equivalent weekly income is £83.20. In the top panel of the table, she is therefore classified in the £80–£99 range. With Child Benefit included in her income, it is calculated as £91.02 per capita equivalent per week, and in the lowest panel of the table, she is also classified in the £80–£99 range.

5.3 Adequacy of Income

The study sample was designed to include mostly women on low incomes. As the details in Table 5.2 show, this has been realised, as the women's incomes fall within a relatively narrow range. The lowest weekly income (per capita) including Child Benefit was £39.85 and the highest £143.57. Median income (weekly income plus Child Benefit per capita equivalent) was £79.70. While it has been established in detail that the sample in this study comprises low-income lone mothers, the more important question, however, concerns the women's *relative* incomes. If their incomes are low, *how* low are they compared with the incomes of families in general? Are the women in the study sample actually *poor*?

To address these questions, a *relative* approach to poverty was adopted by comparing the incomes of the families in this study with a measure of incomes in the community at large. This is a relative income definition of poverty and is based ultimately on the work of Peter Townsend (Townsend, 1979). The approach is summarised in the statement that:

> Individuals, families and groups in the population can be said to be in poverty when they lack the resources to obtain the types of diet, participate in the activities and have the living conditions and amenities which are customary, or are at least widely encouraged or approved, in the societies to which they belong. Their resources are so seriously below those commanded by the average individual or family that they are, in effect, excluded from ordinary living patterns, customs and activities. (Townsend, 1979: 21).

In summary, this approach asserts that poverty must be viewed in a social context. Families are "poor" if, *because of lack of income*, they cannot buy what are regarded as necessities or engage in the activities and customs that are viewed as normal in their society.[5] To apply this approach requires us, first, to document the families' incomes and, second, to describe the actual living standards of the families and how these are determined by their income levels.

The incomes of the families in the study were compared with a measure of incomes in the population at large. It was *not* possible to do this in the appropriate fashion by analysing the incomes in the sample in the light of statistically representative data on household and family incomes in 1993. Such data are not available.[6] In their place, the average per capita equivalent income in 1987 in the ESRI's national poverty survey (Callan, Nolan et al., 1989: 63) was identified. This was £85.50 using the 1.0, 0.66, 0.33 equivalence scale. This figure was then updated by the growth in personal income in the economy as a whole, by applying the growth rate for 1987–92 for Personal Income as recorded in the National Income Accounts (Central Statistics Office, 1994B: Tables 9, 12).

The updated estimate of personal income per capita equivalent is £116.28 per week. This figure allows "poverty lines" for the households in the sample to be constructed. For example, 50 per cent of average income (per capita equivalent) is £58.14; a "poverty line" at this level for a woman and one child (under 14) is £77.33 — the £58.14 figure multiplied by the number of per capita equivalents. This procedure can be replicated for families of different sizes and at different proportions of estimated average income; families can then be assessed as lying "above" or "below" a specified poverty line.

The current exercise entailed a comparison between the actual income figures in the sample, specifically weekly income and Child Benefit, and the estimated poverty lines. The logic of the relative-income approach suggests that incomes may be inadequate to prevent deprivation if they are significantly less than average incomes.

---

[5] There is considerable and contentious body of research on concepts and measures of poverty (for reviews of this literature see Whelan et al., 1993; Piachaud, 1987; Townsend, 1979; Callan and Nolan, 1989). This study confines itself, however, to applying a relative income/relative deprivation approach, in line with the recent work on poverty in the Republic of Ireland (Callan, Nolan et al., 1989).

[6] The ESRI poverty survey data was collected in 1987 and a "re-run" of this was commenced in 1994. Likewise, the Household Budget Survey conducted by the CSO.

However, this methodology does not rely on the choice of one poverty line — it is most appropriately applied when alternative lines
are applied and the results for these lines are compared.

Table 5.3 below gives the results of this exercise. It can be seen
that about one-third of the families fall below the threshold of half
of (estimated) average income and just under 50 per cent below a
threshold of 60 per cent of average family income. The estimates of
"poverty" are therefore highly sensitive to the choice of "poverty line".
In this sample the incomes of the families fall within a relatively narrow range and thus any manipulation of the "poverty line" leads to a
noticeable shift in the estimate of poverty.

**Table 5.3:   Numbers and Percentage of Lone-Mother
Families Below "Poverty Lines" of 40, 50 and 60
per cent of Estimated Average Income**

	Percentage of Average Income		
	40%	*50%*	*60%*
Number	5	17	25
%	9.4	32.1	47.2
1987 ESRI %	7.5	17.5	30.0

Note: See text for definitions.

The final row of Table 5.3 gives some relevant comparison with the
ESRI's national estimates of poverty in 1987 for all households. These
latter figures are based on the original 1987 average income data —
they refer to *households*, and they are based on the same equivalence
scales as were used in this study. At the 60 per cent line the lone-
mother sample shows a poverty risk of 47 per cent compared with 30
per cent and at the 50 per cent line the risk is 32 per cent for the lone-
mother sample in contrast to 17.5 per cent for the national sample.
However, at the more stringent threshold, 40 per cent of average income, the risks are very similar. This may be because of the relative
levels of social welfare payments. At these very low-income levels,
where social welfare income is a central contribution to family income,
the social welfare income of lone-mother families may leave them marginally less likely to fall below an extremely low "poverty line" than
other low-income families receiving social welfare (McCashin, 1993).

Table 5.4 shows the risk of relative income poverty for families of
different types in 1987 — these data are derived from the nationally

representative Household Budget Survey. At a relative income line of 50 per cent of mean income, single and separated lone parents face poverty risks of 35 per cent and 28 per cent respectively. Table 5.4 also shows that large *two-parent* families face a high risk of relative income poverty: 30.2 per cent in the case of two-parent families with four or more children.

Table 5.4: **Percentage of Households Below Alternative Poverty Lines for Lone-Parent, Two-Parent and Other Households, per capita Equivalence Scale 1**

	Poverty Lines		
	40%	*50%*	*60%*
Lone Parent: Single	1.5	35.0	79.9
Lone Parent: "Separated"	15.5	27.6	64.3
Lone Parent: Widowed	—	14.0	42.1
Two Parents, One Child	3.5	13.2	22.6
Two Parents, Two Children	3.4	14.0	22.4
Two Parents, Three Children	4.9	19.8	31.1
Two Parents, Four or More Children	9.9	30.2	43.7
Other Households	3.8	9.7	23.5
All	4.5	13.5	26.8

Source: McCashin, 1993, Table 2.9.

A more focused set of comparisons is given in Table 5.5. This table confines the data to families where the head of the household is out of work or not economically active. In this context, the relative risks of poverty are reversed. These two-parent families face very high risks of falling below the 50 per cent relative income line — for families with one child, the figure is 47 per cent and for those with two the risk is 58 per cent. These very high risks contrast with the figure of 39 per cent for single lone parents and 25 per cent and 19 per cent for separated and widowed lone parents, respectively.

In interpreting the sample data and the existing published data on the risk of relative income poverty it should be recalled that only one type of family — low-income, lone-mother families is included in this study. While the figures for this study quantify in detail the extent to which the low-income, social-welfare dependent families in this study may fall below average incomes, they reveal nothing about the incomes of *other types* of families — such as two-parent families affected by unemployment — who may also be susceptible to relative income poverty.

Table 5.5:   Percentage of Households Below the 50 per cent Poverty Line for Households where Head of Household is Out of Work (2-Adult Households) or Not Economically Active (Lone-Parent Households)

	Number	*%*
Lone Parent: Single	43	38.8
Lone Parent: "Separated"	61	24.8
Lone Parent: Widowed	28	18.5
Two Parents, One Child	92	47.0
Two Parents, Two Children	124	57.9
Two Parents, Three Children	119	67.0
Two Parents, Four or More Children	157	79.4
Other Households	401	39.0
All	919	53.5

Source: McCashin, 1993, Table 2.11.

Such data as are available from published studies suggest that on a relative income basis, lone-mother families largely dependent on social welfare may be no more prone to "poverty" than other families who are also reliant on social welfare because of unemployment, sickness or other contingencies. The reason for this is, in large measure, the relative treatment of one- and two-parent families in the social security/taxation system. Specifically, for all low-income families, social welfare is crucial in determining their incomes. It is critical to note, therefore, that the per capita equivalent income of a lone-mother family with a Lone Parent's Allowance is *higher* than that of a man with a wife and four children who is dependent on Long-Term Unemployment Assistance.[7] Undoubtedly, this social welfare "differential" explains the pattern of poverty risks noted here. From a

---

[7]   For example, the per capita equivalent weekly social welfare incomes in the two illustrations cited, at the time of the fieldwork, were £53.98 and £50.84 respectively.

policy perspective, the issue that arises from the analysis is the need to view the financial circumstances of lone-mother families in the light of the circumstances of *all* families, as suggested in the recent ESRI study.

Before turning from income to actual living standards it may be useful to contrast the relative-income analysis with a more stringent approach to financial poverty. Currently, the social welfare system offers an explicit income guarantee through the Rent Allowance payments made by Health Boards. This provision is designed to ensure that a family's net income *after housing costs* does not fall below the applicable rate of Supplementary Welfare Allowances minus £5.00. In the case of a lone-mother family with one child, the relevant 1992/3 figures were as follows: the SWA rate was £65.50; SWA minus £5.00 was £60.50; if a person's rent or mortgage costs resulted in their net income (after rent/mortgage) falling *below* the SWA minus £5.00 threshold, then a Rent Allowance was paid up to the point where a person's income (net, after housing costs) was brought up to the SWA minus £5.00 figure.

In the study sample, the extent to which the lone mothers' incomes fell below this official threshold was assessed. This assessment was applied only to the 39 of the 53 women who were heads of households and living independently. Of these 39, an admittedly small number, eight families, were *exactly on or below* the SWA minus £5.00 threshold: a percentage rate of 21 per cent. Some of these eight were in receipt of Rent Allowances. This calculation is not, in fact, a measure of the extent of poverty. It merely adopts an official minimum and counts those who are below it. As such, it is a measure of the *efficiency of the social welfare system* in achieving the official objective ascribed to this system. That such a high[8] proportion of these low-income families are on or below this SWA threshold reflects critically on the operation of the SWA Rent Allowance scheme and is a further indicator of the low standard of living of the families in the study. Equally important, it draws attention to the fact that while *current weekly income* is an appropriate measure of families' *resources* it is also necessary to examine what factors mediate the effect of income on living standards.

In Section 5.4, the families' actual living standards are examined, but before proceeding, it is worth recording, again, the statistical

---

[8]   The figure may be overestimated: SWA rules would not permit capital repayments on mortgages as part of rent allowances, and the housing-costs figures in the study may include some capital element; also, one family is counted, which is exactly *on*, but not below the SWA minus £5.00 line.

constraints on any claims that might be made on the basis of the income data. It is clear from available data that a substantial segment of the lone-mother population is in financial circumstances of the type depicted here. However, it is not possible to generalise statistically about the incomes of lone mothers in the population at large. While it has been possible to quantify and describe the incomes of a particular subset of lone mothers, the limits of this exercise reveal the urgent need for a large-scale, statistically representative study of the financial and social circumstances of families.

5.4   Relative Deprivation

There are two dimensions to the relative approach to poverty, based on Townsend's work, that were adopted for this study. As the extended quotation in Section 5.3 makes clear, relative poverty arises where families' incomes are so low that they are, in effect, excluded from customary styles of living. The first element in this approach is income: the extent to which the incomes of families in the study fall below the incomes that pertain in the population at large has been shown.

The second element in this approach is *deprivation*: the extent to which families' low incomes *prevent* them from consuming certain goods, using certain services, engaging in certain activities and so on.[9] It is to this dimension of poverty that we now turn. The ESRI research studies on poverty and deprivation applied the methodology developed in the UK by Mack and Lansley to measure the extent of social deprivation (Mack and Lansley, 1985). This methodology — building on Townsend's original study with its list of deprivation indicators — entails the following steps:

(1)   Respondents in a large-scale national survey are asked whether they own/have access to certain items or engage in certain activities.

(2)   If the answer in respect of any one item is "No", respondents are asked whether this is because they cannot afford it (as distinct from personal choice).

(3)   Respondents are also asked whether they consider the particular item/activity to be a necessity.

---

[9]   There is a complex and controversial literature about whether poverty is best measured *indirectly* by looking at income or *directly* by examining expenditure and consumption (Ringen, 1988; Donnison, 1988; Callan, Nolan et al., 1989).

(4) A list or index of *socially defined necessities* is then compiled, comprising those items that are regarded as a necessity by a (specified) majority of the whole population.

The underlying approach here is to define as deprived those families who do not possess/enjoy a number of items/activities considered essential by most of the population. This approach firmly locates "deprivation" in a social context by measuring the views of the population as to what is considered essential. The definition of "necessity" is not imposed by a researcher: it reflects society's definition and hence is a proper measurement of *relative* deprivation.

Table 5.6 below — reproduced from the ESRI report, *Poverty, Income and Welfare in Ireland* (Callan, Nolan et al., 1989) illustrates the first three steps, (1), (2) and (3) above, in the method. From the list of 20 items it can be seen that many, but not all, are regarded as necessities by a significant majority of the respondents surveyed. For example, 92 per cent believe a fridge to be a necessity, only 5 per cent lack a fridge and 3 per cent lack a fridge because of lack of money ("enforced" lack). A contrary example concerns the activity "ability to save"; here too a very large majority regard it as a necessity, but 57 per cent lack the ability to save and 55 per cent experience an *enforced* inability to save.

The next step is to select from these items a shorter index of items. In its work, the ESRI used two indices, one of which was applied to the small, local sample in this study. This index comprises *14* items — chosen because they meet these criteria:

- Deprivation of the item negatively correlated with income

- Possessed by a majority of respondents (or their households in the case of durable such as a TV)

- Considered a necessity by a majority of the respondents (Callan, Nolan et al., 1989: 112–16).[10]

The 14 items included in this index of deprivation are asterisked in Table 5.6.

---

[10] In his study, Townsend included items possessed by a majority (with three items added); Mack and Lansley included items considered to be necessities by a majority; none of their items was possessed by less than 70 per cent and therefore in their use of this method the ESRI added this condition — possession by a majority — to their interpretation. The ESRI criteria are "extended Mack-Lansley criteria" (Callan, Nolan et al., 1989: 115).

Table 5.6: Indicators of Actual Style of Living and Socially-Defined Necessities

	% Lacking	% Experiencing Enforced Lack	% Stating Necessity
* Refrigerator	5	3	92
* Washing Machine	20	10	82
Telephone	48	31	45
* Car	38	22	59
Colour TV	20	11	37
A Week's Annual Holiday Away from Home	68	49	50
* A Dry Damp-Free Dwelling	10	9	99
* Heating for the Living Rooms when it is Cold	3	2	99
Central Heating in the House	45	30	49
* An Indoor Toilet in the Dwelling	7	6	98
* Bath or Shower	9	7	98
* A Meal with Meat, Chicken or Fish Every Second Day	13	9	84
* A Warm, Waterproof Overcoat	13	8	93
* Two Pairs of Strong Shoes	16	11	88
To Be Able to Save	57	55	88
A Daily Newspaper	45	16	39
* A Roast Meat Joint Once a Week	24	13	64
* A Hobby or Leisure Activity	33	12	73
* New, Not Second-hand, Clothes	10	8	77
* Presents for Friends or Family Once a Year	24	13	60

Source: Callan, Nolan et al. (1989): Table 8.1.

In the study sample, the same information was obtained from respondents about their ownership of TVs and fridges, and their ability to save, buy newspapers and so on. They were also asked whether their lack of an item reflected an inability to afford it. So, to what extent were the families in this study deprived of these necessities? Table

5.7 below presents the results for this study, the original national study representative of all households, and poor households only in the national study. The table shows the cumulative percentages of respondents according to their "deprivation scores" on the 14-item index of deprivation. The scores are simply the number of necessary items for which the respondents experience an enforced lack.

Table 5.7: Percentage Distribution of Lone Mothers and ESRI Survey Respondents on 14-Point Deprivation Index

Deprivation Score (Enforced Lack)	Lone Mothers	ESRI: Poor Households	ESRI: All Households
0	8	28	51
1 or more	92	72	49
2 or more	81	51	30
3 or more	69	38	20
4 or more	50	27	13

Notes: Poor households in the ESRI study were those under the threshold of 60 per cent of mean per capita equivalent income.
Source: Callan, Nolan et al. (1989): Tables 8.2 and 8.7.

Clearly, on this index of deprivation, the lone mothers are much more deprived than the population at large. Notably, only a very small proportion of the study sample scored zero, while about *half* of the national sample did so. At the other extreme, 50 per cent of the study sample had a deprivation score of 4 or more in contrast to a mere 13 per cent of the national sample. Notwithstanding the very small sample of lone mothers, it is distinctly obvious that these low-income mothers experience significantly higher levels of deprivation: they are deprived to a considerable extent of the services, activities and amenities that the majority of the population possess and that a majority of the population consider to be necessary. Further, it appears that the lone mothers are *more* deprived than those households in the ESRI study classified as poor according to a 60 per cent of mean income criterion. Data from the ESRI study on these households are given separately in the right-hand panel of Table 5.7. Contrasting this distribution of deprivation scores with that for the lone mothers, it is clear that the lone mothers are distinctly more deprived than this wider population of poor families.

Additional summary data that contrast the current study sample with the ESRI's national sample are the mean deprivation scores for the enforced lack of necessities. In the current study sample as a whole, the figure is 3.5 and for the ESRI's sample the figure is 1.3.[11] The ESRI study calculated mean scores for each decile of the equivalent income distribution. These calculations yielded a mean score of 2.2 for the lowest (i.e. poorest in income terms) tenth of the population — less than the mean for the study sample. It appears that these lone mothers experience a standard of living that is lower than that of a representative set of families and households at the lowest end of the income distribution.

In this analysis of social deprivation it is useful to distinguish between different aspects of deprivation. It might be argued from a policy perspective that, notwithstanding social definitions of "necessities", some forms of consumption and expenditure are *more* necessary than others. Or, put another way, that policy improvements in income supports might be more forcefully argued if "more basic" forms of deprivation can be identified. The more recent analysis undertaken by ESRI researchers can be adhered to in an attempt to describe more basic forms of deprivation (Callan, Nolan and Whelan, 1993). In addition to the 20 items listed in the deprivation scale, this study followed the ESRI methodology by adding four items to the list as follows:

(1) Whether there had been a day during the previous two weeks when the respondent did not have a substantial meal at all — from getting up to going to bed

(2) Whether they had to go without heating during the previous year through lack of money — that is, having to go without a fire on a cold day, or go to bed early to keep warm, or light the fire late because of lack of coal/fuel

(3) Whether the respondent had not had an afternoon or evening out in the previous fortnight, "something that costs money", and this was stated to be because they had not enough money

(4) Whether the household had experienced any one of the following:

   • It was currently in arrears on rent, mortgage, electricity or gas.

---

[11] This was derived from Table 8.4 of the ESRI study (Callan, Nolan et al., 1989: 117): the unweighted mean of the 10 separate means for the levels of income was calculated.

- It had had to go into debt in the previous 12 months to meet ordinary living expenses (such as rent, food, Christmas or back-to-school expenses).

- It had had to sell or pawn anything worth £50 or more to meet ordinary living expenses.

- It had received assistance from a private charity in the previous year.

These items relate to very basic elements of lifestyle — food, heat, a tendency to indebtedness in meeting essential needs. With these items included, the total scale comprises 24 items. In the ESRI's national survey, the mean score on the (24-item) index was 5.4, ranging from 8.1 for the lowest income decile to 2.1 for the highest.[12] For the study sample, the mean was 7.0. The lowest tenth of the income distribution in the national study had almost 35 per cent with a score of 10 or more on the scale — the corresponding figure for the study sample as a whole was 25 per cent. These comparisons suggest that while the low-income lone mothers in this study are indeed deprived to a considerable extent, their circumstances are matched by other households and families at the very lowest reaches of the income distribution.

However, there may be limits to the analytical value of simply "adding up" scores on a range of very diverse items. A multivariate statistical analysis of the 24-item scale undertaken by the ESRI researchers suggested that the scale could be decomposed into *three* different dimensions, one of which is of particular interest to us.[13] The dimensions were as follows:

- A dimension (titled *"Basic"*) which contained eight items about heat, food, ability to purchase new clothes, indebtedness/arrears, affordability of meat, and so on. This is the dimension also applied to the sample in the current study.

- Second, a dimension comprising *consumer durables and housing items* — access to TV, washing machine, indoor toilet, etc.

---

[12] See Table 2, Callan, Nolan, Whelan (1993): the 5.4 figure in the text above is the unweighted mean of the 10 decile means reported in the original study.

[13] Factor analysis was applied to the 24 items and a 3-factor solution specified: this generated the three factors "basic," "household/ durables", "other". For details of the analysis, factor solutions and item loadings, see Callan, Nolan and Whelan (1993), Table 3.

- Another dimension, which largely captures *leisure and social participation* — could respondents afford a holiday? Did they have a
  hobby? Could they go out in the evening? etc.

The distinction between these dimensions in the national sample is
important for two interrelated reasons. First, the "basic" dimension
may be a good indicator of poverty in the very strict, literal sense:
deprivation in terms of food, heat, clothing and so on. Second, the
three dimensions of deprivation are not as equally highly correlated
with current weekly income. This highlights the possibility that other
measures of income or resources may be more strongly related to
social-deprivation measures and to the distinct likelihood that non-
economic (or non-income) factors such as life cycle, age or household
composition may be related to social deprivation. In the study sample,
for instance, some young single women lived in households with a TV,
phone, washing machine, central heating and so on: their scores on
consumer durables/housing items would indicate little deprivation —
yet their incomes would be low. It is also plausible — indeed the
ESRI's correlations of the various dimensions with income suggest
this — that the "other" dimension (i.e. social and leisure) has the
strongest statistical relationship of all three dimensions with income.[14]
Arguably, this would occur because these activities would be the least
likely to be pursued by those on a persistently low income — or would
be the first to be "dropped" at the onset of financial deprivation. Conversely, with "basic" items it would be expected that families would go
to considerable lengths to continue consumption of "basics" — these
lengths would include borrowing, drawing on family support, reducing other "non-basic" consumption, and thus the statistical correlation
between income and "basic" deprivation would be weakened.

The small sample size in this study does not permit the intricate
interconnections between income and deprivation, and between various aspects of deprivation, to be *quantified*. However, in the next section illustrative material is used in a qualitative attempt to discern
patterns of deprivation in the study sample.

Before shifting the analysis on to the qualitative level, the distinction between different aspects of deprivation can be used to good effect.
Basic deprivation scores were calculated for the study sample — deprivation scores based on the eight items that comprise this dimension of

---

[14]   Callan, Nolan and Whelan (1993) report the following correlations be-
    tween deciles of equivalent income and deprivation dimensions: Basic —
    0.33; Housing/Consumer Durables — 0.22; and "Other" — 0.53.

deprivation.[15] The average score on this scale for the study sample was 1.9. Table 5.8 contrasts the actual and cumulative percentage distribution of scores on this index of basic deprivation for the study sample and for the national ESRI survey. Given the self-selected nature of the study sample, it is unsurprising that such stark differences emerge: only 17 per cent of the low-income lone mothers have a score of zero, in contrast to 68 per cent of the national sample. Likewise, 23 per cent of the lone mothers had scores in the 3 or more range, whereas only 11 per cent of the national sample had these scores.

Table 5.8: Distribution of Scores on Basic Deprivation Index for ESRI National Sample and Lone-Mother Sample

Score	ESRI %	Lone Mothers %	Cumulative % ESRI	Cumulative % Lone Mothers
0	68	17	68	17
1	15	33	83	50
2	7	27	90	77
3 or more	11	23	101	100
Total	101	100		

Note: Percentages may not add to 100 because of rounding.
Sources: See text and Callan, Nolan and Whelan (1993), Table 4.

A more focused comparison can be made between the study sample and the national sample if the comparison is confined to low-income households, as in Table 5.9. The left-hand column of this table takes a basic deprivation score of two or more. Fifty per cent of the study sample experience this level of deprivation, while the corresponding figure for the national income distribution is 17 per cent. The low-income social welfare-dependent families typified in the study sample seem to face a higher risk of high basic deprivation. If the scores for two or more are compared, it can be seen that the percentage for the lowest decile in the national study is 21 per cent, higher than the figure for the lone-mother sample. A similar comparison is not available for scores

---

[15] The eight items are: go without heat; go without substantial meal; arrears/debt; new, not second-hand clothes; meal with meat, etc.; waterproof overcoat; two strong pairs of shoes; a roast or its equivalent.

of three or more. It can be concluded from this analysis that the low-income, lone-mother families represented in the study sample are experiencing higher levels of deprivation relative to the population at large, and, furthermore, that they incur about the same risk as other very low-income households of experiencing *high* levels of basic deprivation.

Table 5.9: Proportions of Lone Mothers and of Low-Income Households in National Sample with Basic Deprivation Scores of 2 or More, or 3 or More

	Basic Deprivation Scores of	
	2 or More	*3 or More*
Percentage of Sample Lone Mothers	50	23
Percentage in National Study	17	11
Percentage of Lowest Decile in National Study	21	—

Source: Tables 4 and 5 of Callan, Nolan and Whelan (1993).

5.5   Patterns of Deprivation

As outlined earlier in this chapter, the relative income approach to poverty requires analyses of both *income* and deprivation in terms of *standards of living*. Separate analyses of these two inter-related aspects of poverty have been given in Sections 5.3 and 5.4. If this study were a large-scale, statistical survey, income and deprivation would be assessed in an integrated analysis — for example by classifying families and households at various "poverty lines" according to their levels of deprivation. This kind of analysis would permit a very close examination of the link between income on the one hand, and deprivation on the other.

However, the very limited sample for this study does not permit such an analysis to be undertaken. The nature of the poverty and deprivation recorded in the study is therefore explored in a qualitative way, first by making some general observations based on interview material and, second, by describing some families' situations in detail.

One decisive pattern can be discerned in the responses women made to questions about the items they could afford and in their free-flowing comments: virtually none of the women enjoyed what might loosely be called "a social life". Almost none of them had had a holiday in recent years, very few of them had a hobby or leisure activity, or even bought a newspaper. These comments made by different women capture this absence of social or leisure activities:

A holiday! I can't remember when I last had one.

I never go out. I don't even go into town on the bus 'cause it costs too much.

My hobby? I can afford a few smokes and that's it — they're my only luxury.

I can't afford the papers. I can get the news on the telly and when my mother comes she usually brings the paper with her.

In contrast to this almost total lack of a social/leisure dimension to their lives, the women for the most part did not comment negatively about their access to durables (TVs, fridges, etc.) or about the quality of their housing. There was 100 per cent ownership of fridges and televisions in the sample and not one woman complained about the *physical quality* of her housing. It is clear from the interviews that these aspects of their living standards are not strongly determined by their own *weekly* income for a number of reasons. In the first instance, half of the unmarried women and a few other women (14 in all) were not "heads of households" but were part of a wider household, in most cases benefiting from the TV, fridge, etc. already provided by the household head (the women's parents, typically.)

In regard to housing, the relationship between weekly income and deprivation was quite varied. A significant segment of the sample were in local authority housing of relatively recent vintage, and probably of good physical quality. Some separated women, however, were finding their owner-occupied homes "a mixed blessing". Many were left with serious mortgage arrears when their husbands left, and the arrears, combined with the difficulty of making repayments on a low income, meant that the effort to sustain their original housing standards was very great indeed. In some of these instances, women commented on their lack of choice, as they perceived it. They felt unable to move house because of their children's schools or because of family support available to them in their present location — "I mean, I can't move house just like that", in the words of one woman. In general, for women who are separated, it is clear that their *current* standards of living are a function, in part, of their *past* levels of income and resources as married women.

Most of the women in the study had primary family networks in their community — as is recorded in more detail in Chapters 6 and 8. For many women, financial and other tangible support from their parents in particular was critical to their arrangements. The support could be in the form of intermittent small-scale borrowing of money — "to tide me over", as one woman explained. Or, more commonly, it took the form of regular buying of clothes and toys for children and frequent provision of meals by parents: "We always go to my mother's house for Sunday lunch — that's one day out of the way." Some women referred to the lump–sum expenses they encounter at Christmas or at Holy Communion or Confirmation occasions. Family support for these expenses was simply a necessity for some women and not an added bonus. The extensive nature of family support in this study has a corollary, however: it reflects the location and type of community in which the study was undertaken and is unlikely to be representative of all low-income mothers' situations.

Two aspects of family structure and its links with financial deprivation in the study are worthy of note:

- The distinction some women made between their *personal* living standards and the living standard of their children

- The differential experience of deprivation according to the ages of the women's children.

In relation to the first aspect, women often made very explicit that their children's living standards were their strict priority — and that their own personal needs were very much secondary. Some women insisted that their children would not have a lower standard of living than others and that the family's economy would be organised to this end. One woman resolutely stated: "No matter what, my kids will have the same as other kids"; some women spelt this out clearly — "I mean, they have to come first, always." The unit of analysis in this study is the *family* and if the focus is switched to the *individual* woman, it becomes clear that some women perceive a stark choice — maintain either their own well-being, *or* that of their children, but not both.

The second aspect of family structure is the impact of the evolving life cycle on the family's living standards.[16] It was unambiguously clear in the interviews that the women with older, adolescent children experienced considerable financial difficulty. They made explicit reference to the impact of their growing children on basic costs for food and clothing. As one woman explained it:

---

[16] The study sample is too small to present meaningful *quantitative* data on the families classified by age of the children.

You know yourself with teenagers. They'd eat you out of house and home — and as for clothes and things, they're just impossible.

Many managed their expenditure so as to avoid a large "weekly shop". One woman did this to prevent her teenage sons eating "everything" the first day: "I never do a weekly shop — it'd be gone the next day. You can't keep them fed at that age." The recent call by the Combat Poverty Agency for Child Benefit and other child-related payments to be tiered by age is therefore strongly reflected in the comments made by the women in this study (Carney, Fitzgerald et al., 1994).

These patterns can be described most effectively by drawing on illustrative case material from the interviews. In the paragraphs below, some such material is set out — first for some single, unmarried women, and then for separated women.

In the case of unmarried women, one very common set of circumstances is that they live in their parents' homes — these kinds of circumstances, as has been seen, apply to some of the young unmarried women in the study sample. This household pattern has definite consequences for the standard of living experienced by the young women and their children.

Ellen's situation is a good case in point. Now aged 25, with a small child, she lives with her parents, two brothers and a sister; her brother of 22 is working, as is her father. Her own income comprises the Lone Parent's Allowance and Child Benefit, a weekly income of £75.75. Although her income is modest, she said she was "not poor" and that her father described the family's finances in these terms: "We are not flush with money, but we manage okay." She says she manages her money "fairly easily": she simply gives her parents an "allowance" of £20 weekly "to cover everything" and her parents pay all the bills, including the weekly groceries. She buys any clothes, toys, etc. for her child separately. At present, she is saving to get married and, in particular, she saves the Child Benefit.

Out of her income she pays, in addition to the weekly £20 "allowance" to her parents, an insurance policy for £5 and a weekly lodgement of £10 into a "Christmas Club"; this leaves about £35 for her own personal needs and any costs in relation to the child. In the house there is a TV, fridge, video and washing machine; and there is a family car. Ellen's level of "deprivation" is therefore minimal. The only item in the 24-item scale which she could not afford was the holiday. Her total scale score was therefore 1, and her score on basic deprivation was zero.

These circumstances illustrate how a lone mother whose household head is in employment and whose eldest child is a subsidiary earner can sustain a good standard of living despite her own *personal* dependence on social welfare. The sample *also* contains young women living at home where there are no earners in the family. In such cases, the women's living standards are still sustained by the wider family economy but clearly not to the same degree.

Ellen's case can be contrasted with that of Róisín, who is 24 and living alone with her daughter of four in a rented house in a Dublin Corporation housing estate. Her income comprises the Lone Parent's Allowance, Child Benefit and (in winter) the Fuel Voucher; a total of £79.88 with the fuel voucher included. By the standards applied in the current analysis, Róisín is highly deprived. In interview, to illustrate her predicament, she said:

> *I got my (social welfare) money yesterday. I have £21 left to last me till next Thursday.*

Out of her weekly income, she spends £15 on a weekly shop, £15 on coal/fuel and £10 on rent (including arrears). She also sets aside £10 per week for ESB bills — leaving just over £25 for all other expenses. She has arrears on her rent and ESB. It is very difficult for her to buy clothes for her daughter: "I saved up for four weeks to get her a dress"; in her own case she never buys new clothes and cannot afford proper shoes:

> *These shoes — they cost me £4 in Dunnes — my jeans are two years old and the T-shirt I have was only £1.99.*

The three-piece suite and the other furniture she has is either "borrowed or presents", and she never goes out socially or on a holiday. In her house, she has a TV and fridge and the Corporation will be installing central heating in the house (with a corresponding increase in rent and a loss of Fuel Voucher). On the total 24-item scale she has a score of 11 and on the index of basic deprivation she scores 3 — reflecting her level of indebtedness for basic amenities and her inability to buy new clothes or shoes for herself. Her own low personal living standard is, in some measure, the obverse of her determination to support her little girl as best she can:

> *There's a clothes shop in Donaghmede with nice clothes. I saved for four weeks to buy her that dress. People were expecting us to look cheap and in tatters. So, because I live here, I make sure I don't give people reason to talk about me. People think because you're a lone parent you shouldn't have anything. But this is my*

home. I have to bring her up.... Food? She loves fruit, but it's expensive. I'll go into town and buy cheaper fruit and cheaper meat.

Róisín gets some financial and practical support from parents: "Only for my mother and father I don't know how I'd get on." Her situation is strikingly similar to that of several other women in the study — resident in Corporation housing, subsisting on a low income, prone to indebtedness and experiencing high levels of deprivation.

To reveal the impact that full-time employment — relative to reliance on social welfare — has on incomes and living standards, the case of Joan can be described. She has a good education, attaining a Leaving Certificate and then training as a secretary. After her daughter — now aged three and a half — was born, she stopped working. However, six months prior to interview she resumed work by taking a FÁS return-to-work course: she now works full-time for a *net* wage of £120 per week. Currently, she lives in a one-bedroomed Corporation flat, the rent for which is £5.30 weekly: this will increase when the Corporation takes account of her wages. On the whole, her circumstances are *not* deprived. Out of the weekly income of £120 she pays £40 for child-minding, £7.80 for bus fares and £5.30 rent. In addition, she assigns her child-minder the responsibility for paying "big bills" such as the ESB, and arranges this by giving her an "extra" £20 to set aside for these bills. This leaves her with £47 out of which she pays £25 to her Credit Union for loan repayments. Usually she has a small amount of money left before pay day: "On Thursday, I might have a fiver left."

According to Joan, she is "no worse off than anyone else", although she also insisted that she "didn't end up any better off" by going back to full-time employment. This she ascribed to the cost of full-time child care — £40 per week for an 8 a.m. to 6 p.m. service. Although her standard of living is modest, she is not deprived in the sense in which that description has been used here: her total (24-item) scale score was 3 and her basic deprivation score was zero. This type of circumstances — full-time employment in office work with a commensurate income — was *not* applicable generally in the sample.

In turning to separated women, it can be seen that the patterns of income and deprivation differ somewhat from those of their generally younger unmarried counterparts who invariably have one young child. Separated women will tend to have more than one child and to have older children. This imposes added costs across a range of needs — food, clothing and housing, for instance. However, some separated women have maintenance from partners or are in receipt of the non-means-tested Deserted Wife's Benefit, which provides a "floor" of income onto which they can add other incomes. For some, these "other" sources of income are essential, however, as their partners have left them to pay mortgages and sometimes to clear off debts. Some of these elements emerge in the cases set out below.

First, the case of Paula illustrates well the predicament of older women with a number of children of varying ages. She is in her early fifties and lives in a rented Corporation house which costs her £15.50 per week. In all, there are eight in the house: herself and seven children, five of whom are dependent financially (the other two are unemployed and on training courses). Her income is from social welfare, £142 plus the £5 Fuel Voucher in winter and £93.20 per month Child Benefit for the five child dependants. In per capita equivalent terms, her income is one of the lowest in the study — just under £46 per week if the social welfare and Child Benefit are combined. She manages, she stated, only with "great difficulty"; and in describing her own financial circumstances said: "Sometimes I think I am poverty stricken."

Her situation is one of acute deprivation — a total scale score of 16 and a basic scale score of 5. This is dramatically highlighted in her own description of her living standards:

> *I don't really eat a lot. Maybe it's subconscious after so long on social welfare. This morning I bought two bags of frozen chips because they were reduced — they're cheaper than real potatoes. If they had not been reduced, I wouldn't be buying them. You get so used to it.*

These revelations about poverty from the comments on food are reinforced by her remarks about clothes:

> *Any clothes I have are given to me — even these ones I have on me. My daughter owns them. It's three years since I bought a pair of shoes and the only holiday we had was subsidised by Parents Alone — four or five years ago.*

Paula is in arrears with rent and ESB and in the last year has had to obtain money from the St Vincent de Paul and from the Community Welfare Officer. She is convinced that the age of her children is the source of her financial problems, as three of her dependent children are over 14. Commenting on the social welfare support for children, she argued:

> *You get the same money for a baby as for a teenager ... at this stage, they want all those personal things. I could manage OK when they were small.... If I buy in bulk it's gone in two days —*

> *it wouldn't last now. So I gave up. It's cheaper to shop daily —*
> *I've tried both ways. Teenagers think it's their right to come in*
> *and have a feed any time they like.*

The combination of circumstances in the above case — large family, older children, social welfare dependence — are not, however, the *only* circumstances that gave rise to high levels of deprivation among separated women. Amy's situation is different in some respects from the case illustrated above but results in an almost equal measure of deprivation.

Amy is in her early thirties and has two small children (aged five and one). She has been separated for only one year and described it as "very, very hard" trying to manage financially. Her former husband was a gambler and an alcoholic and as a result she was left not only with the responsibility of paying the mortgage, but also with large debts. Her weekly income comprises Deserted Wife's Benefit of £95.00 in addition to a Fuel Voucher and a Rent Allowance of £25 per month from SWA to assist with mortgage arrears. From this income, she pays £50 weekly in mortgage payments, a "minimum" weekly shop of £16, £7 for special soya milk for the baby and £2 for a return bus fare to town. The remaining £35 or so must suffice for fuel and coal and all other bills. Currently, she is in arrears on her ESB and gas accounts; she paid only £40 off her most recent ESB bill of £80, and obtained £50 from the SWA service to pay off against an outstanding gas bill of £258. Amy's lifestyle is very frugal, as she explained:

> *I wait till I run out of stuff before I buy. I don't drink tea or cof-*
> *fee, so I just have hot water. My mother brings her own tea and*
> *coffee that she drinks when she's here. We live on fish fingers*
> *and beans. I can't afford steak or meat for Sunday.... I don't do a*
> *big shop. I just make a dinner out of nothing.*

She has a three-bedroomed semi-detached house with central heating that she now cannot afford, and has a telephone that was recently disconnected because of non-payment of bills. Amy is clear that her biggest financial constraint is the mortgage: "I could see myself selling this house — I just can't afford it." On the measures of deprivation used in this study, she has a scale score of 12 on the total (24-item) scale and a very high score of 5 for basic deprivation, reflecting her indebtedness and inability to buy food, fuel and clothes. Her income after housing costs, it should be noted, is less than the official rate of SWA minus £5.00. This type of situation — a young woman with children, financially captured by high housing costs — resembles the circumstances of some other women in the study.

As with single women, those separated women with earnings, or with combinations of income, manage to obtain an adequate living standard with little apparent deprivation. For example, Beth, who is aged 42, has three children aged 16, 14 and 10. Her weekly income is derived from a full-time traineeship which yields her about £80, net, per week; in addition, she receives £90 per week from her former partner. From this weekly income of £170 and Child Benefit combined, she pays £57 per week on her mortgage repayments and saves a little money. She describes her circumstances in this way:

I probably will be okay. I'm a survivor. I don't see myself as poor.

Her financial arrangements after taking up the traineeship had only just settled at the time of interview and she expressed some uncertainty — especially about the clothing and school-related costs of her teenage children. However, she had a clear strategy: "I know the £90 is for certain things like the mortgage. I have to live on what I get after the maintenance." The net effect of all this is that her basic deprivation score was zero and her total scale score was a mere 3. In Beth's case, she is able to earn additional income partly because her mother-in-law, who lives across the road, provides free after-school child care for her children.

Beth's situation illustrates an experience that applied to other separated women. Those who managed to "top up" welfare income (or maintenance) with employment — even modestly paid employment — obtained a significant higher standard of living than those who were welfare-dependent, and they expressed and articulated this experience in the interviews.

Finally, Figure 5.1 offers a framework for considering the influences that shape the link between low income and social deprivation, and for summarising some of the detailed case material given in Chapters 5 and 6. As the figure suggests, there is a strong underlying influence running from low income to social deprivation. However, the influence of low income on deprivation is affected on the one hand by a cluster of factors labelled "High Needs/Costs" and, on the other, by countervailing factors labelled "Extra Resources". For example, two women with the same low income might experience different levels of deprivation if the children of one are older and "more costly", and the children of the other younger and less costly. Similarly, women with families who are nearby and who receive extensive "in kind" support may experience less deprivation at a given level of low income than women who have no such supports.

Figure 5.1: The Link Between Low Income and Deprivation

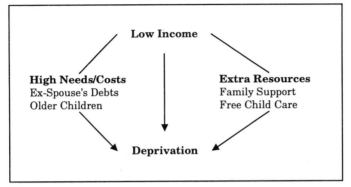

In Chapter 6 the value of Figure 5.1 as a framework will emerge. There the focus is on a more rounded analysis of the women's financial circumstances, and detailed interview material is presented to show more fully the connections between income, deprivation and the lives of the women as a whole.

6: Living in Poverty

6.1   Introduction

That many of the women in this study are poor is evident. The extent of their poverty and the fact that for many it is a continuing situation impels us to pose a wider question. How do women experience, perceive and manage their situations? This chapter describes first how the women managed *financially* — the strategies they adopted to cope. It also attempts to convey how they *viewed* their circumstances and how their expectations, hopes, and practical supports helped them to manage personally and psychologically.

This chapter therefore contains material on the women's financial affairs — their "budgeting" arrangements and so on — as well as on their use of social services and family support. It also contains the responses women gave to open-ended questions about how they perceived their own situation. To provide a context for this analysis, the chapter outlines in some detail the circumstances of a number of women, and then discusses some general issues which arise from these cases. This illustrative material is *not* being advanced as typical or representative. Rather, it attempts to portray the diversity of the women's circumstances and the complex ways in which their financial situation is related to their living standards and to their lives as a whole.

6.2   Case Studies

In each of the cases information is given about the women's incomes and their expenditure. Then, for each case, there is an outline of their broader family context, their views about their own financial situation and their experiences of the State's Social Welfare and Community Welfare services. A summary of some relevant characteristics is given in Figure 6.1 as a guide to the cases.

CASE 1 refers to Ciara who has been separated for four years. Her children are aged 11 and 9 and they live in her owner-occupied house. At time of interview her weekly income comprised £92.00 from Deserted Wife's Benefit. In the terms of Chapter 5 she is "poor": her weekly income combined with Child Benefit is below the relative income poverty threshold. She is moderately deprived, having a score of 3 on the basic deprivation scale and a score of 7 on the total scale.

Ciara's husband left her with a mortgage to repay: the monthly repayment for this is over £100 but she has renegotiated a repayment of £80 monthly. Like other women in the study she managed her resources by not doing a "big weekly shop". Her itemised previous week's expenditure was as follows:

Item	£
Mortgage	20.00
Loan Repayment	10.00
Gas/ESB	10.00
Children's Clubs	3.75
Petrol	10.00
Total	53.75

She pays £20 weekly off her mortgage and also pays £10 per week on an outstanding loan — her husband left some loans unpaid. In addition, she sets aside £10 towards gas and ESB bills; her son and daughter are in the scouts and a local majorettes band which cost £3.75 weekly in total. The balance of about £40 weekly is for general

Figure 6.1: Summary of Characteristics of Some Lone-Mother Cases

Case	Marital and Family Status	Housing and Household Position	Weekly Income Source(s)	Poverty Line	Deprivation Scores
Ciara	Separated. Two Children Under 12	Independent Household, Owner-occupier	Deserted Wife's Benefit and Rent Allowance	Income Below 60% Line	Total Scale, 7 Basic Scale, 3
Paula	Separated. Five Dependent Children — All Over 12	Independent Household, Local Authority Tenant	Lone Parent's Allowance	Income Below 60% Line	Total Scale, 7 Basic Scale, 5
Leona	Separated. Four Dependent Children — Aged from 7 to 17	Independent Household, Owner-occupier	Deserted Wife's Benefit, FÁS Scheme	Income Above 60% Line	Total Scale, 1 Basic Scale, 0
Ellen	Single. One Child Aged 4	Part of Parents' Household, Local Authority Tenant	Lone Parent's Allowance	Own Income Below 60% Line	Total Scale, 1 Basic Scale, 0
Dana	Single. Two Children Under 4	Separate Household, Local Authority Tenant	Lone Parent's Allowance	Income Below 60% Line	Total Scale, 12 Basic Scale, 4
Joan	Single. One Child Under 4	Separate Household, Local Authority Tenant	Earnings	Income Above 60% Line	Total Scale, 3 Basic Scale, 0

shopping such as food — she does this on a daily basis. She keeps her Child Benefit income separate: "I try to use that for the kids."

Ciara's family is directly involved in her finances. Her mother, who lives very near, bought her a car and pays the tax and insurance on this, while she herself pays for the petrol. Also, her mother adds £5 every week to the £10 she sets aside for gas and ESB bills, and her mother's mobile home at the coast is available for her use for holidays. Ciara also described how she and the children regularly eat in her mother's house and how her parents' support was given without any interference in her personal life.

> *I go to Mammy's on Sunday for dinner. I am lucky, as I say. If we were up in Mammy's and we are there early, I have a bit of dinner with Mammy, you know, which means I only have to cook for the kids, you know. I am lucky that I have somebody that can give me a hand or a help out, you know. They are like a back-bone there and I must say they never got involved in all the trouble — they just said "well, whatever decision you make we will stand by you...."*

Ciara was emphatic that her own social welfare income was inadequate for her needs and stressed, as she saw it, the rationale for increasing payment levels:

> *They could do with giving us just that little bit more, you know, because if you're married and your husband's coming in with his wage and if you have a part-time job, there is something extra coming in. I mean, even if the man is working, he is taking home well over £100 a week. Do you know what I mean? But they still expect you to live on less than that and still have all the bills. I am not saying that they should be giving you £100 or £200 a week, just a little more, you know.*

One recurrent theme in the interviews, which Ciara voiced, was a general tendency to put children's needs first — with direct implications for mothers' own welfare. As Ciara explained: "I try to make sure that they don't miss out on what two-parent families get." She followed this "children first" strategy even in the allocation of food:

> *What I would probably do would be if there wasn't a lot I would kind of do without the dinner myself maybe and give it to the children. I make sure they have got enough, you know?*

She was strongly critical of one local Community Welfare Officer (CWO): she had been refused help with her mortgage repayments and it took a number of visits to obtain help with the costs of a child's confirmation. In her recollection of this CWO, she remarked that "I don't think he is really friendly. I don't think he is really nice — I just don't think he is suitable for the job."

By way of contrast, she praised the Social Welfare Office. While relying on SWA on an interim basis, she applied for a social welfare payment. She received this within six weeks and described the official: "She came and she was quite nice. She made you kind of feel at ease." When asked about the cohabitation rule applied to social welfare payments for lone mothers she claimed that it was irrelevant to her personally, as she had no interest in a new relationship. However, she could see the logic of such a rule and actually proposed a policy change: that women who cohabit should have only the *personal* portion of their social welfare payment revoked, while being allowed to retain the Child Dependent Additions portion.

CASE 2 is Paula, referred to in Chapter 5. She is a middle-aged woman who has had 10 children in all. She now has five dependent children, all of them teenagers, and has been separated for 11 years. She has been out of the labour market for a long time, has minimal formal education, and she is a local authority tenant. Her weekly Social Welfare income in the week before interview was £144; in addition, she received the £8 fuel voucher. In the previous week she spent her income as follows:

Item	£
Rent	16.00
Coal/Fuel	25.00
Curtain Club	3.00
Insurance	7.00
Vegetables	7.00
Total	58.00

Her *itemised* expenditure is small because, in her words, she "never does a big, weekly shop. If I buy in bulk its gone in two days — it wouldn't last."

Her weekly income is below the poverty line and she experiences a high level of deprivation, with a basic-scale score of 5 (the highest in the sample). She was candid about her living standards:

> *Sometimes I'm poverty stricken. You have to look for the cheap-*
> *est, you have to compare the prices in two supermarkets. I don't*
> *really eat a lot. Maybe it's subconscious after so long on social*
> *welfare.*

She never socialises, buys clothes or newspapers for herself. It is three
years since she bought herself a pair of shoes, and four years since
she had a holiday — it was a holiday subsidised by Parents Alone.
Also, she continually denies the children money for the cinema, discos
or entertainment: "You haven't got it — simple. But it leads to conflict
in the house." Her Child Benefit money, and the extra weekly income
of £25 from her son on the dole is spent on large bills. Currently, she
owes the ESB nearly £260, and in the past year she approached both
the local CWO and the St Vincent de Paul Society for help.

Paula recalls that when the children were smaller she could "manage OK", but that it is now very difficult with the children as teenagers.

As regards the administration of welfare payments, she was refused
help during the year prior to interview as a result of the 1992 "cuts"
imposed on "lump-sum" payments though SWA. She argued that:

> *They [the local CWOs] are not left with a lot of power to help*
> *you. If my lights were cut off, where would I go? The next op-*
> *tion is a money-lender. They are saying "Keep away from*
> *money-lenders" — but they don't help.*

In 1982, when her husband first left, she received a "split payment" —
that is, a portion of his unemployment payment — and then applied for
a Deserted Wife's payment. This took seven months to be put into effect, worsening an already bad financial situation. She recalls the Social
Welfare Officer's visit to her in relation to the Deserted Wife's claim:

> *From the time I applied till the time I got the money it took*
> *seven months. It can be a very traumatic time. They sent out a*
> *man. I will never forget him — the personal questions. If I had*
> *known about this I wouldn't have applied. He almost asked me*
> *how many times I had sex — it was that personal!*

She was clear that her husband had been "a father in name only" and
that she was "much happier" on her own. The independence of having
a personal social welfare entitlement was one of the positive aspects
of her life: "You have your own book and your own money."

When asked about the cohabitation rule in relation to Social
Welfare, she claimed that it did not directly impinge on her because:
"Having been in a bad relationship, I would be slow to go into a new

one." However, her general view of it was that it was unfair: where a recipient is cohabiting "it doesn't mean he is handing you up the money". She felt that it does affect whether women go into a relationship — because if women embark on a new relationship "you could lose your own book" (social welfare book for weekly payments).

CASE 3 is Leona, introduced in Chapter 4. She is distinctly not "poor" or deprived. Leona is in her forties and has five children in all — four of these are financially dependent on her and are aged between 7 and 17. She is an owner-occupier, buying a private house with a mortgage from Dublin Corporation. Her weekly income comprises a Deserted Wife's Benefit and net earnings from her full-time job on a local community project. Her net income in the week prior to interview was £248; her expenditure in the previous week was as follows:

Item	£
Rent/Mortgage	30.00
Weekly Shopping	90.00
Child Care	25.00
Gas	20.00
ESB	20.00
Total	185.00

The balance of over £60 after her necessary expenditure allows her to save — she has no arrears or debts and is putting money aside to add an extension to the house. Her non-dependent daughter of 19 "helps" financially, but essentially keeps her income separate. On the whole, she claims that financially she manages "very easily".

When invited to assess her own circumstances, she emphasised that she was "not poor now", but her frame of reference was shaped by her past experience and future prospects. She recalled graphically how, six years ago when her husband left and she was relying on SWA, she had "scrimped and scraped", baked her own bread, confined the whole family to porridge for breakfast, and eked out a meagre life. Her most telling illustration was of walking into Temple Street Children's Hospital one snowy winter's day, and walking home — a return journey of almost 10 miles — with a small child in a pram: she could not afford the bus fares:

> *Well, I walked everywhere. I remember when my eldest daughter was diagnosed as having epilepsy and the babies were very small. I used to walk in the snow to Temple Street Hospital*

*from Coolock and stay there all day and then come home and
boil potatoes and a few sausages or something for myself and
the small kids. All day we were in the hospital. We'd bring in
bread and have a package of crisps or something during the
day. But I was always guaranteed a cup of hot tea and the
nurses and staff were very, very good to me and I would walk
home in the dark and by the time I'd get back I would just heat
up a hot water bottle and we would all get into the bed together and then throw the hot water bottle into their bed and
when they got warm I would put them back into their own
beds so I was saving on coal.*

This initial period of reliance on SWA continued for two years, and
she only became aware of her entitlement to Deserted Wife's Benefit
when a Department of Social Welfare official visited her in relation to
her husband's application for Unemployment Assistance. Six weeks
later she received her Deserted Wife's Benefit and this resulted in an
increase in income of £40 a week:

*It was an extra £40 a week. It was great. I could buy biscuits,
and I could buy apples to make apple cakes, and make the dinner with meat, you know.*

She contrasts her current situation with this initial period of dire
poverty as a lone mother. The future, however, is uncertain. First,
one of her children, will be "going off" Child Benefit soon and, second,
the job she is in is temporary. In her case she was adamant about the
independence she enjoyed: "I can come and go as I please" and listed
the freedoms she exercised. Her freedom was such that the prospect of
another relationship would not interest her: "My home life now is my
own life and I wouldn't like to share it." She related her personal preferences in this regard to her views about the social welfare cohabitation
rule. For *young* people separated at an early age it was unreasonable,
she believed, to restrict their freedom and privacy:

*There is other younger people than I am who want to have a
second relationship and I feel that they should not be denied a
second relationship.... I mean they didn't make the mistake — in
most cases it was their partner, but they are being penalised.
That's an invasion of privacy for the social welfare to do — that
you can't have sex with somebody.*

This woman came from a large family — she has nine brothers and
sisters. Two of her sisters live a mere 20 minutes walk away, and the

remainder are all abroad. Her parents are dead. As she works and her sisters also have families, they do not see each other frequently — every six or seven weeks. However, this lack of social contact and personal closeness does not mean that practical support is missing. On the contrary, she felt reassured that her sisters were there. They helped in crises and emergencies, bringing her and one of the children to a hospital appointment recently at an awkward hour.

CASE 4: This is the case of Ellen, mentioned in Chapters 3 and 5, who is 25 and lives with her parents. She has a child of four and plans to marry a man to whom she is engaged. This relationship is a "new" relationship which commenced a year or two after her child was born.

Ellen receives the Lone Parent's Allowance — this is her only weekly income. She would be "poor" if her *own income* were considered in isolation: the LPA and Child Benefit combined give her (and her child) an income below the 60 per cent of mean income threshold. However, she is *not* deprived, as her score on the basic deprivation scale is zero and on the total scale is only 1. She apportioned her previous week's income, as follows:

Item	£
Contribution to Household	20.00
Insurance	5.00
Christmas Club	10.00
Total	35.00

The balance of her income was not spent. In fact, she explained, she sets aside most of her income every week, as she is saving for her future marriage. Her contribution to the household covers all her essentials — food, heat and so on. She is not involved at all in the management of the household's finances — this falls to her mother.

When talking about her financial circumstances, she usually referred to "we" — the economy of the entire household. According to her, the household does not have financial difficulties and her father, who is a full-time employee, believes that the family manages financially. Her financial reference points outside the household were her friends with whom she grew up. In comparison with them she felt restricted and was conscious that the deprivation she experienced as a single mother was the lack of freedom to travel and socialise: "Like all my friends, they have all been to Spain and Greece, all things like that. I know a holiday isn't everything but it's a part of my life I never had".

Ellen had not applied recently for SWA and expressed quite puni-tive views about the cohabitation rule and people's general over-reliance on social welfare, as she saw it:

> *No, I don't think it is fair if they have their book and they have someone living with them that has a full income. I don't think that it is right. Like, they are being greedy, they get everything. They have their own flat, they get their ESB bill paid, they get their fuel, they get this voucher, them vouchers, they get all these different conces-sions and it is the likes of people that really need it can't get it, and they have someone living with them that brings in a full week's wages. I think that is very wrong.*

Ellen's child is part of the wider family and she receives extensive practical support at home. Her parents are very involved with her child, as are her brother (aged 22), her teenage sister, and small brother (aged 10).

CASE 5: The case of Dana is very different in key respects from that of Ellen above. As recorded in Chapter 3, she is a single woman of 19 who lives independently with her two small children as a tenant in a local authority house. In income terms she is poor. Her only weekly income is the Lone Parent's Allowance, and her regular disposable income comprising the LPA and Child Benefit is below the 60 per cent poverty line. She is also deprived: her score on the basic scale is 4 and on the total scale is 12. Her high deprivation scores derive from the fact that she had arrears on rent and ESB, that she had to borrow to meet ordinary living expenses, and that she has recently been short of food or fuel; overall her life style is frugal — she cannot afford new clothes, newspapers, or a social life of any kind.

In the week prior to interview she received £86.40 from her LPA and fuel voucher, which she spent as follows:

Item	£
Rent	5.50
Weekly Shopping	25.00
Insurance	5.00
Loan Repayment	15.00
"Duvet" Loan Club	10.00
Credit Union	20.00
"Piped" TV	2.00
Total	82.50

Her expenditure is very close to her total weekly income. Usually, she explained, "I get paid on Thursday and when I have all my bills paid I have £3 left. And I can say 'that's mine'."

As she lives independently, she has had to equip a house, and consequently a lot of her weekly income is pre-empted by loans and repayments. She owes both the Corporation and the ESB arrears. In the case of the ESB, her local CWO paid off part of the last bill on a "once-off" basis but she is in arrears again. The rent arrears are difficult to deal with. Her rent to the Corporation was being deducted directly from her social welfare until recently as part of an administrative pilot scheme. This scheme ended and she now has to "hold on" to her rent from Thursday ("social welfare day") until Monday: the Corporation will only accept the rent on "rent day". Her monthly Child Benefit money is allocated to the gas bill or to any arrears on loans.

In her own view, she is badly off. When asked whether she found it difficult to manage, she said that she had "a lot of difficulty". When asked whether she would use the word "poor" as a description, she said:

> *I am always saying "I'm broke" ... I don't have the money to go out and buy what I want, what I need. I just buy the same things each week.... Half their clothes seem to be going too small for them.*

Her only outlet is a weekly trip to bingo with her mother: they share the cost of the game. Her parents live in the same estate and she sees them regularly; one sister of 21 will occasionally lend her money and a younger sister or her mother will baby-sit for her on request. Her mother and sister would be her support in an emergency.

Dana is still in regular contact with her former boyfriend who comes weekly to see the children. She is not involved in a relationship with him now, however. On the whole, she was not interested in marriage, which she partly ascribed to the *financial* impact this would have:

> *When I see other people getting married, they end up living on their money and if he's on the labour that means living on his labour, and I'd be worse off than I am now. I'd be no better off.*

This is a clear instance — but unusual in the context of this study — of a woman who perceives that the relative social welfare incomes of lone mothers and couples is a strong deterrent to marriage. However, in this case it is also true that her mother actively discourages her from marriage: "My Mam's always saying to me, 'Don't ever get married, don't ever get married ... Just live with him for a while.'"

CASE 6: This final illustration concerns Joan, a single woman in her mid twenties with one child aged 3, some of whose circumstances were reported in Chapters 3 and 5. She lives with her daughter in a local authority flat and works full-time. Her net weekly income in the week prior to interview was £120 — that is, gross pay less tax and PRSI. This income was spent as follows:

Item	£
Rent	5.30
Child Care	40.00
Bills	20.00
Credit Union	25.00
Bus Fares	7.80
Total	98.10

Her necessary expenditure leaves her with a surplus of just over £20. The largest item is the cost of full-time child care while she works. A close friend is her paid child-minder — she gives this friend £20 per week "for bills", to ensure that she has money set aside for ESB and other commitments.

According to the poverty standard applied in this study, she is not poor. Nor is she deprived, having very low scores on the scales of deprivation. She does not feel poor and described herself as "no worse off than anyone else". The benchmark she used for assessing her circumstances was the lower income she had when on social welfare — although she described herself as "not much better off" since going back to work. (She had not heard of Family Income Support (FIS) and was vague about whether she was receiving the Lone Parent Tax Allowance).

Her worst problem since having her daughter was accommodation. At first she lived with her sister with whom "I don't get on". Then she tried to get a private rented flat, intending to use the SWA rent allowance, but her experience was of poor quality, high prices and rejection by landlords of low-income tenants on SWA rent allowance.

> *Once they found out you were a single parent they didn't want to sign the forms. I went to loads of places before I got one. Their prices are ridiculous — the reason they charge them is because the welfare is helping them.*

She used the influence of a local TD to have her "housing points" reassessed and after 18 months obtained a flat in the area she hoped for. Her mother is deceased and her father and sister live locally. However, her father has not accepted her situation, and since her sister and she do not always agree, she has little emotional or practical support from her family.

She is uncertain in her views of marriage and sees the logic of the cohabitation rule in social welfare. However, in her view, she also sees the point of view of recipients that the Lone Parent's Allowance is "their own" entitlement. She claimed to know "a few girls" who were receiving the payments and who would not get married "because they can't afford to". Her perception of these situations was:

If she gives up her book, he only gets an extra amount for her every week on his social welfare per week — there's no way they'll do it [get married].

6.3   Poverty and Social Welfare

The descriptive summary of the women's income levels and sources in Chapter 5 and the case material given above vividly reveal how sparse are their incomes and living standards. Clearly, the first general issue to arise from this material is the adequacy of the social welfare payments. Confirmation of the importance of this issue can be found in the pattern of responses to two formal questions put to the women.

First, when women were outlining their incomes and how they coped financially they were asked to describe whether it was difficult/very difficult ... easy/very easy to manage financially. A very large majority of them stated that it was either very difficult/difficult to manage — as the details in Table 6.1 show.

Table 6.1:   Do Women Find it Difficult Managing Financially?

Managing with	Number	%
Great Difficulty	23	43
Some Difficulty	15	28
A Little Difficulty	6	11
Fairly Easily	7	13
Easily or Very Easily	2	4
Total	53	99

Note: Percentages do not add to 100 because of rounding.

Second, at the end of the interview, women were asked an open-ended question about what comments or suggestions they had regarding Government policy. A very frequent suggestion was to increase the level of social welfare payments.

It may seem a rather obvious conclusion to offer, but there is no doubt that most of the women would have benefited considerably from a higher level of income support. In policy terms, the level of social welfare support of lone mothers must be viewed in the light of the social welfare system as a whole — not least because the extent of poverty among lone mothers may also be found among other groups in the population. The most balanced policy conclusion, therefore, is that the incomes of families on social welfare, of whom lone-parent families are one type, should be significantly improved. The evidence of existing studies (Commission on Social Welfare, 1986; Callan, Nolan et al. 1989; Nolan and Farrell, 1990) is that households *with children* have a higher risk of poverty than non-family households. A general increase in social welfare payments on which families of all types depend would therefore be an important improvement.

A range of recent studies (Blackwell, 1989; Nolan and Farrell, 1990; Callan, 1991) have outlined how Child Benefit in particular could be improved. This study showed how crucial Child Benefit is to the finances of low-income lone mothers — being paid less frequently, the mothers were able to use it for bills or for items specially for children (notably clothes). This study does not offer any basis for advancing any *particular* reform of Child Benefit — it merely highlights again that a general improvement in Child Benefit would have a beneficial effect on the type of low-income lone mother included in this study. However, the detailed case material does raise the specific question of the *structure* of child income support. The interview material for this study supports the view that child income support should be tiered according to the age of the children — with a higher payment for older children. This was recommended by the Commission on Social Welfare in relation to Child Benefit — some of the case material given above and in Chapter 5 strongly echoes that proposal. However, there are counter arguments against an age-differentiated Child Benefit, as the *Report of the Child Benefit Review Committee* recently pointed out (Department of Social Welfare, 1995A).

In relation to the delivery of social welfare payments, one aspect of their administration emerged as a significant issue in the interviews. This was the length of time that it took for separated and deserted women actually to receive their payments. It can be accepted that the delivery of these payments might be slower than other payments because of the complexity of the maintenance obligations and the time that it takes to investigate these. Nevertheless, some women were waiting many months for their payment. A summary of these data is given in Table 6.2.

Table 6.2: How Long Women Waited to Receive Their Social Welfare Payment

Time	Number	%
1 Month or Less	7	19
2 or 3 Months	18	49
4 or 5 Months	3	8
6 or More Months	9	24
Total	37*	100

* Sixteen cases missing or not applicable.

In this waiting period, women claim SWA from their local Health Centre as the case-study evidence shows. However, the SWA rate is less than they would be receiving from social welfare and, while they receive "back money" in respect of the delay, the waiting period can result in women sliding into arrears and debts. Many separated women are left by their spouses with debts and commitments, and these escalate over the weeks and months while women rely on SWA — the lowest level of payment. The experiences recorded in some interviews highlight the need for administrative arrangements that are more local, more integrated, and therefore speedier than the present dual system of SWA — Social Welfare.

The final point to note here is that not *all* women in the study rely exclusively on social welfare for their income. In particular, as Chapter 7 will show, some women work full-time or part-time, and a very small number receive maintenance. As one of the illustrations above shows, a woman living independently who has full-time work, even at modest earnings, can have a living standard that keeps her above the poverty line. It is important, therefore, to note that improving social welfare payments is not the *only* route out of poverty for lone mothers — paid employment is another route. The small sample for this study does not allow cross-tabulation of the risk of poverty according to employment status, but the impressionistic evidence in the interviews is that women who have limited earnings, as a *substitute* for, or in *addition* to, social welfare, have higher standards of living. Policy should therefore focus not alone on the level of social welfare payments, but on using income maintenance, training and other policies to facilitate women to obtain paid work. This view is broadly supported in the research and policy literature (Millar and Glendinning, 1989; McCashin, 1993).

6.4   Budgeting and Financial Management

The interviews conveyed a strong picture of women engaged in a continuous and, at times, complex process of financial management. Perhaps the most striking aspect of this process was the manner in which the women "pre-empted" their weekly incomes to medium-term commitments. As the case studies show, they assign portions of their income to advance payments on gas, ESB, and loan commitments, and then "spend" the remainder on daily necessities. This pattern of financial management has mixed consequences. It undoubtedly allows the women to plan — in the sense of ensuring that potentially large bills are anticipated in advance. However, it also means that daily necessities cannot always be afforded.

Inescapably, many women had very low *personal* standards of living. While they manage within limits to pay bills such as rent and ESB, they have very little "personal" finance for relaxation, leisure or social life, or clothes. What was striking in some interviews was the somewhat apologetic way in which some women "admitted" to some very inexpensive personal expenditure: "I have to have my smokes to keep me sane," to quote one woman; or "I go to my adult education course, no matter what," to quote another. Even at the most personal level of clothing, some women relied on borrowed clothes or presents from their families.

Housing costs were critical to the women's financial welfare. In the first place, as one of the case studies illustrates, many single women do not have an "overhead" cost on their income in the form of a rent or mortgage repayment, as they live in their parents' home. At the other extreme, as a further case shows, other women are attempting to meet a mortgage repayment out of a considerably reduced income — sometimes paying additional repayments in respect of mortgage arrears. In between these extremes, women who are paying local authority rents have housing costs that are low relative to their incomes — weekly rents in a range around £5 per week applied to some women in the study. A definite problem mentioned by some local authority tenants was that "rent day" was not the same as "social welfare day". Dublin Corporation was reported as refusing to accept weekly rents on any day other than rent day. One woman mentioned that even her *arrears* would not be accepted on a day she offered them: "it makes it that much harder again to manage," she commented.

Regular receipt of Child Benefit and discretionary access to SWA "lump sums" were an integral part of how the women on social welfare managed their affairs. With Child Benefit it was straight forward: all of the women had it clearly and regularly "earmarked" either as a contribution to larger bills, or as a specific source of funds for the needs of children. Some commented that it was useful to have a separate monthly source of income, which allowed them to pay bills, for example. Discretionary "lump-sum" payments were a different matter. The worst financial problem women faced was the size of ESB, or rent, or mortgage arrears. Some women who had been refused "lump sums" simply could not understand the refusal; conversely, women who had received such payments remarked on how essential this "fall back" was to them.

The fieldwork took place shortly after the restriction on SWA exceptional-needs payments had been repealed. A number of the women commented on this and a few had been victims of the restrictions. It is difficult in a policy context to see how the restrictions could have been justified. What the interviews show is that women resorted to SWA "lump sums" for *very particular* reasons — for example, spouses ceasing, unexpectedly, to offer maintenance. As long as the mainstream social welfare payments remain at their current levels, it is difficult not to envisage a role for the discretionary SWA exceptional-needs payments.

Finally, it is important to note that although women "managed" financially, in the sense that they had financial routines, the women least well off spoke of the constant strain and stress involved. One woman spoke of this as a "struggle", another said it was "always a hassle". These descriptions would be typical of how some women experienced their financial responsibility. This financial burden, especially for separated women, was the converse of the freedom and independence that they also experienced. In other words, the women in general, and those women who had experienced difficult relationships in particular, sometimes linked their low incomes to their experience of financial *control*: "It's not a lot, but at least it's mine," in one woman's words, or, in the words of another, "I'm not worrying about him being out spending". This sense of control is part of a wider sense of freedom reported by many of the women — this is analysed more fully in Chapter 8.

6.5   Perceptions of Poverty

The case material given earlier shows that the women, although tending to be critical of aspects of the social welfare system, had quite limited expectations and narrow frames of reference against which they evaluated their own experience. A number of elements emerge here. First, women were likely to define their own experience in terms of their *immediate* past, or likely future changes. For example, those women who had moved from relying on Social Welfare to a mix of Social Welfare and a training allowance reported how much "better off" they were; likewise, women who had spent an interim period on SWA were pleased finally to receive their Social Welfare payment, and might comment, as did one woman: "At least I can get by on this, now." These highly individualistic assessments of their circumstances result in women having limited expectations — at least by the standards of society at large.

To the extent that women ever offered a relative view of their situations, it was in one of two categories. Either they emphatically accepted that they were "poor" or "badly off" and used such words, or they were optimistic about the fact that things could be worse or that "other people are worse off."

A number of mechanisms can be identified in women's behaviour, which helped them to sustain these perceptions. One or two women explicitly avoided situations that would place their limited choices in a social context: for example, one woman stated that she "never goes into town — It only reminds me of what I haven't got"; other women mentioned how they minimised contact with friends or family members as it made them realise that not everyone shared their circumstances. These examples suggest that the women on the very lowest incomes may *need* to have narrow and personal assessments of their living standards if they are to survive psychologically, long-term, on a minimal income. Some develop these assessments and expectations in a relatively deliberate and conscious fashion.

6.6   Social Welfare and Relationship Choices

One of the most contentious and complex aspects of public debate about lone mothers is the impact of the social welfare system on the family *choices* women make. This debate can be seen in the kind of concerns expressed publicly by politicians, as outlined at the beginning of the study. Equally, there is a body of analytical debate (see Murray, 1984, Brown 1989A, Brown 1989B, Wilson and Neckerman, 1988) focused on the role of social security in determining women's choices about families, marriage and relationships.

This study does not lead to a definitive view on the complex issues involved here, but a number of preliminary points can be made. First, as was illustrated in Chapters 3 and 4, women who where "choosing" lone parenthood seemed to do so for quite specific reasons related to their relationships, marriages, and so on. On the whole, it is probably safe to assume that social welfare per se does not determine women's choices. The rise over time in the extent of lone parenthood is probably best explained, therefore, first by reference to broad social changes in values and attitudes, and, second, to general socioeconomic factors in the labour market and employment generally as they affect women. But once a woman becomes a lone parent, does the social welfare system *then* affect her choices? The interview data for the study are somewhat ambiguous on this point.

One of the cases given earlier seems to support the view that single women may decide not to marry because they are "better off" alone on social welfare. This case was of a girl who had a boyfriend, living separately, who compared her *household* living standard if she married, to her current *personal* living standard. Clearly, if this set of experiences and perceptions had been widely found in the interviews, then a relatively firm conclusion might be offered. But at most only three or four offered views along these lines. A number of other points must also be noted.

First, many women expressed great satisfaction from the personal independence and freedom they experienced — a satisfaction that was based on their experience of relationships and not solely on the "financial freedom" conferred by a State social welfare payment (see Chapter 8). This applied to single women and separated women.

Second, women on the whole were generally quite disinterested in relationships and marriage. But this disinterest was only rarely expressed in the context of the relative social welfare entitlements of couples and lone mothers. Therefore, it can be argued that women first arrive at a strong preference about relationships. Social welfare *facilitates* and, perhaps, *reinforces* these preferences, but it is difficult to see how it could create these preferences. In this context, the question must be asked in the light of the material in Chapters 3 and 4 whether it is a policy *problem* that the social welfare system may be affecting women's choices, and, if so, what that policy problem might be. Many of the women in the study had experienced difficult, perhaps violent, relationships over a period of time. If the social welfare system facilitates them to make a choice, which would otherwise be very difficult, this system may therefore be viewed as a "success".

It should also be noted that the relative circumstances of lone mothers and couples is shaped by the adult-plus-adult-dependent structure of social welfare payments generally. If this kind of family-based structure persists, the social welfare system will always face the task of meeting the income needs of lone-parent families, while simultaneously avoiding any perceived "bias" or "discrimination" against two-parent families.

The issue of cohabitation raises similar questions. It is by no means clear whether the social welfare legislation per se deterred women from embarking on relationships. There was an almost uniform indifference about relationships among the women, as Chapter 8 confirms. Both separated and single women, aside from their attitudes based on experience, were also able to cite objective obstacles to new relationships — having children, lack of a social life, age, and preoccupation with their problems. However, if future, more representative research were to suggest that social welfare restrictions per se did prevent women entering longer term, stable relationships it would offer an argument for reconsidering the cohabitation "rule" — that it restricts choice and that it blocks a route out of poverty for some women.

Finally, as the cases above illustrate the women do *not* generally reject the principle of the cohabitation rule. One case above is cited as strongly supportive of the rule and another as seeing "both sides". Those women who criticised the rule often explained that men who are involved in relationships do not necessarily *financially* support their partner.

6.7   Family Support

Many of the separated women lived near the partners and families, and the young, single mothers were by and large in the community in which they had grown up (Tables 6.3, 6.4). The case material highlights the variation in family support among the women. At one end of the continuum are those women who live with their parents and effectively *share* the households' living standards. In some cases, such as the one outlined above, this results in a good standard of living and a sense of financial well being and security. However, income information

Table 6.3:   Location of Women's Mother

	Number	*%*
Decreased/Emigration	10	19
In Ireland — non Dublin	3	6
In Dublin	7	13
Near	19	36
Respondent in Mother's Home	14	26
Total	53	100

Table 6.4:   Where Do Respondents' Brothers/Sisters Live?

	Number	%
None	6	12
At Home with Respondent*	12	23
One Near	10	19
Two Near	12	23
Three or More Near	12	23
Total	52**	100

*   Women living in parents' home with one or more brother/sister.
** One missing case.

was not obtained about household members where women were in the wider household. This highlights the reality that some of the women, although vague, pointed out that their parents too were dependent on social welfare. In short, the impact of the "wider household" setting on young, single mothers can be varied: if the parents, for example, are also poor then the extent of *financial* support is limited.

The case material on family support more generally highlights the fact that having parents or family *near*, is not a guarantee of extensive emotional or practical support. Clearly, for some women their parents are critical to their day-to-day régime and are an indispensable financial fall back. But for other women nearness is *not* coterminous with closeness or financial support, as one of the cases suggest. The parents and families of these women also face constraints and, furthermore, tensions and disagreements within families can cut across the need for support. That parents and sisters are the most common source of help is clear from the summary information in Table 6.5. However, not all

Table 6.5:   Who Would Help Respondents in Emergency?

	Number	%
Parents	27	51
Sister	14	26
Brother or Other Relative	7	13
Friend	4	8
Other/None	1	2
Total	53	100

the women in the study *are* in their community of origin; some are in this situation, but family circumstances limit or eliminate the prospect of support; some who do receive support are conscious of it and in one woman's words "do not take it for granted".

7: Employment

7.1   Introduction

This chapter looks at the role of paid employment in the women's lives: whether they were at work at the time of the interview and what their aspirations or plans were in relation to paid work in the future. There are two principal reasons for focusing on this question in the research. First, lone mothers face the dual task of providing both parental care and financial support for children — in two-parent families these tasks can be, and very often are, largely divided between the parents. This may pose a dilemma for lone mothers: to which of these primary roles do they ascribe most importance? The study attempted to ascertain how women themselves viewed work and, in particular, whether their current employment status actually reflected their essential needs and preferences.

Second, the actual and desired employment situation may have important implications for social policy, notably in social welfare and child care. It has been pointed out that in the development of social welfare and other policies for lone mothers in Ireland the *assumption* that lone mothers are — and should be — full-time mothers has influenced the formulation of policy (McCashin, 1993). For instance, in 1972, in its deliberations on social welfare issues affecting women, the Commission on the Status of Women considered and then recommended the introduction of an allowance for unmarried mothers.

> We consider that there should be some financial support available to an unmarried mother who keeps her child, particularly when the child is very young and she cannot resume employment. We recommend, accordingly, that an unmarried mother who keeps her child should be entitled to a social welfare allowance at the same rate and on the same conditions that apply to a deserted wife, for a period of not less than one year after the birth of the child *(Commission on the Status of Women, 1972: 153).*

The role the Commission envisaged for the proposed allowance was one that provided an income for the period when "the child is young and she cannot resume employment".[1] In this analysis non-participation in the labour market is associated with the age of children and is not assumed to be a permanent, inevitable status for

---

[1]   Two other aspects of the Commission's recommendation which we need not comment on here are (a) that the allowance is envisaged as facilitating women to retain custody of their child and (b) that the allowance is for a "a period of not less than one year" — that is, a temporary allowance.

all unmarried women with children.

However, when the allowance (and the corresponding allowance then in place for Deserted Wives) was introduced, it appeared to *assume* that full-time mothering, on a permanent basis, was the appropriate social role for all lone mothers. *All* lone mothers, irrespective of the age of their children were entitled to the payment; furthermore, the amount of income women could earn without loss of allowance was small and remained unchanged over a long period of time. Nor was there any statutory assessment made of child-care costs for working mothers in determining access to the payment. This pattern of provision effectively separated social security from work. When set in the context of an absence of child-care services and of generally inferior conditions for women in the labour market, the social welfare system arguably may have helped to create a pattern of long-term exclusion from the labour market and dependence on State social welfare payments (McCashin, 1993).

This line of argument has direct implications for public policy. If the structure of social welfare has had the kind of consequences outlined, then it has also contributed to the significant growth in public expenditure on social security payments, and institutionalised the dependence of many women on social welfare as their sole source of income. From the point of view of this research, the essential question is whether the women have preferences in relation to paid work and, if so, to what extent these are being fulfilled or frustrated by social welfare and related provisions.

To address these issues, Section 7.2 outlines the *current* labour-market status of the women in the sample. Section 7.3 gives a qualitative account of how women view the role of paid work in their lives as a whole. This account is focused on the question referred to earlier: whether women's preferences are facilitated or impeded by public policy arrangements — as they perceive and experience them. Section 7.4 contains an analysis of the most direct and immediate policy that might impinge on the women's perceptions and decisions about work — social welfare policy. This discussion would not be complete without some commentary on the changes in the 1994 Budget to the means test for the Lone Parent's Allowance. As this very specific and very recent policy initiative has a direct bearing on the lives of low-income lone mothers who are depending on social welfare, it is commented on in detail.

7.2 Current Economic Status

In official analyses of the Irish population and labour force a *Principal Economic Status* measure of the labour force is adopted. Respondents to the annual Labour Force Survey and to the Census are invited to describe their "Principal Economic Status" in terms of one category from a list that includes categories such as: "Retired", "Permanently Sick and Unable to Work", "Unemployed", "Engaged in Home Duties", and so on. The respondents to the Census and the Labour Force Survey assign themselves to one of these categories and this forms the basis of the labour force "participation" profile. Thus, the total of those who are Unemployed and those In Work is taken as comprising the Labour Force (that is, Labour Force "participants") and the total of the Retired, Permanently Sick, those Engaged in Home Duties, Students, etc. comprises those not in the labour force.

Descriptions of these Principal Economic Status type figures as they affect women provide the basic calculations of women's "participation rates" in the labour force. Typically, analyses of these data in Ireland for recent years reveal a rise overall in women's "participation rate" in paid work outside the home and, in particular, a significant rise in the past two decades in the participation rate of married women (NESC, 1991; Blackwell, 1989B). A recent critique by Fahey (1993) of this approach to an understanding of women's relationship to paid work has pointed out that this concept has a gender bias. It assumes that women have "Principal" statuses, whereas for many women "work" and "home duties" may *both* be "principal" statuses. Informed by this critique of standard measures of women's level of employment participation, the women were not asked for their "principal" or "main" activity. The subject of "jobs" was explicitly raised with women by asking them "as regards jobs, are you at present ...?" A list of possible responses was then suggested: "Full-time Mother", "Full-time Mother, but occasional 'one-off' jobs"; "In regular paid part-time work"; "In regular paid full-time work"; or some "Other" category that they were asked to specify.

As will be shown below, most women described themselves as "full-time mothers". In the interviews this question was used not only to classify women according to current economic status, but also to open up discussion on the subject of employment. The women were all invited to talk about their preferences regarding their future status and how they thought they might fulfil, or fail to realise these preferences. The women were also asked to reflect on their views and experiences of combing paid work with their roles as mothers. In short, the description of their *current* situation was not assumed to be a direct reflection of their fundamental preferences or aspirations.

Table 7.1, reproduced from the relevant panel in Table 2.4 (Chapter 2), shows the classification of the women in the study based on their responses to the question outlined above. Most of the women described themselves as full-time mothers, and small proportions described themselves as full-time employees or part-time employees. A number were on training courses (for which they were receiving a training allowance); two women said that they worked "at home", keeping foreign students and doing child care for other mothers; while one woman actually used the description "unemployed". The central finding — that the majority of these women are out of the paid labour force — is common to studies of lone mothers in the UK and was also reported for Ireland in the ESRI's publication in 1993 (McCashin, 1993). Within the limits of the sample size, it is not possible to quantify differences in labour-force status of various categories of lone mothers or to analyse these differences. The interview material can, however, be used to give a qualitative analysis of the role of paid employment in the women's lives and of women's aspirations in relation to work.

Table 7.1:   Self-Reported Employment Status of Lone Mothers

	Number	*%*
Full-time Mother	30	57
Full-time Employee	7	13
Part-time Employee	7	13
Training	4	8
Unemployed	1	2
Other	2	4
No answer	2	4
All	53	101

Note: Percentages do not add up to 100 because of rounding.

7.3   Employment — Preferences and Perceptions

Before reporting any specific interview material on the role of employment in the women's lives, it is useful to note some of the key themes that emerged in the research literature (NESC, 1991; Blackwell, 1989B; Wong, Garfunkel, McLanhan, 1993). First, the trend over time has been for an increase in recent decades in many countries in the participation of married women in paid work outside the home. Second, against this backdrop of an overall rise in women's participation, a differential persists between women at different stages of the family cycle — notably, in some countries, women with young dependent children are less likely in time to be in paid employment. Third, levels of education and training — and consequently the financial return to work — have a significant influence on the likelihood of women remaining in the labour market. Fourth, there are considerable differences across countries in the labour-force participation rates of lone mothers in particular. Irish and British rates, for instance, are low by international standards, while the rates for Scandinavian and some continental European countries are high. These differences arise to a considerable degree from the employment and social policy régimes that affect women in different countries (Lewis, 1993).

An immediate point to note about the Irish experience, as reported in the ESRI study (McCashin, 1993), is the low rate of labour market participation. This pattern is replicated in the local sample for this study, with 15 of the 53 women being in paid employment, either full-time or part-time — or unemployment (a "participation rate" of 18 per cent). What cannot be documented is whether this rate has been changing over time. Therefore, there is no evidence as to whether or not the British experience of a *decline over time* in lone mothers' work participation may apply to Ireland (Dilnot and Duncan, 1991).

Some of the factors identified as key influences on labour market behaviour in the international research emerge also in the local interview material for this study. What the study attempts to do is to convey the perceptions women have of the decisions that they have reached, and to understand — through their eyes — why they have made these decisions. This form of analysis allows an understanding of how the women interpret their experience of the labour market and offers some insight into the actual impact of current and alternative policies on women's lives and choices.

To report the interview material, a typology is used that captures the broad range of experiences and perceptions found in the study. First, the experience of women who are in *full-time paid employment* can be examined. What is striking about the small number of women in the study who are paid employees is the diversity in their circumstances and in the meanings they ascribed to paid work. Jackie, for example, is 41 years old and has two children aged 12 and 9. At secondary school, she obtained her Leaving Certificate and left at the age of 18. Having completed a secretarial course, she took up office employment and remained in employment until her late twenties when her first child was born. She was at home with her children full-time for eight years, and in 1989 participated in a FÁS return-to-work course. Her placement on this course was in a nearby hospital where she was kept on after the course ended. She is now a regular staff member, employed as a medical secretary and "bringing home" about £140 per week net.

She portrayed her employment commitment as quite a difficult one, for two reasons. First, she works full-time, primarily because she needs the money: when she first returned to work on a trainee pay rate her financial circumstances were bad — she owed repayments to the Building Society, and no maintenance was being paid by her husband:

> At first I was only on £80 to £90 per week and the Building Society was threatening to repossess. If I had a choice, I'd be out there part-time maybe. My prime commitment is to the kids: I only go to work because of the financial ropes around my neck.

Second, as the quotation makes clear, her children are her first consideration. Initially, when she resumed work a local child-minder looked after the children at very low cost for a year and a half. However, the minder, as she recalls, "let me down suddenly", and she had to make new arrangements. This, she feels, affected the children's confidence. Her second and current arrangement involves a next-door neighbour who helped her out of the predicament at no cost by agreeing to take the children after school and "to keep an eye on them" on days when they were not at school. However, Jackie feels obliged to come home every day at lunch-time to check on the children and then return to work. In addition to the financial pressures and the child-care concerns, she describes the job situation as "stressful":

> The job is stressful now — I'm tired and find it stressful. I'm temporary so I have minimum pay and minimum holidays. The job now is demanding — I'm a medical secretary — I saw about a hundred and eighty public patients today. You take a lot of abuse in an average day.

A complete contrast in experience is offered in the circumstances of another woman employed full-time. This is Leona, in her early forties, with four dependent children ranging in age from 7 to 18 — her financial circumstances were detailed in Chapter 6. She had married in her early twenties and given up her job — she had left school at 13 without any qualifications. Nine years ago, she and her husband separated, and some years later she became involved in the Parents Alone Resource Centre. This led to her participation in adult education classes and a variety of part-time courses in the area of community work and adult education. Her gradual re-education had brought her to the status first of a part-time employee in a local Community Development Project, and, at the time of interview, a full-time employee.

When asked about her experience of combining the roles of mother and employee, she was emphatic:

> *I love my job. I love being out doing work in the community. I see what I am doing now as part of community work and I work very much hand in hand with the school the two boys go to.... The only two children that have to be minded are the two youngest. They are in school till 2.20 and they are minded till 4.30, so I have the whole evening to spend with them, and the weekends. I love my work and I love my family but they are a separate entity. My work is for myself and my time at home for the children, being a mother.*

She receives a net wage weekly of £120, which supplements her Deserted Wife's Benefit, although she did not in any way ascribe her satisfaction with her employee status to financial considerations.

These two cases represent "extremes" of experience among women engaged in full-time paid work. One reported considerable stress and anxiety caused by a combination of child-care worries, financial pressures and the nature of the employment, and the other expressed considerable satisfaction with the freedom, status, and identity conferred by a full-time job. Other women who were employees reported some of these elements in varying degrees and combinations, although not with the same intensity. These other cases include the following:

- Joan, mentioned in Chapters 3 and 6, who is single and has a small child. She "always wanted to work". She has a Leaving Certificate, worked as a secretary before her pregnancy, and returned to work six months prior to the interview. Joan claimed that it was "not really worthwhile financially" as the child-care cost of £40 is paid out of a net wage of about £120.

- A separated woman in her late thirties with four children of school-going age who has an aunt minding the children for a mere £20 per week. Without this willing aunt, this woman would be, in her own terms, "in massive trouble" with child-minding — she now works full-time on a local community project and the wage of £112 (net) supplements her Deserted Wife's Benefit. She described herself as having "good training and experience" for work, having been educated to Inter Cert standard and worked before marriage as a Dental Receptionist, Quality Control Worker and then a Civil Servant.

- A woman of 37 with two children, one 13 and the other 11, who returned to Ireland from the UK two years ago having divorced her husband from whom she now receives no maintenance. Although at the time of interview she was a "a full-time mother" she was planning within two weeks of the interview to open her own catering business now that her children's ages permitted her to work. She has no formal educational qualifications, but trained in the catering area in the UK. She attributes her willingness and keenness to establish the business to her training: "I have a skill", and to her long-felt preference for independence: "As a child I always had the old notion: when I get my place, I won't be working for anybody else."

The second group of women comprises those who had made a choice to be *full-time carers of their children* or to work for only limited periods of time outside the home — because of the needs of their children, as they perceived them. In these cases, women were, of course, conscious of other considerations — such as income — but they ascribed their decision to be full-time mothers or to take limited part-time work *primarily* to issues affecting their children. A clear case in point here is Alice, a 19-year-old single woman living in her parents' home with her son aged two and a half. She left school at 15, having completed her Group Certificate, and worked in pubs and shops until she finished work when her son was born. At present, she is at home with the baby but has applied for a course in a local community adult education centre. This would be for three mornings only and occasionally at weekends. Her plan is to use the allowance for child-care costs, which forms part of the trainee payment, to pay her sister to mind the baby. Her preference as regards work she expressed as follows: "I want to do something where I can be around the baby and be involved in work." She was clear, however, that full-time work which kept her from the baby was not something she would consider: "I would have to have options for minding her or I wouldn't take a full-time job. I mean I already have one." Her intentions regarding the planned part-time course were clear:

> *The way it works is that, if I asked my sister to mind the baby, I would have to pay her because I would be doing this course three times a week and probably at weekends and you would be going away on weekends. So what they do is, they pay you to have your*

child minded. I wouldn't be anything out of pocket because the money they give me I would give to my sister, because it's only three times a week. But if it was a full-time job that would be different. I would have to leave her with a crèche and I don't want to do that.

Delia is another case of a woman who made a clear and explicit choice in favour of limited part-time work. She is in her early thirties and separated from her husband. At the time of interview, she was living independently with her 6-year-old daughter in a small owner-occupied house. Delia had completed her secondary education to Leaving Certificate standard and worked in "good jobs" — as she termed them — in banks and the civil service. After her marriage to a chronic alcoholic and gambler broke up, she resumed part-time work having taken a course in counselling. Her part-time job is in a counselling agency (mornings only) during the September to end-June period.

In outlining her mix of limited part-time and caring work at home, she at first explained that her decision was based on *financial* considerations:

Well, financially it is a maximum situation for me in relation to the amount of effort I have to put in and the amount of work I have to do. I get Deserted Wife's benefit and I have that part-time job. So I have to pay tax on it: if I earned more, I'd be paying more tax. I'd have to pay a baby-minder and I'd have to work much more myself. I mean there is a lot of work to be done here, I have a big garden out the back, a lot of extra work really. So this is a maximum situation for me, an optimum situation really in regard to money and effort.

However, when directly asked how important child-care issues were in her decision to limit her involvement in paid work, she clearly emphasised the needs of her daughter as the main consideration:

Child care and the taxation system and the mortgage — all those things matter. Also, I feel that emotionally, Susan needs a lot of security. She likes to know that I am coming home, that I am here. I would say that is nearly the biggest one — her emotional security — and then my financial position.

This theme of the primacy of children's needs ran through many of the interviews. It is important to note that while the theme recurred time and again among women with young children, it was not *confined* to them. In fact, this category of women comprises women in quite diverse situations as the examples above, and below, suggest:

- A single woman aged 24 with a 4-year-old daughter, living in a rented corporation house with her daughter — she had a full-time job for three months during which time her little girl was in a child-minder's home from 8 a.m. to 6 p.m. at a cost of £40 per week, but gave this up because her daughter was getting upset; she now says: "My role now is to be Leona's mother ... people are saying "You're sitting around the house" — but I love having her here. I hate when she's at school even!"

- Beth, whose financial situation was described in Chapter 5, is a separated woman in her early forties with three children aged 16, 14 and 10, and she works part-time; her mother-in-law lives "across the road" and on some days gives the children lunch after school; on the days when she is working, she is home at 4.30, but she is emphatic that she will not work full-time: "I don't want to work full-time because of the kids — and anyway I need more training.... I wouldn't like them to come home to the house every day without me there".

An important variant on the kind of cases noted above concerns those who expressed their choice as a dilemma: they felt quite torn and found the choice not to work a difficult one. For example, one woman articulated her decision not to be at work in this way: after her marriage broke up, leaving her alone to care for her small boy, she was financially obliged to work, she felt. However, as time passed, she became conscious that, although she liked working and needed the money, she felt that her son needed her, and she gave up work. Recently, she was tempted by an offer from an employer — an offer her friends encouraged her to take: "You have to think of yourself." But in this situation, which she described as "a Catch-22 situation", she opted to remain out of paid work: "I brought him into the world and I have responsibility for him". Furthermore, she was conscious as a separated woman that if she worked her son might grow up "not knowing he had a mother or father" (her emphasis).

Similarly, Amy, whose severe deprivation was illustrated in Chapter 5, is a young separated woman with two small children, who had obtained a Leaving Certificate and worked in a building society up to the time her children were born. She described herself as a "full-time mother" at the time of interview. However, she viewed her situation as one in which she could not work because of the children's ages. This she found very difficult: "No, I'm not working.

Its cracking me up. It's driving me mad."

The third category can be described as *unemployed* in the conventional sense. These women had actively looked for work and at the time of interview were still anxious to find work and in the process of searching for a job. What is significant about these women is that when asked a simple "descriptive" question as to their current status, they almost all categorised themselves as "full-time mothers". One of the women described herself as unemployed. In other words, the descriptions the women used as to their current status were a poor guide to their actual preferences and aspirations.

The clearest case of these circumstances is Barbara who is in her mid-thirties, lives with her 5-year-old son in a rented local authority flat, and receives the Lone Parent's Allowance as her only source of income. She had lived abroad for some years and returned to Ireland about a year prior to the interview after her marriage broke up. Barbara has an Inter Cert and considerable experience of secretarial and office work in Ireland and abroad. She was quite clear about her preoccupation with finding a job. In response to a query about whether she was doing any paid work, she replied:

> *No, no, I'm looking. Every week. I've been for interviews — it is very, very hard. I didn't realise how hard it can be. I really didn't. I thought after a couple of months ... I knew I wouldn't get anything immediately, but I thought after a couple of months I should get something. There is just nothing and then my age doesn't help.*

She was definite that she would have accepted a full-time job offer, although she had a son below school-going age: "I would have put him in a full day-care centre which I had his name down for — it was locally." Despite her lack of success in getting a job, she was still active in her search — she said, when asked if she was still looking for work:

> *Oh yes! I am — I'm writing away and all. I kept them all. I have about that much rejects. But you've gotta keeping going, you can't let that knock you down. You've gotta get a lucky break some time. I mean, I'm not the only one, like you know.*

Similarly, another young woman of 30, with a 6-year-old daughter who is now attending school, was keen to work despite a lack of success to date in obtaining a job. Finola, who was mentioned in Chapter 4, is living in social welfare rented housing with her daughter and is being maintained by her husband from whom she separated two years ago. Now that her daughter is at school, she is anxious to work: "I'd love to work because I have so much time on my hands when she's at school." She said that she had tried to obtain further training — her only training to date is secondary education to Leaving Certificate — but was refused a place on a FÁS course because she had a child:

> *I want to get retrained. I've tried FÁS and they've refused me because of having a child. I can't get on them courses. That's what I'd like — to be retrained. It's very frustrating wanting to work and not being able to.*

This category of "unemployed" lone mothers includes not only young women with small school-going children, but also some middle-aged women with grown-up children, who are persistently looking for work. For instance, Daphne, who recently separated, has four children ranging in age from 18 to 10. She was married for over 20 years and during that time she was out of the paid labour force. Now, however, she has begun to look for a job assiduously, partly as a result of the growing confidence that she has acquired in counselling since her marriage break up. She did a return-to-work course about a year ago and now says:

> *I am beginning to look for work. I am getting my self-confidence back slowly.*

When asked what her view might be if her search for a job led to an offer of full-time work, she replied:

> *If you asked me that before Christmas I think I would have said that I would hold back, but now I think I would go for it.... It's only in the last month I'm thinking of me now.*

This group of women who are actively looking for jobs can be naturally contrasted with a category of women who are *deterred* from even considering looking for paid work by a combination of age, lack of training and education, and the length of time that they have been out of paid employment. Women in this latter category are middle-aged, with little or no formal education or training, and out of the paid work force since their marriage or the birth of their first child. Paula is a very typical case in point. As the material in Chapters 5 and 6 showed, she has a low income and is quite deprived. Aged 53 and the mother of 10 children (five of whom are still financially dependent on her), she has been separated for over 11 years and relying solely on social welfare for her income during that time. Despite her very difficult financial situation, she cannot envisage seeking paid work. When discussing this possibility she said:

> *At this stage in my life I wouldn't like to go back to work — because of my own age and the kids are still young. Physically or mentally, I don't think I could cope with a job. It's very hard at my age to get a job.*

Although the women in this category are remarkably similar in terms of age, education levels and time out of the labour market, it may be advisable not to see an overly deterministic link between these characteristics and the choices they make. Other women in the study with similar characteristics made different choices. For example, there are some middle-aged women with very limited formal education, who had withdrawn from paid work after marriage, and who are now full-time or part-time employees. With the limited sample size, it is not possible to contrast such categories in detail. It is possible to suggest on the basis of the interviews, however, that women who avail of services such as PARC, or who used counselling or other similar supports for their *personal* situations, then developed an interest in the world of paid work and a sufficient level of confidence to enable them to re-enter formal employment or to attempt this despite the obstacles.

Finally, there is a clearly identifiable group of women whose orientation to paid work is negatively affected by the *financial* implications of taking up employment. These financial implications arise from the impact of an increased, earned income on their social welfare income, and from the costs of attempting to earn an income — for example, child care and bus fares. It is clear that some women experience a type of *unemployment trap*: they had either withdrawn from paid work or would not contemplate paid work because, *as they perceived their situations*, they would gain little, or actually lose, by staying in work or taking up work. The analysis for this study is based on the women's *perceptions* and not on the detailed factual arithmetic of their incomes or of their actual entitlements and benefits. The study did not attempt to ascertain whether women's assessments of these issues (how much tax they might pay, what reduction in social welfare would ensue and so on) were in fact correct. Rather, it recorded their perceptions and experiences and looked for their own explanations for their decisions.

A vivid illustration of their circumstances was given by Rita (see Chapter 3). She is a single woman of 19 with a baby of six months, living at home with her mother and brothers and sisters. She left school at 15 with her Group Certificate and worked in a nearby clothes factory as a machinist. At the beginning of the interview, she mentioned that she was giving up work the following week. Her net weekly earnings were £105, out of which she paid child minding and other work-related expenses, and she estimated that it would be more financially advantageous to claim half of her unemployment benefit (based on her PRSI record) and the Lone Parent's Allowance. In relation to her weekly earnings of £105, she pointed out:

> *That is after tax. I have to take £30 out of that for a child minder and I have to give my Ma money, dress the baby and feed her and that. Like, you are not coming out with anything, so if I was on the unmarried mother's (allowance) like, I would be able to claim my labour — half of my labour — for a year and then I would still be coming out with £100 and I wouldn't have to pay a child minder.*

When asked how important it was to her to spend time with her small baby, she clarified that it *was* a factor in her decision but that she would continue working if the financial outcome were different:

> *I want to spend more time with the baby. That is what I am saying like — if I was coming out with more, like that I'd say stick at it for a while. Like I am not gaining anything and then I am not seeing her an awful lot, you know, so....*

Rita's entitlement to some unemployment benefit would not apply to many women, but her perception of the financial implications of work were clearly echoed in the views expressed by other women in a variety of circumstances. For example, Sally is a lone mother with three children, living in a rented corporation flat. She obtained her Leaving Cert at secondary school. However, she has virtually no experience of paid employment, as she had her first child while at school and has been caring full-time for her children since her first child was born. Her hope is to return to work, but she clearly perceives that the child-care and ancillary expenses associated with work are obstacles. She first expressed the view that she would work in these terms: "Like, babysitting, family wise, if I wasn't paying a professional baby-sitter...." When asked if the cost of child care was an obstacle, she elaborated:

> *Yeah, the cost of child care, and as well as that I know my tax-free allowance is good, but you can only earn so much and then it's taken out of your allowance book. And you've got the cost of*

> *travelling and the cost of meals away from home. And I suppose*
> *if it wasn't financially feasible, I mean if I wasn't coming out*
> *any better, it's just ... the hassle of arranging child care, working,*
> *coming home, late nights, then it just wouldn't be worth my*
> *while.*

These litanies of the "costs" of work were common in some of the interviews, although it is also clear from the other categories identified
that other factors — age of the children, lack of training and so on —
intrude on women's decisions about paid work. These unemployment
trap cases, however, are distinguished by the importance the women
ascribed to the *financial* costs/benefits of paid work relative to remaining out of the labour market. One of the "costs" of work could be
deemed to be more important in the women's lives — child care.
Women frequently quoted a figure based on their own experience or
gave a precise estimate of child-care costs. Other instances of this pattern include the following:

- Kay (see Chapter 3) who returned from Canada with her child
  having parted from her boyfriend, and who contrasted the Irish
  and Canadian contexts in terms of the comparative difficulty of
  working in Ireland: "In Ireland — you can't work here. It's the price
  of child care."

- A separated woman of 30, with twins under 4 years of age, who
  simply stated when asked about work: "Love to. I'd love to get a job"
  — she was clear about the financial constraints implied in her child-
  care obligations: "I'd have to be taking home a hundred and fifty
  pounds — that's not a lot by the time you pay your child minder."

- A single woman in her early twenties with a 3-year-old child, who
  gave up work because of the small extra income she gained after
  child-care costs: "I had to pay baby-sitting money plus the money I
  was giving my Mam already — it kind of didn't work out that I
  was doing it for any real extra money — I was only £10 better off."

As explained earlier, the identification of different categories of
women is based on the women's perceptions and experiences. In the
case of those who felt that they experienced an unemployment trap, it
is important to note that some of the women's perceptions of the tax
and benefit system were actually inaccurate. It is clear, for example,
that not all women knew of their potential entitlements in regard to
the Lone Parent's Tax Allowance and Family Income Supplement and,
consequently, these perceptions might be amenable to policy change if

greater awareness and improved take up of entitlements could be achieved.

It should be realised that there is no evidence to suggest that women in low-income *two-parent* families do not feel similarly constrained in their choices. The public policy context in which married women, for example, make decisions about employment is also one in which the impact of taxes, benefits, and child-care costs may loom large. In considering the policy implications of the research for this study, it would be prudent to see obstacles to labour market participation among low-income mothers as a *general* problem, of which the problems of lone mothers are a specific and acute manifestation.

The analysis of the women's perceptions and experiences of work focused on the *differences* among the women in the study. These differences, need to be viewed in the context of one, almost universal, finding. All women in varying ways, and to varying degrees, are *positive* about paid work, and some are enthusiastic. There is no evidence that the welfare system has corroded women's underlying preferences and aspirations to have a job when their family circumstances permit. The patterns of "non-participation" which were described should be viewed as *responses* to constraints and circumstances, rather than wilful disregard of the potential benefits to women and their families of earned, independent income.

The material on employment was presented in a way that highlighted the relationship between the women's current situation and their preferences and aspirations. In some cases, these clashed — as in the cases of women who, although currently "housewives", were actually unemployed and keenly searching for work; in other cases, these were in some form of equilibrium — where, for example, women had contacted a mix of paid work and family life which suited them. Women's decisions about employment emerged as quite complex: they brought a range of considerations to bear on the decisions they made. The broad categories used to record their experiences and perceptions have not been summarily described with distinct labels, as they cannot be viewed as clear, discrete categories.

7.4 Social Welfare and Employment

The last section analysed the views and aspirations of the women in relation to paid work. One feature of that analysis was the perception among some women that the "costs" and "benefits" of going to work were such that they felt it was not worthwhile. In expressing these views, women did not offer *precise calculations* — nor was any attempt made to obtain them. They offered instead general perceptions that once the cost of child care is taken into account on the one hand, and the deductions from earnings on the other (such as income tax and PRSI), the financial return from work was minimal or negative. It was also observed from the interview material that the women did not rigidly demarcate these financial aspects of work from the child-care aspects: both sets of issues feature in their decision-making processes.

It is necessary at this point to look at the *actual* interaction of pay, child-care costs, deductions from earnings and so on. Is the interpretation of these intricacies held by some of the women in the study distorted, or is there in fact an "unemployment trap" which effectively prevents them from re-entering paid employment? "Unemployment trap" refers to a situation in which a welfare recipient's net income, would *decline* as a result of taking up employment or of increasing the amount of income earned from (say) part-time employment.

If such an "unemployment trap" prevailed, policy issues of efficiency and equity would arise for consideration. There are potential *efficiency* losses in the economy if these poverty "traps" affect the incentive to work and thereby increase public expenditure on social welfare payments. The question of *equity* is involved in that some persons out of work might obtain higher net incomes than persons in work. This discussion is entirely hypothetical. Any empirical analysis of the poverty trap is critically dependent on specific assumptions about the taxes and benefits included in the analysis and how their "value" is quantified. For example, is the loss of a medical card entitlement and other *non-cash* benefits to be incorporated in the calculations? If so, how can the value of the medical card and other benefits-in-kind be expressed in monetary terms?

While it is arithmetically possible to generate "unemployment trap"-type scenarios across a range of categories (such as the unemployed, low-paid employees, lone mothers), it is essential to identify how *intensive* and *extensive* the illustrative scenarios are. An intensive poverty trap would occur where an actual decline in net income corresponded with a move into employment or an increase in the amount of part-time employment. A less intensive scenario would apply where a welfare recipient's net income would remain unchanged or increase only marginally after moving from "welfare to work". Extensiveness refers to the degree to which any hypothetical situation actually applies to the relevant population. In the case of unemployment payments, for example, a potential unemployment trap for people with large families receiving long-term unemployment assistance (UA) and living in local authority tenancies can be identified. This situation, however, is not extensive: only a small minority of the unemployed are married with a number of children, only some of these are local authority tenants, and not all of them will be in receipt of long-term UA. As much of the comment on this question is based on illustration, rather than on statistically representative data, it is important to assess how extensive, in fact, any illustration is likely to be.

The above cautionary comments apply to the illustrative material on which Figure 7.1 is based. The figure attempts to assess whether an "unemployment trap" arises in the case of lone mothers receiving the social welfare Lone Parent's Allowance (LPA). This allowances is means tested: if a woman takes up employment, it may result in a reduced LPA. Her net pay might be affected by the payment of tax and PRSI on her gross earnings, and she may have to incur child-care costs to go out to work. The figure shows a range of gross earnings on the vertical axis and net income on the horizontal axis. Two graphs are included: one which assumes the implementation of the 1994 Budget's alterations to the means test for the LPA and one which incorporates the pre-1994 means test.

Until the 1994 Budget the means test was relatively restrictive: it disregarded only £12 of earned income before a reduction in the LPA was effected and the reduction was a "£1 for £1" reduction — or a "marginal tax" on additional income of 100 per cent. In response to the criticism that this means test, in conjunction with the interaction of tax, PRSI, child-care costs and other means tests, offered a powerful disincentive to its client population to obtain earned income, the means test was altered in the 1994 Budget so that the first £30 per week of income is disregarded in assessing net income (that is, income after social insurance, child-care costs, etc). A further significant change introduced in that Budget was that after net income has been identified and the new disregard applied, only 50 per cent of the balance is considered as income, offsetting the amount of the allowance to which an recipient is entitled.[2]

Figure 7.1 compares the impact of these two means-test régimes. The payment rates for 1994/95 were applied and the impact that

---

[2]   There were two further budgets since the fieldwork for this research was completed. Three key features of the 1995 Budget of particular relevance to lone parents were: weekly social welfare payments were increased by 2.5 per cent, Child Benefit was increased by £7 per month per child and a commitment was made to the reform of Deserted Wife's Benefit and Lone Parent's Allowance. In the 1996 Budget, welfare payments were increased by 3 per cent, Child Benefit by £2 and the Government decided to proceed with the introduction of a new One-Parent Family Payment Scheme which will replace the existing Lone Parent's Allowance and Deserted Wife's Benefit Schemes. This new Scheme will come into effect on 1 January 1997.

these means-test régimes would have on the net income of a lone parent with one child was contrasted. The calculations incorporated the intricate, inter-related changes in income tax, social insurance, the LPA, family income supplement and child-care costs. Net income in the figure refers to the income a lone mother is "left with" after she has received whatever cash allowances she is due and has paid tax, social insurance and child-care costs. The impact of local authority rents or medical card eligibility are *not* included, nor is any account take of travel-to-work costs.

Figure 7.1: Unemployment Trap, 1994/95 — Lone Mother, One Child

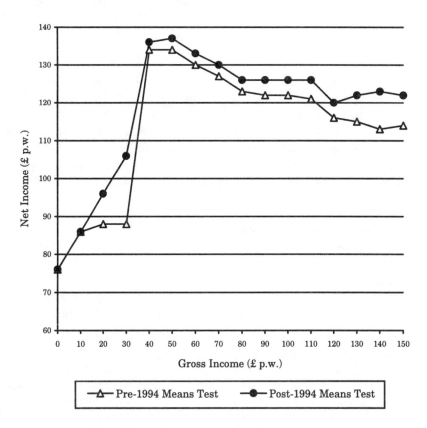

It is important to recognise that the interactions involved *are* complex. A woman who increases her earned income significantly might find that she becomes liable for income tax. Likewise, a move across the £60 p.w. earnings threshold in formal, contractual employment means that an employee becomes liable for social insurance contributions. On the benefits side, an employee who works 20 hours or more per week is entitled to claim Family Income Supplement. However, if after a period of 52 weeks in receipt of FIS, a claimant's income has increased, the FIS payment is reduced by 60 per cent of the increased income. FIS pays 60 per cent of the gap between the relevant target income and actual income. However, when gross income rises, 60 per cent of the increase in gross income is withdrawn from FIS. It is not difficult to see how the combined effect of the means tests, taxes, and PRSI and child-care costs can, in principle, generate an "unemployment trap" which might deter welfare recipients from seeking work, or accepting a job if offered one.

A summary of the calculations on which Figure 7.1 is based is given in Table 7.2. The first point to note about the figure is that at

Table 7.2:   The "Unemployment Trap" for a Lone Mother and One Child, 1994/95 Gross Income and Net Income on Alternative Means-Test Scenarios

Gross Income £ p.w.	Pre 1994 Means Test Net	Post 1994 Means Test Net
0	76	76
10	86	86
20	88	96
30	88	106
40	134	136
50	134	137
60	130	133
70	127	130
80	123	126
90	122	126
100	122	126
110	121	126
120	116	120
130	115	122
140	113	123
150	114	122

Notes: See text.

all gross income levels the *net* figure for the "post-1994" line is marginally higher, indicating that the impact of the relaxed means test
has been to improve the return on increased earnings relative to a
pre-1994 means test. A second and more striking, feature of the table
is the very marked improvement in net income at low levels of gross
earnings. Where gross earnings are assumed to be £20 or £30, the
new means test results in a much sharper increase in net income
than would otherwise be the case: this is a direct outcome of the
more generous means test. It is important to note that for both
graphs, it is assumed that at £40 per week the client works at a
minimum of 20 hours and therefore qualifies for FIS — this explains
the steep slope of the lines at that point.

However, it is clear from the graph that once a claimant begins to
attain higher gross incomes, the slope of the net/gross relationship
alters dramatically, even under the new means-test régime and the
net income line *declines* as gross pay rises. How could this occur? It is
assumed that at the very lowest levels of income no child-care costs
were incurred but that these gradually increased to £20, £30 and £35
over a range of gross pay from £40 weekly — it is also assumed that
these costs were off-set in full in the means assessment. The higher
LPA and pay are now assessed against FIS which is steeply withdrawn. In addition, once the £60 threshold for gross pay is exceeded,
PRSI is paid, and further up the income curve (£134 p.w.) the ancillary levies must be paid. Finally, the role of income tax must be noted:
at higher levels of gross pay the combination of the LPA and earned
income draw the claimant into the income tax net.

The net impact of this analysis is that the *reformed* means test has
improved the potential return on earned income at very modest levels
of gross pay. In short, the potential return on low-paid employment
for recipients of the LPA is actually quite high: their net income rises
steeply as they increase their gross pay. However, this gross pay–net
income relationship does not apply across the entire range of incomes.
On the contrary, a more general *poverty trap* persists which can be ascribed to the interlocking effects of the means tests for FIS and the
LPA, as well as the normal impact of social insurance and income tax
on earned income. The "Poverty Trap" at higher levels of gross pay
refers to persons in *employment*. It shows the impact of an increased
gross income on net pay and it should be distinguished from the specific "unemployment trap" which refers to the effect of a switch from
"welfare to work". The more general phenomena of the "poverty trap"
at the income levels identified on Figure 7.1 is one that may apply to
all those affected by FIS in particular. Analyses by Blackwell (1989A)
and the NESC (1990) have documented this poverty trap.

In conclusion, some lone mothers clearly perceive that the costs of returning to employment or of increasing their earnings outweigh the benefits. An analysis of social welfare, PRSI, child-care costs and so on shows, however, that at the lower end of the gross-pay scale there would actually be proportionally large increases in net income for lone mothers who would attempt to take up full-time or part-time employment. Therefore, there does not appear to be an "unemployment trap": the changes made in the 1994 Budget have helped significantly in these respects and are to be welcomed. A "poverty trap" does affect those whose gross incomes require them to pay PRSI, tax and child-care costs, and to lose FIS. This is a general, and well-documented feature of the tax/benefit system.

The fact that some women's perceptions of the social welfare/tax/child-care nexus are at variance with the objective system is of some significance. The fieldwork for this study was undertaken before the 1994 Budget, but the reported perceptions would also be at variance with the pre-1994 situation. A number of complementary lines of explanation for these perceptions — which would require substantiation in further research — might be considered.

Clearly, the respondents' views might simply reflect the well-known problems of non-take-up of means-tested benefits and a lack of knowledge of entitlements to, for example, the Lone Parent's Tax Allowance or the Child Care deduction in the LPA means test. The interviews suggest that some respondents appeared not to be aware of FIS or of the tax allowance for lone parents. However, the women may also be expressing more deeply ingrained social attitudes. Women might perceive their personal income "choices" in this manner if they were simply reflecting the view, which is popularised to some degree in the media and in public and political debate, that the welfare system is a disincentive and that it does not "pay" social welfare recipients to take up work. The interviews for this study provide no basis for this argument.

There is a further line of argument: that welfare recipients are concerned not only with the amount of any change in their income, but also with the likely stability and security of their incomes. How long an increase in income might last might be considered important, if the increase required a recipient to forego more secure sources of income. Here also the interviews for this study are unable to provide any evidence, but it has been clearly revealed as an important aspect of the UK tax/benefit system (McLoughlin, Millar and Cooke, 1989).

8: Being a Lone Mother

8.1   Introduction

The aim of this chapter is to capture the *experience* of lone mother-hood. Chapters 5, 6 and 7 focused on the financial and economic aspects of the women's lives. Here the emphasis was shifted to examine how women felt about being lone mothers and how it had affected their own and their children's lives. The material in this chapter draws on the very general, open-ended questions put to the women about the positive and negative aspects of their situations, about the impact of their situation on their children and the responses of their families and communities to their situations.

It is important to note that the distinction employed between the "economic/financial" dimensions (discussed in Chapters 5 and 6) and the "personal/social" dimensions (discussed here) is somewhat artificial. Many women integrated these two aspects of their lives in outlining their experiences and feelings. For example, most of them would begin their account of what it "feels like" to be a lone mother with an emphatic statement that "the money is the worst problem" (in one woman's words), but would then proceed to mention loneliness, or family support, or "the compensations" such as independence and freedom. However, for purposes of condensing and presenting the material it seems useful to classify the women's experiences and perceptions in this way.

8.2   Independence, Freedom and Loneliness

The single most common aspect of their lives as lone mothers mentioned by the women was the freedom their circumstances conferred. This sense of freedom has a specific financial meaning: some women reported that having the sole responsibility for their families' finances was a "compensation" for their low *levels* of income. This was a feature of the women's experience of poverty. However, this experience of independence and control extends beyond financial matters, as will now be shown.

Many of the women when invited to talk about their lives as lone mothers actually used the words "independence", "freedom" or "confidence". They instanced activities such as "adult education classes", "learning a language, "getting involved in the community" as examples of how much more confident they felt in the absence of a partner. This analysis applies in particular to many separated women, and applies in a somewhat different way to the young, unmarried women. Greater involvement and activity is one form of an enhanced sense of freedom and independence: another form is the increased degree of day-to-day choice they experienced. For example, women mentioned their exclusive control over the children, or the household routine — "simply being able to decide to switch on the telly or when to have the dinner", as one woman expressed it.

Some of the women, as was illustrated in Chapters 3 and 4, had experienced particularly difficult, and even violent relationships. For these women, the sheer *absence* of violence and conflict compounded a sense of freedom and independence: one woman gave a list of things she had "started to do" and ended it by noting the "sheer peace and quiet" she and the children now enjoyed.

While their financial situation was the most severe deprivation — and the most common deprivation — of lone parenthood mentioned by the women, they also mentioned "loneliness". For many women, "loneliness" was the converse of independence, and in the interviews many expressed their experiences in that fashion. For instance, one woman, when asked to summarise how it felt to be a lone mother, started by saying "It's very lonely" and then went on to explain how much "more freedom" she now had. Other women presented this mix of experience in the opposite way: one spoke initially, at length, about the "peace", "freedom" and "independence" and then added "but it's lonely at times". The experiences of the women below illustrate well how this compound of independence on the one hand and loneliness on the other is experienced.

Betty, for example, is aged 27 and has been separated for four years. The background to her marriage breakdown was outlined in Chapter 4. She and her two children (aged 6 and 4) live in her parents' house with her parents and her sister of 24. She has been separated for four years. When asked whether there were positive things about her situation, she couched her views in terms of a comparison with marriage:

> Yeah, there are actually. I keep telling people that say that they are getting married, "Don't do it!" I feel that I can be my own person, that there is no one to answer to. As long as my kids are OK I can do what I feel like. They come first, obviously, but once they are looked after, say if they are in bed asleep by nine o'clock and I decide that I want to go out, once Samantha is there to baby-sit, I don't have to say to anyone that I want to go out. You don't get any of the hassle that you get with husbands or fellas. You don't have any of the fights like, "You said this or that". At times I think that I'm better off on my own.

She was then asked if she actually compared her own situation with that of married people and she replied:

> *Yes, sometimes. A lot of my friends are married and they say, "Stay the way you are, don't ever...." I mean you can't get married again in this country, but I don't know if I would be prepared to live with somebody again.*

Her explanation for why she feels as she does was:

> *Because I think that I'm too used to my freedom. I can come and go as I please. But there again, having said that, you can't say for definite if you met someone, what would happen.*

This woman is considerably younger than most of the separated women. She lives in her parents' home and in the area in which she grew up. In her case, therefore, she did not mention loneliness as an issue for her.

> *Loneliness? I get out a little. I don't really stay in and if I am in, there's always somebody here. My friends are quite welcome to drop into the house at any time.... One of the friends that I grew up with — she is still single, so I would go out with her and my younger sister. She is still single, so the three of us would go out together. And there are a couple of friends that I wouldn't go out with, but I would drop down to see them and they would drop up to see me.*

Clearly, Betty's circumstances — family support, a network of friends, and some social life — are not found in all instances. To see how women who are older and have more children and more responsibility view their situation, the case of Christine, who was introduced in Chapter 4, can be looked at. She is 37 and has four children aged between 13 and 5. Since she and her husband separated two years ago she has been solely responsible for the children. Her parents are deceased and she relies on an aunt to mind her children while she works — she has taken up full-time work on a community project. When asked whether it was difficult being a lone parent, she focused on the loneliness she experienced and balanced this against the peace and independence that she also felt.

> *Being on my own, loneliness is very difficult because a person needs somebody to talk to, even if they just sit there and listen and let you ramble on and I suppose the closeness of somebody, when you need them, you know, when the kids are gone to bed then you go to bed. I mean, I have read more books in the past two years than I have ever read! But having said that, I enjoy*

the peace and quiet, I enjoy the space and I sit back at times and I look around and I say "I know there is bills and I know the debts are there — I know the four kids still have a long way to go, but it is mine and no-one can take that away from me any more."

Likewise, when the possibility was raised that there might be positive aspects to her situation, she again linked the experiences of loneliness with the various types of independence that she had begun to experience:

Oh yes, definitely. It has made me realise that there is a whole world out there and I am still young enough to get out and enjoy it and that I can do more for my kids by being in the workforce. It will take a while if this job doesn't last over the year but hopefully it will. But I don't intend to go back, to reverse, staying at home, I don't. I find the kids are more positive with their attitude in everything. They know that things are getting a little bit better. I'm not roaring and screaming half as much, I'm not crying night after night which I did for a long time, for what reason — I don't know if it was because I was feeling sorry for myself or my marriage gone down the tubes, but if I was honest, my marriage went eleven years ago, rather than two years. I don't know, I think to be on my own, I appreciate the fact that I have a brain and a mind and I can make conscious decisions about my life. The loneliness is subsiding a little bit.

These inter-related themes of loneliness and independence were echoed time and time again in the interviews — especially among separated women, as these other examples reveal:

- Daphne, separated for three years with adolescent and adult children, who claimed that: "There are many positive aspects. Now we have peace. I have my own financial independence. I've started to use my own name again.... But the separation is for life and you lose family and the kids lose cousins."

- A woman in her forties with three children, who has been separated seven years, having been married to a man she described as "an alcoholic", and who stated that the difficulty of lone parenthood was that it is "lonely, yes, very lonely", but who also listed as very positive "the peace I have", and "the right to make decisions". She described her ability to cope on her own: "There is a great sense of worthiness about it, you feel a person in your own right."

While the experience of loneliness and independence was a dimension of the experience of *all* of the women, there are identifiable factors which shape the experiences of particular women and which give rise to variation among women. First, it appears that the women with particularly difficult relationships behind them tend to emphasise their acquired freedom and peace of mind. As Paula, who had 10 children by her husband, and who was separated 11 years ago after a difficult marriage, exclaimed: "I'm as happy as Larry on my own. It's no sunshine but up here (pointing to her head) it's great!" Conversely, one woman in the sample — aged 30, with three small children — did acknowledge that she had acquired "more confidence", but the relationship between her and her husband, and between her husband and her children, she described as "good". She expressed an interest in a reconciliation and, far from emphasising the strong feelings of independence, she talked of her loneliness: "The loneliness is the worst."

Second, some women, when talking about their sense of loneliness, placed this in the context of coping alone with their children. For some, this was arduous and difficult over a long period of time; for others, it was easier than coping *both* with children and with their husbands. Within the limits of this study, it is not possible to classify the women's experiences in this respect. The interview material suggests, however, that the factors that may affect the women's experience of parenting alone — and which in turn therefore affect the more general sense of "loneness" — include: the number of children, their ages, the gender mix, the past and current relationship between the children and their father, and the availability or otherwise of a network of support within the extended family. (Clearly, the parenting task is also shaped by the impact of the father's absence and departure — a factor examined separately later.)

To illustrate how the parenting burden varies from one woman to another, two cases can be contrasted. One is Paula, in her early fifties with five dependent children, separated a long time from her husband. She was quite clear that despite the financial hardship and the sole responsibility for the children, her exclusive responsibility is not an added burden: "It wasn't a huge change when he left — I was always the one with them anyway — he was never there." Although this woman's parents are dead, she has two sisters living near and is "very close" personally to one. In contrast, Barbara is in her thirties and has one child of four. She said that it was "hard being a lone parent" and difficult "having to do everything". This woman has only one brother (who is chronically ill), no sisters, and although her parents "can baby-sit, sometimes", she cannot rely on them for much support because of their age and ill-health. The source of the parenting difficulties arises not just for women with small children. Other women with teenage children referred to the difficulties when the children "get older" and expressed concern about boys in particular — "not having a father around".

Third, some women lost their partners suddenly and completely involuntarily. These women experienced very intense and prolonged feelings of loneliness. Two of the women in the sample for this study are widows — both of them widowed in their thirties, and left to care for a number of children. One such woman, Fidelma, graphically described how isolated and lonely she felt when her husband was killed in a road accident:

> *It was terrible. For ages afterwards I couldn't do anything about his death without vomiting. I even had a few breakdowns. And I went to a psychiatrist in 1984 — he just gave me tablets and I just said after a while "f*** this" and tried to pull myself together.*

This illustration serves as a reminder that women who lose husbands through widowhood experience the same practical problems as other lone mothers, but do not have the "compensation" of having shaken off a difficult relationship. Likewise, widows' children suffer a permanent, total, and unexpected loss, whereas children of unmarried and separated lone mothers may have continuing contact or a relationship with their father.

However, if separated and widowed women experience varying degrees of freedom on the one hand, and loneliness on the other, how does this apply to the largely younger unmarried women? The younger single women adopted a different frame of reference — one that hinted at a feeling of ambivalence and contradiction. These women sometimes referred to their peers, friends or sisters and noted how much less freedom and choice their own circumstances, by comparison, allowed them: "It's not the same with a baby — I can't just get up and go." The experience of being a lone mother for these women is one of *loss* of freedom. However, these women also contrasted their situation with *married* women and expressed their satisfaction at not being married and not being "tied down", as one woman described her married friends. It appears then that the unmarried parents implicitly identify a continuum. One extreme of this is marriage with all its constraints, and the other is being single (without children). Some then perceive themselves as being in the middle: not as tied down as married women, but equally, not as free as single women.

The circumstances and attitudes of Sheila illustrate this perception very clearly. As described in Chapter 3, she is aged 23 and has a 2-year-old child; she lives in her parents' home with both of her parents and an adult brother. Prior to this, she had lived with the father of her child, whom she still meets regularly. In the context of talking about her boyfriend, she explained that when their living together did not prove successful she moved home to her parents' house, and she contrasted this choice with the alternative of marriage:

> *I feel that when you're not married, in the situation I'm in now, where I have a baby and I was pregnant before I was married, and had a baby before I was married, and went through the baby stages, you know, she being two, you know, it worked for me for this length of time, not being married. I can come and go, not that I can come and go when I want, but when things were so bad when we were living together, I could say, "Well, I'll go home now." And I went home. It's a better environment for me and for the child. I wouldn't like to be married and having to stay there. I wouldn't like having to do that. So that's a disadvantage of marriage, like, you can't just get up and go. I don't know really. You have to stay and make it work.*

However, when asked about the enjoyable aspects of being a mother, she went on to describe how the restrictions of being a mother contrast with the greater freedom her young, single friends enjoy:

> *It's different. It's very different. Although still I'm actually tied in so many ways. Although I have an awful lot of freedom compared to most people, I do have an awful lot of freedom. Friends of mine would say, "Right, I'm going." I have to say, "Well, I'll let you know tomorrow." 'Cause I've got to go home and say, "Mam, would you mind looking after her?" They'll say, "No problem." And then I say, "Fine", and I wait to see if I've got paid. Do you know what I mean? So you're still tied. You can't just get up and go off on a holiday. Well I suppose I could, but I wouldn't just do that. My mother would say, "Right, go ahead, I'll look after her for you." They're really very, very good. But you still can't.*

Later in the interview, she talked about her independence relative to the independence she perceives that she would have, if married:

> *Yeah. You can be independent on your own. Even though you have a child, you still have your independence — well, I still have. Anyway, I think maybe if I was living with him or we were*

married, you wouldn't have that kind of independence. You can't just get up and kind of walk out the door around to your friend, or whatever. You know what I mean? You're kind of responsible to two people. You're responsible for the child during the day, and when she's gone to bed, then you'd have to listen to him. I don't have to listen to him.

It is clear that her view of lone parenthood as an alternative to marriage is founded both on her experiences of a specific relationship and on general impressions formed in her social milieu:

A few people will say, "Get married, it's great. It's brilliant." But the majority of people would actually say, "Don't — why fall into the trap of marriage? You're so young. You've a lot of life ahead of you. Just because you have a kid, your life doesn't end, you've only one child." Do you know what I mean? Like, if you get married, you'll end up with four or five. So they kind of say, "Just think, in two years she'll be going to school. Look forward to the life you'll have when she's four. You'll be off sunning yourself in Spain or wherever." That's the attitude most people have. "Don't get married, you've only one child. Are you crazy? I wouldn't get married if I was you. All the time and there you are with the life of Reilly." That's the way people look. Now, I wouldn't think that way. There is good points to living with someone, and whatever else. But I don't know, I wouldn't like to be married. And I actually would prefer if, God forbid, anything ever happened to my mother and father, I would actually prefer to live on my own in the house, with my daughter, rather than to be living there with him. It's kind of your house. You can do as you like, you know. Like, it's not his house or our house, where he can come in and....

It is important to appreciate that not all the unmarried women offered such fully worked out accounts of their own situations. However, the elements that feature in Sheila's remarks are echoed in varying degrees in almost all of the interviews. First, the sense of loss of unrestricted bachelor freedom was mentioned especially by all of the younger, (teens and twenties) single women: Róisín, for instance, told of her sense of frustration when her sisters and their friends invited her to go out at weekends: "When my sisters and her friends come on Saturday and say they're going out, I think to myself 'You cow' — they're always asking me."

Second, with the exception of two women, one of whom is engaged, the unmarried women adopted distinctly negative dispositions towards marriage. This was common across both categories of single women — those who had lived with their partners and experienced a marriage-type relationship and those who had not. These quotations from various women illustrate this perception:

> *I don't really feel the need for a male companion — "been there, done that" — you know, what I mean?*

> *I don't think I could get married. It doesn't work, I don't think.... My parents — they don't really have conversations ... and my mother — she's just bitter now.*

> *There's that kind of house-bound feeling because you're married. There's also the responsibility of looking after a house and raising the kid, and him out at work, or if he's on the labour he's in the house all day, hanging around your feet.*

Third, like their separated counterparts the single women were positive about the independence they enjoyed and the sense of satisfaction at achieving things alone. These quotations from a variety of women reflect this sense of freedom and achievement:

> *I enjoy it. I'm bringing up a four-year-old the way I want to.*

> *You've got total control over your own life — no compromising with anybody.*

> *The kids will be brought up decent — I'm going on a course that I want — for retraining.*

Finally, in relation to the single mothers, the experience of loneliness was, for many, the obverse of their freedom and independence. Their experiences are somewhat similar to those of the separated women. Before illustrating these experiences it is useful to note the ways in which the unmarried women and separated women differ in this respect. On the one hand, the unmarried women who talked of loneliness linked the experience to coping with children — so did their separated counterparts. On the other hand, half of the unmarried women lived in the parental home. Most of them grew up and went to school in the area and had peer-group contacts, and some had boyfriends. These circumstances mediate the impact of their lone parent status on their experience of that status.

The situations of two women allow a comparison of how these various factors shape the experiences of women. First, the situation of Rita, aged 19, who lives with her original family in a rented corporation house. She has a small baby of six months and at the time of interview was about to give up her job in a local factory. Unusually in the context of this study, she has a continuing relationship with her boyfriend, who is involved with their child and was supportive throughout the pregnancy.

Rita was generally quite positive about her situation. Like all the unmarried women in the sample, she recorded her newly experienced loss of freedom. However, she did not admit to loneliness or isolation or to difficulty with the baby. On the contrary, her older friends at work "shared the pregnancy" and take an interest in her and the baby. At home, she has the interest and support of her family and her boyfriend, who suggested that they get engaged, and calls to see her and the baby every day.

When asked to talk about the difficulties of her situation, she mentioned the baby's age, and the associated problems of sleeplessness, teething and so on, and the physical tiredness this caused. However, even when pressed to consider whether she ever felt lonely or isolated, she was emphatic: "No, not really." On the contrary, while she referred to the fact that "you haven't got the freedom just to do what you want", she described her network of practical support. Her mother collects the baby from a crèche early in the afternoon and minds her until Rita comes in from work. In the evening, she is free to go out after the baby has settled, because "there is always somebody here" and her sister, whom she described as "baby mad", is "great with her" (the baby). Her mother's friend has knit all of the baby's cardigans, and because she was the youngest girl in her workplace (a clothes factory) to have a baby, her friends in work, who mostly live locally, have taken a great interest:

> They all love to see her in the factory — like I am kind of the youngest out of the factory that ever had a baby like. So all of them in the factory are her aunts. They all love her.

Rita's case conveys a sense that she and the child are part of an immediate network of family, friends and locality which is highly supportive. While no other case offers an extreme contrast to these circumstances, other women's experiences are somewhat different. Cathy, mentioned in Chapter 3, is 32 and lives in her own accommodation with her 6-year-old child. She works part-time in a local centre. In her situation she has to be highly independent and self-sufficient. Her parents are deceased and although she has two siblings — a brother and sister — who live nearby, she does not rely on them for support. In her sister's case it is because "we have different opinions — we don't see eye to eye"; and in her brother's case it is because he is also "badly off". When Cathy talked of who she relied on for baby-sitting support, friendship or emotional contact, it was a close friend, also a single mother, living nearby.

Cathy's child's father is not in contact, having effectively rejected her when she became pregnant. Her network is therefore relatively small, comprising her friend and her colleagues at work who have encouraged her to stay in work, and allowed her flexibility in combining work and child care. Against this background, she experiences a sense of isolation, both in terms of personal and emotional support as well as in practical matters such as baby-sitting.

> *A childminder is five pounds. Now in saying that I have found that recently it is really hard to get a childminder. I mean, I can't get my friend because she herself would be in, so she would be minding her son.... Sometimes it is a case of you would love someone to knock on the door and say "Right, come on, come on out for a night, just, you know, don't worry about the money." I mean it is you who are dealing with ... you have everything. You are dealing with finance, you are dealing with emotions — both your own and the child's. You are dealing with things that come up for the child in school, in playtime, their complexes, their friends and also the questions that are asked....*

While Cathy also talked about the positive aspects of her status, it is clear from a comparison between her experiences and Rita's that the extent of contact with, and support from, family, partner, and wider networks is an important factor in shaping the experiences and perceptions of individual lone mothers.

8.3   The Impact on Children

In public debate in the research literature on lone-parent families the issue that has generated most controversy is the supposed effect on children of living in a one-parent family. No attempt is made here to review the complex and controversial literature on this subject. Nevertheless, it is useful to set out some of the questions that arise in this area of research.

Gee's recent review of work in this area identifies two broad approaches to understanding the impact of lone parenthood on children (Gee, 1993). First, a socialisation or social-learning model emphasises the roles that parents play in socialising children, providing role models, and offering practical and emotional support. This approach would examine lone parenthood from the perspective of "inadequate" socialisation. It would hypothesise that in lone-parent families, because of the absence of one parent, the custodial parent is placed under severe stress and, consequently, supervision and discipline might be inconsistent. Furthermore, one role model would be entirely absent and children might have an emotional over-involvement with one parent. This type of analysis would then compare the "outcomes" — such as psychological adjustment, educational attainment, levels of anti-social behaviour — between children from one-parent and two-parent families and ascribe the observed differences to the difference in family structure.

Early research on children in lone-mother families was substantially influenced by this perspective. As Gee's and Ferri's recent reviews point out, this research was often based on clinical samples, or samples of children referred to medical and social services for assessment or intervention. A second broad approach can be loosely characterised (Gee, 1993, Ferri, 1993) as a *socioeconomic* model. The emphasis here is on the economic deprivations affecting lone-parent families: these deprivations are hypothesised as being the underlying differences between lone-parent and two-parent families.

For example, in this model, differences in outcomes, such as behaviour, educational performance and so on, are acknowledged, and their link to socialisation and parenting within the family is admitted. However, the reasons for these "parenting" differences are seen as largely economic. Maternal poverty requiring mothers to work would result in lower levels of child supervision; children would assume adult roles at an early age in response to family poverty — working part-time or supervising younger children, for instance. Therefore, economic deprivation could *indirectly* affect children's lives through the impact on socialisation and parenting, and *directly* affect them also because of poorer diet, inferior housing and lesser access to services and amenities (See Acock and Keecolt, 1989; McLanahan, 1985).

Naturally, the kind of research that would be required to disentangle these influences is substantially more large-scale and complex than the study reported here. In the first instance, it is clear that any study that attempts to identify differences associated with changes in families' circumstances must take a longitudinal approach. If there are differences, they may only emerge after a long period of time, as in the case of educational attainment. Further, and as a corollary to this, it is important to observe children at several points in time, rather than just *after* the onset of lone parenthood, and to avoid the assumption that their observed levels of educational attainment (for example) can be ascribed to a change in family status per se. For example, some studies have revealed that children in lone-parent families who score poorly on psychological tests or educational indicators also scored poorly when their families were intact. In other words, the *process* of family conflict and family dissolution can evolve over a period of time and affect children at an early stage. Therefore, the *event* of lone parenthood (divorce, for example) is not the factor affecting children (see Cherlin et al., 1991; Elliot and Richards, 1991). Logically, this leads to the conclusion that if children are deleteriously affected by parents' unhappy marriages, then their parents' formal separation or divorce could result, after a period of time, in an *improvement* in the children's situation.

This line of reasoning raises a practical policy point. Is it valid in discussing family policy to compare children in one type of family (one-parent) with children in another, as the basis for asserting that one type is, in general, "better"? This kind of general comparison informs some of the research as well as the popular debate in Ireland and elsewhere about the social impact of lone parenthood and the implications of legalising or liberating divorce. The implications of the research cited above is that such comparisons may be inappropriate, at least in the context of understanding the impact of marital breakdown, separation and divorce. Specifically, it can be argued that the benchmark against which the circumstances of children in lone-parent families should be compared is how they would have fared if the marital conflict had continued and the family remained intact.

Additional cautionary notes about the research on the impact of lone parenthood on children are required. As Ferri (1993) notes, some studies compare average results for one- and two-parent families on a range of criteria — education, socialisation, health, behaviour, and so on. However, this form of comparison ignores the fact that there is variation *within* the categories one- and two-parent families and that other aspects of family structure impinge on children's circumstances — such as age of children, life cycle, number of children, household composition, and contact with extended family. Finally, studies vary in the outcomes they attempt to explain. Some concentrate on educational and economic outcomes — such as unemployment rates or educational participation rates among the adolescent and adult children of lone parents. Others focus on the relative incidence of relationship difficulties or personal problems among adults brought up in lone-parent families (Amato and Booth, 1993). The extent to which differences between the children from lone-parent families and two-parent families are identified is critically dependent on which particular outcomes are observed.

The body of research that is particularly relevant in this context is that derived from the UK National Child Development Study (NCDS). This study began as a longitudinal Survey of more than

17,000 births in Britain in a week in March 1958. These children were studied on a longitudinal basis by means of regular follow-up surveys; the sample size has permitted comparisons to be made between children in different types of families, and has facilitated the study of quite specific sub-groups such as adopted children or children born outside of marriage. The availability of these data has spawned a whole series of studies on lone-parent families, the most notable of which are Ferri's, *Growing Up in a One Parent Family* and *Coping Alone* (Ferri, 1976A; Ferri, 1976B).

Space does not permit a detailed review of the findings of these studies. In the context of the small local study being reported here, perhaps the most significant aspect of the NCDS series is the consistent finding that lone parents' *material and economic* circumstances are of critical importance in explaining the social, educational, and other experiences of their children. Ferri's recent summary statement (Ferri, 1993) of the findings regarding the socialisation of children in lone-parent families is as follows:

> Briefly, the results have revealed the significant contribution of the disadvantaged circumstances suffered by lone parent families (including low income and housing difficulties) in explaining the poorer overall performance of their children.... A tendency remained for children with divorced/separated parents or lone fathers to have done less well than their counterparts in intact homes, but the differences were comparatively small in magnitude. The contribution of socioeconomic factors to developmental differences are inextricably linked to issues of policy and support. Thus, the disadvantages suffered by lone parent families in terms of income, housing and weakness in the labour market are amenable to change through social policy measures aimed at strengthening the lone parent family as a child-rearing environment (Ferri, 1993: 12–13).

Unfortunately, there is no body of research on families in Ireland that can provide a context for the material in this study. One recent small-scale study contained some comparisons between lone-parent families and two-parent families who were assessed as part of a longitudinal study (Richardson, 1991). When the children were a year old, the 109 single women and 80 married women were compared in a number of respects. First, very high proportions of all women viewed the parenting role positively; when asked whether they would have made the same decision about having the baby and parenting it, a *higher* proportion of single women than married women said with hindsight they would have made the same decision (90 per cent: 75 per cent). Not surprisingly, very high proportions of fathers in the married cases were involved in parenting (90 per cent) and rather low proportions in the unmarried.

As regards coping with children, a "surprising result", in the author's description, was that more married, than unmarried women had problems coping at the end of the first six months and at the end of the first year. Richardson points out that these patterns may not persist through time.[1] Nevertheless, she ventures the following conclusion:

> ... the results do not indicate that for this group of women, at this time, the differences combine to put the single parent family including lone single parents at one year in the life cycle of the unit at a disadvantage in comparison with the marital family unit. Overall, the results for these mothers in this study do not give a profile of single parent families at one year beset by a multiplicity of inequalities that combine to make it more difficult for them to create adequate homes for themselves and their children.

The tentative findings from Richardson's Dublin study reflect those from the study by Phoenix of young married and unmarried women in London (Phoenix, 1991). The evidence of this study also rejected any argument that the status of "lone motherhood" per se had any negative effects on child development.

Turning to the present local study, it was not possible within the confines of this local, small-scale, qualitative exercise to attempt any comprehensive assessment of the impact of lone parenthood on children. Two sets of issues were addressed in the interviews, and these will be dealt with in turn.

Women who had been married and are now widowed or separated were asked an open-ended question as to what effect, as they perceived it, the loss/departure of their father had on the children. Among these 30 women a clear pattern of responses emerges. In one group, the women were unambiguous and emphatic that their children's welfare had *improved* as a result of their father's departure or continuing absence. A second group gave a more qualified response: that one child who had a particular relationship with the father was affected, but that other children were totally unaffected. These patterns can be illustrated with the case material.

First, the case of Pat can be taken as an illustration of definite "improvement" after the separation of parents. She has three small

---

[1]   Obviously, other limitations on these results should be noted: the study is local, the sample is small, separated women are not included, and the independent effects of income and family variables are not analysed.

children and lives in an owner-occupied house; aged 30, she has been separated almost two years. Prior to the separation, she stated, she and her husband had argued a lot and a separation was the only resolution possible. As regards the children, a 4-year-old boy and twin baby girls, she outlined how she tried to explain the situation to her oldest child:

> *Well, I sat with Darren and I explained to him what the situation was as clearly and as easily as I could and he seems to have taken it quite well. The two girls now ask for him a lot but I just say "Well, no — Daddy is not coming home tonight and you might see him tomorrow." Sometimes he drops up during the week. I don't think that it has affected them. I was very worried that it would. I went down to Darren's school, etc. and explained to the teacher, but he seemed to be happy because the way I said was "Darren," I said, "you will have to understand that it is better for Mammy and Daddy not to live together and not be fighting," I said, "I don't want to fight with you all the time." He looked at me and said "Yes, OK". He basically accepted it, because we couldn't even look at each other at one stage.*

When asked would she go as far as to claim that the children benefited from their separation she was definite:

> *Yes. You see the children are content because they were afraid of him, because he has a fierce temper. Not that he would ever physically hit them, but he would shout at them and he was so tired coming home at night time, if they kind of woke up during the night he would be like a bull, whereas he doesn't do that any more. He has a lot more tolerance towards them and seems to kind of realise what he is missing. Unfortunately it had to happen this way.*

In short, the absence of parental conflict in the home has, in her estimation, improved the children's situation. This is a case where the father, who lives nearby, visits the children regularly and now, according to Pat, has a *better* relationship with his children than before the separation. However, this scenario of the father remaining involved may not appear to be a crucial factor, as other cases in this category are situations where all contact with the father has been severed. For instance, Jackie said of her two children (aged 12 and 9) that the effect on the children of their father's departure was one of "great relief". She went on to explain that he was an alcoholic and at times threatening and violent in his behaviour:

> *They never knew when he would come home. We used all sleep in*
> *the same room and they would say, "I hope he doesn't come*
> *home." They still remember the violence. You could almost touch*
> *the tension when he was here. When he walked out the door, so*
> *did Alan's asthma. When he left, the whole atmosphere changed.*

This category of improvements in the children's overall well-being (as
perceived by the mother) is easily understood. Children could only
have benefited from the ending of conflict and tension between parents in the home. *All* of the cases in this category are instances of that
type of situation. What emerges from the women's accounts — as illustrated in the two cases — is that the women focused on the *past*
and on the *marriage* as the source of children's difficulties. The very
frame of reference they adopted in considering what impact the separation might have had was one that stressed the separation as the
solution and the prior marital conflict as the problem.

Some women were at pains to differentiate in their responses the
impact between the individual children. Women in this category would
typically identify one child who was affected — perhaps the oldest
child with the best-established relationship with the father, or the
child most attached to the father. This pattern applies to women with
a number of children across a wide age span.

Noreen's account is a good case in point. In her late thirties, she
has five children two of whom (aged 18 and 20, a girl and a boy) have
now left school and are working. She has been separated for nine
years — her eldest child, a boy, was 12 when she and her husband
separated after a difficult and sometimes violent marriage. Her account of the impact of the separation is straightforward: her eldest
son, was affected both before and after the separation, but the other
children were not:

> *The eldest young fella is very rebellious. I've been trying to con-*
> *trol him. It's still a problem. He tried to take over. At one stage,*
> *he went to live with his father and came back here at weekends.*
> *So I made him choose. He was twelve when he [the father] left*
> *— but the damage was done because of the violence. Women are*
> *there for men — that's his attitude now — he got that from his*
> *father.*

In contrast, she described the other, younger children as "very happy".
She had explained the family circumstances to their teachers who
never recorded any difficulties. These other children "don't even remember their father".

Beth's case is very similar. She has three children — a boy of 16, a girl of 14, and a boy of 10. She has only been separated for a year; her elder son was 15 at the time of the separation. In this case the son identified with his father:

> *The eldest son was affected. He took his side and he blames me — I pushed him out, he says. Now he's mitching from school and he's gone downhill an awful lot.*

This pattern of one child being upset and the others less so is the single most common type of response women offered. Were there, however, any instances where children were reported as being psychologically very distressed or disturbed in their behaviour? Women reported few such instances. In two interviews, mothers recalled their adolescent sons being quite disturbed. One such case was the son of a widow who, as she recalled, "never cried, but he blamed me for his father's death. Once he attacked another young lad." Only one mother of young children instanced a small child requiring some form of professional intervention. The child was eight at the time of separation and was "very loyal" to his father. His mother recalled that he had "screamed, 'Don't go, don't go'. He had to go to a child psychiatrist".

This impressionistic material falls a long way short of the quantified, representative data in the international research. The purpose in using the illustrative material is to highlight how the women themselves defined the impact of their marriage breakdown on the children and to identify a focus for future research. A key issue for further, more representative research is to establish more firmly that the impact on children is a process that takes place over the history of a marriage, and that separation per se may not be an important factor in explaining the effects on children. Clearly, more specific measures of child-related effects are required — the effect on children's educational performance, their physical health and their psychological development are priorities for research. The illustrative material tentatively suggests that one common research finding may apply also in Ireland: that the response of children to being in a lone-mother family varies according to the age and gender of children. Notably, adolescent and pre-adolescent boys may be more overtly affected by their father's departure than girls and younger children. Finally, one issue, not explored here, which merits investigation is whether the structure of the wider family, and in particular the support of grandparents, in any way ameliorates the impact on children of being in a lone-mother family.

The second issue tentatively addressed by the study in looking at children in lone-parent families was the parenting involvement of the

unmarried women. In their case, the question of the departure of the
father and its impact on children was not as generally applicable as in
the case of separated women. What is of interest, however, is how these
women fared in their basic parenting tasks. In Phoenix's larger study,
she constructed a formal profile of how young mothers "parented", by
focusing on six specific indicators, as follows:

- Was the baby welcome, when born?

- Was the baby breast-fed?

- Did the baby receive the officially recommended injections etc.?

- Did the baby develop any long-standing illness?

- What were the mothers' feelings for the children?

- How did the mothers feel about their coping with the children?

The most interesting finding in Phoenix's study was the absence of any
significant difference between young (under 20) unmarried and married women on these criteria (Phoenix, 1991). In the present qualitative study it was not possible to apply this "checklist". Instead, the
women were invited in an open-ended fashion to describe their feelings for the children, and they were questioned about how they would
spend time with them, and how much actual "parenting" they did.[2]

A detailed analysis of this interview material reveals four general
findings — all of them applying in one degree or another to the experience of all of the women:

(1)   The women spend a very large proportion of their time with their
      children engaged in basic caring — feeding them, playing with
      them and so on — although the two full-time employees are
      clearly different in this respect. It is important also to note that
      this applied as much to the women living with their parents as to
      those in their own accommodation. This preoccupation with basic
      care of these children is the obverse of what was also reported
      above — their sense of relative lack of freedom. Simply, their
      child is their main focus of activity.

(2)   All of the women explicitly mentioned a distinct element of en-
      joyment and pleasure in fulfilling routine parenting tasks.

---

[2]   How this information was obtained obviously varied form one woman to
      another. But for each woman a picture was obtained of: who fed the baby,
      who put the child to bed, who gave the child lunch, the daily routine of
      parent–child interaction.

(3) More women — but not all — admitted also to elements of strain and tiredness from the demands of being a mother.

(4) Some women gave clear expression to feelings of pride and responsibility about their role. While no one woman used the word "status", some deliberately stressed the value that they placed on their work as mothers, and did so in a way that suggested that they felt society at large also valued this.

To illustrate these themes we return to Róisín. She is aged 24 and living alone with her 4-year-old daughter in a house rented from the corporation. The background to her circumstances is that she was involved in a continuing relationship when she got pregnant and "was engaged". In her account, she had: "wanted to get married and assumed all along I would get married." She does not work outside the home and her routine is built around her daughter, in the following way: she brings her to school, returns home, cleans up the house, returns to the school later on in the day to collect the child, brings her home and gives her lunch, goes to her mother's or her sister's house for the remainder of the afternoon/evening, returns home in the evening, gives her tea/supper, puts her to bed, and then stays in for the evening.

She volunteered her feelings about what her role entails:

> *I enjoy myself. People say, "Do you not get bored? — I say "NO!" I chase her around, I play with her and I really enjoy her — I miss her when she's at school.*

However, she acknowledged that it was "hard" when she noticed how much social life her single sister had, and she was very frank about the demands made by a small child:

> *At night I just crash out on the sofa. It's hard. Every sixteen-year-old should be given a child to mind — that way they'd never get pregnant!*

When she was pregnant, she placed considerable importance on the pregnancy, and this has continued as a sense of responsibility about being a mother:

> *I did everything to have a stress-free pregnancy — being pregnant was my job.... My role now is to be her mother. People say, "You are sitting around the house", but I love having her here.*

When talking about the financial strain of being a lone mother, she expressed determination to provide well for her daughter:

> *People think because you're a lone parent you shouldn't have anything. But this is my home. I have to bring her up.*

A variant on these experiences can be found in Carmel's situation. She is 23, and she and her 3-year-old child live in her parents' house with her parents and three adult sisters. Exactly as in the case above, she was able to detail how her routine was built around caring for the child. She gives the child breakfast, brings her to play school, collects her, usually gives the child her lunch and then plays with her. Weather permitting, she would then "go out for a walk or to the shopping centre", return home and, having fed the child again, would go through the full routine of bed-time preparation. Almost always, she stays in after the child has gone to bed.

In this instance — and this recurred in most cases where the women lived with their parents — the mother did not go out a lot. On the contrary, she explained that when she goes out, she usually brings the child with her. Her mother, by arrangement, baby-sits "once a week", and occasionally she leaves the child with her mother during the day. Her mother insists: "Just don't be long, don't delay." She does not ask her father to baby-sit. This brings out the reality, explored again below, that living at home is not a situation of infinite or even completely spontaneous support. The situation is a negotiated one in which the unmarried younger mother does not feel she ought to expect her parents or siblings to carry a lot of responsibility on her behalf.

Most of the time, she claimed, she enjoyed her role but she too was frank about how demanding it was on her.

> *Most times I enjoy it. Some days are just — you would love to just get out and be able to sit down and not have to worry. Like, I mean, I can never sit down and watch something on telly even if it is only on for half an hour. He is constantly over reading stories or playing with something or "Show me this" or "Get this" or "Get that". Like you would love kind of a day or a couple of days just, but most days now it's fine.*

The evidence here of extensive practical involvement and strong positive feelings about their role and their children echoes the findings of the most recent work in the United Kingdom on teenage, working-class single mothers (see Schofield, 1994). These women identify strongly with the role of mother and, while freely acknowledging the stresses of parenting alone and the financial constraints, they were optimistic and cheerful about their lives and those of their children, and determined to cope well as parents. As one participant in the study — a young, single woman with three children — stated: "In the beginning it was hard. But now five years down the line.... I suppose you just become more confident in your own situation. I know I'm doing a good job."

One final point for future research arises from these findings. If young, poor women express positive feelings about parenting alone outside marriage, is this associated in any way with the broader social and economic factors that have contributed to the growth of this form of family? Might it be argued, for instance, that developments in the labour market — especially high long-term unemployment among young working-class men and women — have excluded some young women from the alternative routes into adulthood? If young women cannot become economically independent through work, or if prospective husbands are prone to unemployment, does single motherhood offer an alternative means of acquiring both financial autonomy and an acknowledged social role? (See Moss and Lav, 1985, for the UK and, Wilson and Neckerman, 1986, for the US).

In the Irish context, there can be no presumption as to the likely findings of research on these questions. The fact that single motherhood has been rising rapidly in Ireland and that it occurs disproportionately among poorer, working-class women is itself sufficient justification for researching the link between the labour market changes and single motherhood. However, any future research would need to start from a recognition that the rise in non-marital births in Ireland started before the serious deterioration in the labour markets. Furthermore, in a previously conservative, Roman Catholic society, the changes that this study is considering could have taken place only if significant changes in values and attitudes, and improvements in state policies, had also occurred. The task for future research, therefore, is to show how the interaction of long-run social change, more fundamental changes in economic and employment conditions, and the State's response to these forces, have combined to alter the context in which young women make choices about their lives. For the women in this study, the context is one of material disadvantage and personal stress, on the one hand, and independence and personal fulfilment on the other.

8.4   Lone Motherhood — A Case of Stigma?

Earlier studies in Ireland of single mothers and deserted wives (Darling, 1984; O'Higgins, 1974), and in the UK of divorce and lone parenthood more generally (Marsden, 1973), have recorded the stigma that many lone mothers experience. By "stigma" what is

meant here is that they experience being stigmatised or labelled in society by overt remarks or social behaviour that has the effect of separat-
ing them from society at large. The aim was to ascertain whether this
was a general experience among the women in the study.

Women were asked whether they ever experienced being set apart
by people treating them differently, by excluding them from conver-
sation or social events, or by neighbours or family members treating
them negatively when they became lone mothers. As a generalisation,
the answer to this line of questioning in the interviews was, "No". Almost all women stated that they could not recall any such experience,
as the following quotations from different women illustrate:

> *No stigma, none. I have good neighbours and I'm not isolated or
> cut off* [separated mother, in local authority housing estate].

> *I've never had any hassle — or any exclusion or hostility to me*
> [separated woman in block of corporation flats].

> *Stigma on me — NO! Definitely. I never mix with the neigh-
> bours but that's privacy not hostility* [single woman in corpora-
> tion house in a large estate].

> *That used to happen. People used to look down on girls that
> weren't married, but I found that when we got this group to-
> gether, we made it a mother and toddler group. It wasn't sin-
> gle parents which a lot of people maintained it was for ... be-
> ing in that mother and toddler group made me realise that
> at one stage we would have been singled out "they're unmar-
> ried mothers"... In this group it doesn't say married or sin-
> gle.... I think now it really doesn't make a difference to people*
> [23-year-old single mother, living with parents, talking about
> a mother and toddler group).

> *I like it here. I don't feel any stigma. The neighbours are OK;
> they stick to themselves* [single mother from Cork who moved to
> Dublin and now lives in a private rented flat on the Northside
> of Dublin].

In recording a general absence of overtly discriminatory or stigmatising behaviour, it is also important to note the qualifications that
women themselves offered to their assessments. Two or three women,
for instance, mentioned *particular individuals* who had said or done
something; one example is of a separated woman whose children were
insulted ("he called them bastards") by a neighbour. Otherwise, she

said, the area was "fine — we drop in and out of neighbours a bit"; a second instance was given of a clerk in the post office who is "usually friendly — but when she saw my lone-parent book there was no more smiles or 'please' or 'thank you'." These were specific incidents.

A further qualification is that the criteria for identifying labelling or stigmatising behaviour are quite limited — the experience of overt behaviour of this type. Very few women recorded this type of experience in their daily lives in the community. However, this does not mean that people receive strong, practical support from neighbours or that they have positive, extensive involvement with their neighbours. On the contrary, many women live within reach of their original families and therefore experience their families — notably their parents — as their mainstay in a financial, practical and emotional sense. This emerged clearly in Chapter 6. Neighbours, on the other hand, were most usually described in neutral terms: "They're OK around here — we all stick to ourselves", in one woman's words. Therefore, the absence of generally stigmatising, negative behaviour should not be taken to mean that women commonly felt that there were widespread, generally positive attitudes to them.

An additional qualification in the women's accounts was their recognition that social behaviour and social rituals still revolve around couples. Many women remarked on their occasional sense of isolation, or of feeling different at family and community events, when the predominance of couples is highlighted for them again. For example, one separated woman with two children, in her own words, "borrowed a brother for the day" to accompany her when one of her children was making his Holy Communion. This, she said, made her and her children look like all the other families. Likewise, another woman recalled how she felt at a twenty-first birthday party: "uncomfortable — everybody else was there with their husband or wife."

8.5   Young Single Mothers at Home

One of the important aspects of the social situation of lone mothers is the extent and type of contact with and support from their parents and wider family. This contact and support in some cases takes the "extreme" form of living with parents. At a national, representative level, it is difficult to be precise about the extent to which lone mothers reside with their parents. Analysis of 1986 Census data suggested a figure in the region below 20 per cent, but the figure is a distinct undercount (for technical reasons) of the extent of household sharing (McCashin, 1993). Among single mothers there is almost certainly a high proportion who reside with their parents and who make this arrangement during the pregnancy (see O'Hare et al., 1985; Richardson and Winston, 1989).

In this study, there are 53 women in all, of whom 23 are unmarried. Of these 23, 11 — or 48 per cent — were residing with their parents. In the research literature, the phenomenon of young single mothers in particular living with parents is generally considered a situation of "support". So too in this study. Most of the young single women, either living independently or living with their parents, considered their parents to be supportive and — for some — their emotional and financial mainstay. The importance of their mothers to young women was shown clearly in Chapter 3 in regard to support for their decisions about the pregnancy. The material on their financial circumstances in Chapter 6 showed the key role that parents' practical help plays in their lives.

However, the interviews with single women revealed another dimension to the experience of unmarried women in their parental home — a sense of ambiguity, lack of choice, and tension about the situation. Before drawing on interview material, some general points about these types of circumstances should be noted. In the first place, some of these young women returned to their parents late in the pregnancy or after their child was born because of housing difficulties — most notably expensive, poor-quality rental accommodation. Others returned because of extreme difficulties with their boyfriends — such as abuse, or abandonment.

Second, all single women living in the parental home play two potentially conflicting roles — that of mother and that of daughter. For the younger women, it might be quite stressful if they are simultaneously experiencing the authority of their parents and trying to develop the individuality, confidence and judgment required to be a parent.

Third, a specific difficulty that might arise is the control their parents might want to exercise over their daughters' relationships. Some of the young women were still involved with the fathers of their children, some of whom lived locally, and these relationships might be disapproved of by parents, and hence be a potential source of conflict.

Fourth, the functioning of the parent–daughter–child arrangement must be viewed in the light of the low income levels of the women themselves and of their original family. As will be shown, some of the women were living with their parents and brothers and sisters in circumstances that give rise to overcrowding — or, at the very least, restrictions on space, or sharing of space in bedrooms.

Finally, however positive, welcoming, and supportive a girl's original family might be on the arrival of a baby, as the girl and the child become older the initial enthusiasm might fade and the girl might develop a preference for independent arrangements.

Some of these concerns are reflected in the case of Carmel, cited earlier, who is aged 23 and living with her 3-year-old child in her parent's home. In all, the household comprises seven persons: she and the child, both parents and three adult siblings (two sisters, one brother). She had become pregnant in England when 20 and returned to live in Dublin in a flat with her boyfriend. As she recalls it, she came to live again with her parents for two reasons: her mother pressurised her to return home when her boyfriend left, and she was unhappy about the cost and quality of her flat. The flat cost £55 per week (in 1990) for "two rooms and a shower" and she did not know "would I be able to afford to stay there on my own". She recalls clearly:

> *She told me to come back home and I didn't want to move back home. I didn't want to move back home. I would have rather stayed — not actually in that place, but somewhere. I just did not want to go back to my parents' house.*

In her account, she and her mother "don't really get on at all". Her mother took control of the baby and, furthermore, she and her baby have been sharing a room with her two adult sisters:

> *She kind of took over with Peter when he was small like you know "You are doing this wrong", "You are doing that wrong" — just straight away came in and kind of took over completely and I didn't kind of want that. Plus room-wise, I was in the bedroom with my two sisters and then there is myself and Peter and we are kind of juggling the bedroom around trying to fit in a lot, and this, that, and the other, and it was really kind of crowded.*

When asked whether she would now prefer *not* to be in her parents' home, her reply shows clearly her essential preference to be independent, and her recognition of limited housing options:

> *Definitely. I'm at the stage that even though we don't get on and I would give my right arm not to be in the house, I still wouldn't get into the situation of moving in with somebody just to get out of the house, or renting somewhere that I couldn't afford and be totally, like, just paying the rent and maybe not have enough to eat or something. I'm not that desperate to get out of the house.*

It emerges that she had applied to the corporation three years previously for accommodation and after a year and a half had pursued her request. Her preference was for a flat/maisonette locally, but she was told that she would need more "points" and was offered the prospect of two other locations. These she refused because she would not "feel safe" in these locations. For the future, her strong desire is to be an independent parent in her own home, but she foresees considerable obstacles to procuring her own housing:

> *That's the most important thing to me at the moment — to get somewhere to live and bring up Peter as my son and not my mother's. I am getting kind of that he knows like at the moment if he wants something and I say "no", he just knows that if he just walks over to somebody else, that kind ... you know, I have to get him out of that, and just for him to have his own room, and just have his own space, and for me to have my own space, rather than constantly kind of toppling over each other in the house. I will either have to try and rent somewhere, maybe try and get a job and rent privately or that's about all I can do, rent privately, get a flat or try the Corporation again but I don't think I will have much luck with the Corpo from the sounds of it, from the impression I got like. The amount of people on the housing lists and the amount of years they have been on it.*

Carmel's case is a distinct reflection of an absence of choice that can be ascribed to a shortage of suitable housing. Other elements in her circumstances such as the poor relationship with her mother, and the extreme overcrowding, do not appear in all of these cases, but the issue of housing most clearly does. Eleven of the 23 single women in the study are living with their parents: of these, only four offered an unambiguously positive account of being "at home", and seven offered accounts which, in varying degrees, echoed the experiences given in the case just illustrated.

The following are some other comments made by various single women living at home:

> *My mother finds it a bit difficult with us all in the house. I used to get hassle from my mother: "Get a house". Now because the relationship* [with boyfriend] *is over, I'd like to get a place of my own — its claustrophobic in the house. I'd like to get a flat* [19-year old, living with both parents and large family — total household size of 11].

> *Somebody with two children can get houses. I have only the one. He* [corporation official] *told me to get pregnant again — or get married.... There's myself and the baby in a double bed and my*

sister in a single bed in the room.... Things would be much eas-
ier for me to get on with the things I want to do. If I was in a
place of my own, there wouldn't be as much hassle (23-year-old,
living with parents and family — total household size of nine).

The maisonette [the Corporation gave] *was right beside my*
mother's, so I took it. When I got it, it was a burnt-out flat — the
Corporation didn't do any repairs. I couldn't light a fire.... I
went to a TD and he said "Hand back the keys and fight for
your points back." That's three years ago and I'm still waiting
for my own place! It's really my mother, because she's not a well
woman. And Nora [daughter] *can do her fair share of scream-*
ing at the same time. Its older we're getting, not younger.... If I
had my own little place for the two of us, I'd find it would be
much better [29-year-old, living with mother and three brothers
— total household size of six].

Clearly, the availability of affordable housing for low-income lone
mothers is the issue that arises for research and policy in the future.
These data are case illustrations from one local area. Nevertheless,
they confirm the view already expressed in the *Lord Mayor's Com-*
mission on Housing (Dublin Corporation, 1993) that low-income single mothers do require improved and increased housing provision.

Finally, it must also be clear that, even on the limited evidence offered, the widespread practice of young women sharing the parental
home is by no means a freely chosen arrangement. Nor is it, for all
mothers, an unambiguously supportive situation.

9: Overview and Implications for Future Policy and Research

9.1   Introduction

In this chapter a brief overview is offered of some key themes that
emerged in the study and the policy and research implications for the
future are considered. Of necessity, this discussion relies not solely on
the material gleaned in this study, but also draws on other work, both
national and international.

While the small-scale, local nature of this study must be acknowledged again here, it should also be noted that this is not a general
impediment to policy commentary and recommendations. Precisely
because the study concentrates on one, relatively homogenous group,
it is possible to identify some of the *impact* of current policy. The policy commentary of his report is therefore distinctly relevant where it
is focused on policies, structures and services that do not vary from
one area to another. For example, social welfare entitlements, and the
judicial maintenance system are invariant national systems, the operation of which has been observed in a context that is likely to be
shared by a specific segment of the lone-mother population. It is
therefore permissible to advance policy arguments about these national systems as they affect the kind of lone mother included in this
study. However, this chapter will refrain from any form of *statistical
generalisation*, as has been the case throughout the book.

9.2   Overview of Findings

The first outstanding pattern to emerge in the study is the degree to
which women chose to be lone mothers — albeit not in circumstances of
their choosing. This aspect of women's situations revealed itself in a
number of ways: the determination of unmarried women to keep their
children; the conviction among separated women that they would be
better off without their partners; and the strongly critical stance that
women adopted in their views of marriage and relationships with men.

Second, and as a logical extension of the above, women's experience of, and search for, independence and control are defining characteristics of their lives as lone mothers. Some young women living at
home with their parents keenly desired to establish themselves as
autonomous families — notwithstanding the support, both emotional
and practical, that their current situation offers. Separated women enjoyed the experience of daily independence in the home and their enhanced opportunities for personal development, community participation, and improved freedom to obtain re-education and training.
Financial autonomy is a central aspect of the women's experience —
an autonomy that is connected with their independence from their
boyfriends and husbands.

Separated women clearly assessed the *amount* of their income, partly in the light of the *control* that they exercised over their income. Newly acquired control over their income was a distinct positive reward for the low level of income that they endured. This control extended as far as an unwillingness to become dependent, in whole or in part, on any maintenance that they might procure from fathers or husbands. Women who had become financially independent in response to their partner's financial neglect or exploitation would not risk such a situation again. This insistence on financial independence is compounded for many women by a clear perception of the costs and benefits of renewed reliance on financial support from men: they might obtain limited and uncertain financial support, but at the considerable cost of finding the men involved, and then persuading them to pay. In some instances, this might prompt renewed, unsettling and conflictual contact between the women's children and the man involved.

Third, for the lone mothers in this study — but clearly not for all lone mothers — this experience of choice and freedom takes place in the context of poverty. Many of the women have incomes and living standards that are very low relative to the prevailing standards in Ireland today. Their levels of personal consumption are very low; they lack a social life for the most part; and they simply cannot afford many of the usual items and activities that are widely enjoyed — newspapers, books, a weekend or holiday away, occasional new clothes. Some women experience not merely relative deprivation, but also acute *basic* deprivation: they are sometimes unable to meet basic costs for rent, electricity, etc., and find themselves in debt or relying on charity, to obtain money for food, fuel and housing costs.

The role of employment in the women's lives is the fourth major theme to emerge. Few of the women in the study were in full-time paid employment, and a small number were in part-time employment. Work, and the financial autonomy as well as the scope for personal development it might offer, was central to the women's lives. This is not to say that all women keenly desired to work on a full-time basis — some did, others were explicit in their preference to put their children first for the moment, and others again were deliberately combining work outside the home part-time with caring for their children. Women experienced an unemployment trap: they desired to be in work but the tax/benefit system and child-care costs, as they perceived them, presented obstacles to working. There is no sense, however, in which women's receipt of State social welfare payments has fundamentally displaced an interest in work or self-reliance.

The women's orientations to work were part of the wider autonomy that they experienced. For women in paid work, either it underpinned their autonomy by giving them an independent income, or it increased their growing sense of confidence and freedom more generally. Among women not in paid work, there was often a clear perception that once they had penetrated the education/training system again, or identified a suitable niche, they would actively seek to become employees again.

Fifth, and finally, the women's experiences and perceptions are inescapably linked in many ways to the lives of their children. Some were compelled, from within either a marriage or a non-marital relationship, to end their relationships, partly in the interests of their children. Likewise, when allocating resources within very limited family budgets, the children's needs were invariably put first. In decisions about employment outside the home, the impact on children was a prime consideration. The continuing, relentless, sole parenting involved for many women is undoubtedly demanding, although this had its compensations for some women in the form of secure and very much improved relationships with children. Overall, the emotional and physical demand of lone parenting was the converse of the independence and freedom that women valued so much in their situations.

9.3   Public Policy and Lone Mothers

Women were asked at the end of the interviews to state what Government policies could be changed to improve the circumstances of lone mothers. Their responses were recorded and classified into broad areas, as summarised in Table 9.1. The pattern of responses is unsurprising: the single most common issue raised was child care. Next in importance was social welfare payment levels. What the public policy response might be to the concerns expressed by the women and to the policy issues emerging in the study is the subject of most of the remainder of this chapter.

Before considering specific policy issues, a general point should be made. Policies affecting lone-parent families may be policies that do not affect other types of families — judicial maintenance issues, for example, are not relevant to the general circumstances of two-parent families. Conversely, other policy topics such as Child Benefit impinge on *all* families with dependent children, of which lone-parent families are only a small sub-set. Some issues, such as the level of social welfare payments, are relevant to *poor* families — some, but by no means all, of whom are lone parents. In the discussion, therefore, the range of families that might be affected by any proposed policy change is identified.

Table 9.1:   Women's Suggestions about Improvements in Policies and Services

Suggestions	Number	%
Increase Social Welfare Payments	13	17
Other Social Welfare	4	5
Improve SWA Service	4	5
Child Care for Working Mothers	16	21
More Housing	9	12
Poverty Trap — Incentives	5	6
More Information about Rights	4	5
Family Law, Legal Aid	4	5
Access to Training/Education/Work Schemes	6	8
Miscellaneous	12	16
Total*	77	100

*   This is the number of suggestions made by the 53 respondents.

9.4   Social Welfare Policy

All women in the study were, by definition, recipients of Child Benefit, and most were also in receipt of a weekly Social Welfare payment. This fact, combined with the reality of financial deprivation among the women and their expressed emphasis on social welfare as a policy concern, naturally requires a range of issues about current social welfare policy to be considered.

Adequacy of Social Welfare Payments

The circumstances of many women in this study highlight, yet again, the relative income poverty of families dependent on social welfare. This situation is almost certainly as applicable to two-parent families as to one-parent families: recall here that the published comparisons of poverty rates (McCashin, 1993) reveal that "ordinary", two-parent families dependent on social welfare, and larger two-parent families in general, have higher risks of poverty than one-parent families. For many women in the study, the standard of living afforded by their social welfare payment was simply inadequate. Therefore, an essential and priority recommendation is an improvement in social welfare rates. At the time of writing, the LPA payment rate for a woman and one child is IR£77.70 per week[1]: A *general* policy of significantly improving social welfare payments would therefore be of considerable benefit to lone mothers.

Structure of Social Welfare Payments

Two issues command attention here, the first of which is the means test for the Lone Parent's Allowance.[2] As outlined in Chapter 7, the women were interviewed before the recent changes in the means test. The women's perception of the combination of benefit withdrawal and tax/PRSI rates was, for some, a disincentive to being in paid work. Since the fieldwork was undertaken, the means test has been altered — a higher disregard of means has been incorporated and the rate of benefit withdrawal has been reduced to 50 per cent from 100 per cent. Also, the administrative discretion to disregard child-care and travel-to-work costs has been published and streamlined.

According to the analysis in Chapter 7, this initiative has potentially significant benefits for low-income lone mothers. For those women in low-paid employment or part-time employment, or those considering the take up of such employment, the return from work is now undoubtedly greater. At the very lowest levels of gross pay, the impact of the means-test initiative has been to improve considerably the return from employment for lone mothers on social welfare. However, if the benefits of this improvement are to be realised, the changes in the means test must become widely known and understood, and the take up of Family Income Supplement and the Lone Parent's Tax Allowance must be complete.

If the focus of policy in the future is to enhance further the prospects for women of entering and remaining in employment, what should the next step be? The implication of the evidence in this study is that the cost of child care is the most impenetrable obstacle faced by some women. As the study shows, women were quick to point to child care as one of the barriers to paid employment — it was the barrier to paid employment which women were able to quantify and

---

[1]   This is the rate that applies after the increases in the 1995 Budget are put into effect.

[2]   Following the 1996 Budget, the Minister for Social Welfare announced the introduction of a One-Parent Family payment. The Scheme will amalgamate the existing Lone Parent's Allowance and Deserted Wife's Benefit. Recipients will be allowed to have earnings of £6,000 a year and still qualify for full payment. The payment will come into effect on 1 January 1997.

which many of them had experienced directly.

This leads to the conclusion that a more explicit, statutorily based recognition of child-care costs in the means test should be considered. The women would benefit in particular from a narrowing of the element of *uncertainty* about the effect of a change in their work status. One relatively simple way to achieve this would be a firm entitlement to a fixed-rate disregard per child per week (perhaps differentiated between full-time and part-time employees). In this way, women would have an exact knowledge of how their child-care costs would impinge on their net income. Currently, because of the absence of a statutory basis and explicit criteria for the child-care disregard, women are unclear about their prospective circumstances. A change such as that proposed would be more visible, whereas any undoubtedly beneficial changes in taxes, PRSI, and the means test would require claimants to have a detailed knowledge of "the system" and how it would affect them.

In relation to the tax/benefit system more generally, the analysis showed that a poverty trap persists at relatively modest levels of gross income. The complex interaction of income tax, PRSI and FIS is the reason for this, and may affect a wide range of lone-parent and two-parent families (see Blackwell, 1989; NESC, 1990). An analysis of this issue is beyond the bounds of the study. However, it is clear that *general* social welfare/taxation policies that would reduce or eliminate this problem would also have benefits for lone mothers.

At this point, the question must be asked as to whether the encouragement to take paid work *should* be a central element in policies affecting the incomes of lone mothers. The criticism has been made (McCashin, 1993) that heretofore the assumption underpinning policy was that lone mothers would not be in the labour market, an assumption that was reflected in the absence of child-care policies, lack of access to training, and an inhibiting means test. Recent policies — such as the improvement in the means test — suggest that policy is now shifting towards facilitating, if not encouraging labour market participation. The strategy suggested here is to facilitate paid work further through the specific proposals given above, but to avoid the *requirement* or assumption that all lone mothers should be actively oriented to the labour market. This is suggested for a number of reasons.

For a labour-market-type income-maintenance strategy to work effectively, two conditions would be required to hold: first, an enormous expansion in direct state support for, or provision of, child care; and second, a considerable improvement in the availability of employment. Sweden, where these conditions *do* apply, is the country which, correspondingly, achieves a higher level of work participation and a low level of poverty among lone mothers (McCashin, 1993; Millar and Glendenning, 1989). Apart from the conditions that might be required to sustain a labour-market-type strategy, it must also be noted that in an Irish context there are likely to be limits to the extent to which women will respond to policy measures geared at employment. Our interviews are a powerful reminder that some women are consciously choosing *not* to be employed for sustained periods of time, in the interests of their children. However, as the interviews also suggest, many women already adopt a strongly positive orientation to paid work. The challenge for policy is to build on that orientation by removing obstacles to employment for women, while simultaneously facilitating and supporting women who choose, or need, to remain outside the realm of paid work.

The second general aspect of the structure of social welfare is cohabitation. Historically and currently, women cohabiting with partners are deemed ineligible for any of the lone-parent payments, and recipients would have their entitlement terminated if found to be cohabiting.[3] Two sets of views can be found in the comments of the women in the study, which mirror the arguments in the policy debate. On the one hand, it is argued that it is unfair to penalise women who are cohabiting. After all, it is suggested, women are for the most part not being maintained financially by cohabiting partners. Furthermore, cohabiting couples are not legally obliged to maintain each other, as husbands and wives are.

On the other hand, it is pointed out that *married* persons' social welfare payments are affected by their spouses' incomes — a principle of aggregation underpins the treatment of married, as well as cohabiting couples. Simply to abolish the cohabitation rule would introduce a serious inequity between married and cohabiting couples, by excluding the income of a cohabiting partner from consideration, while retaining it for married persons. It is by no means clear how these opposing perspectives can be reconciled or whether current policies require review.

As Brown has argued in the context of the UK's system, one widely accepted rationale for abolishing or mitigating the cohabitation rule can be advanced (Brown, 1989 A and B). It might be accepted that movement into new or reconciled two-parent families is a desirable objective — not least because it may enhance the opportunity to escape

---

[3]   By which is meant women deemed to have a social, sexual and financial relationship with a partner — that is, in a relationship which is a marriage in all but legal formality.

from poverty. If this were agreed, and if it could be clearly shown that the cohabitation rule per se was a deterrent to women attempting long-term stable relationships, then the cohabitation rule could be seen as negative and self defeating in its impact. Our study is too small and unrepresentative to offer it as support for this line of argument. As was seen in Chapter 6, however, some women did link their prospective loss of entitlement to their views about new relationships — but these women were few. However, most women's desire for independence, in both the general sense and the financial sense, arose from their experience of relationships in the past and from the social, domestic and personal freedom that they were enjoying. It could hardly be claimed on the basis of this study, that the social welfare payment system per se was the factor determining women's personal choices in these matters.

Further research is required on this issue. If in future studies support were found for the reasoning outlined above, it would emphatically point to the abolition (or some amelioration) of the cohabitation rule. It must be accepted, however, that outright abolition would require to be combined with an adjustment to the way in which married partners' entitlements are dealt with. The complexities raised by this issue are beyond the scope of this study, but it is clear that some way would have to be found to make the entitlements of married women more "individual" and independent than they currently are. (For discussion of the arguments about "aggregation" or "individualisation", see Department of Social Welfare, 1991; Cousins, 1995.)

Social Welfare — Administration

As was seen in Chapter 6, there was no *general* evidence of women criticising the Department of Social Welfare's services or the administration of the Lone Parent's Allowance and Deserted Wife's payments. What does merit comment, however, is the duration of time that elapsed from the point of application to the point of receipt of a relevant payment. For many, this time period extended over several months. In the interviews, most women themselves did not necessarily comment critically on this. They were able to recall that while waiting they had received SWA and eventually received retrospective payments (minus SWA paid) when their allowance was put into effect.

The financial details reported in the interviews suggest that there is a danger that this time lapse can trigger indebtedness and poverty. Some separated women, for example, waited months for their payment to be effected, while in the meantime they struggled on SWA, deferred payments on ESB, rent and other commitments, and slid into financial disaster. Their payment, when it arrived, would be at a higher level than the SWA, but not sufficiently high to recover the lost financial ground.

It must be acknowledged that the financial circumstances of lone mothers may be innately more complex than those of other social welfare claimants. However, if the pattern of delay in payments reported here is representative, it must raise questions about the administration of the payments. No specific solution is proposed here, but the general arguments of the Commission on Social Welfare (Commission on Social Welfare, 1986) in favour of localised, integrated delivery of services should be noted. If SWA were fully integrated into the mainstream social welfare services and all of the services — or at least the assistance allowances — were administered locally, it would obviate the need for the two-tier system of SWA-to-Social Welfare Payment and speed up the process of claiming. The material in this study merely highlights a more general argument already advanced about the desirability of more local access to, and administration of, services.

In the context of an integrated, local service, lone mothers should be able to apply locally, receive a lone-parent payment immediately (subject to basic eligibility and to follow-up assessment of the claim), and then have their payment and entitlement confirmed (or otherwise) at a later point. It is difficult to accept that the processing of LPA and similar payments often requires the involvement of two agencies (DSW and Health Boards), two sets of personnel, the administration of two eligibility tests (LPA and SWA), and the receipt of two different levels of payment.

Child Benefit

All of the women in the study were recipients of Child Benefit. It was central to their financial arrangements and one of the mechanisms that enhanced their autonomy. Child Benefit, however, is a very modest proportion of the total income of families. Therefore, it was not surprising that in their policy suggestions women did not focus on it: they stressed instead the need to improve the weekly social welfare payment.

Notwithstanding the women's lack of policy proposals for Child Benefit, it is important to consider the implications of possible reforms of Child Benefit for the incomes of lone mothers. (For a selection of proposals, see Commission on Social Welfare, 1986, Chapter 13; Nolan and Farrell, 1990; Callan, 1991; Department of Social Welfare, 1995A.) Any overall increase in the rate of Child Benefit payment would benefit *all* families, including lone-mother families. However, significant increases would be relatively costly, and this raises the question about whether a more selective approach to Child Benefit would permit substantial increases in Child Benefit for *poorer* families.

This approach has now been thoroughly researched (Callan, 1991). In summary, it has been demonstrated that (in a revenue-neutral reform) a substantial increase in Child Benefit, of the order of 40 per cent, could be afforded, if Child Benefit were taxable.[4] The effect of such a reform, in brief, would be an increase in the incomes of low-income families, a decline in the incomes of high-income families, and no net change in the income of middle-income families (see Callan, 1991, for details). If it is acknowledged that the incidence of family poverty is high, and that a more targeted approach to Child Benefit could have a significant impact on reducing poverty, the merit of such a policy is clear. A strategy of "increasing and taxing" Child Benefit would result in a significant improvement in the incomes of *low-income* families — both one-parent and two-parent families.

A second set of broad issues about Child Benefit concerns the *overall structure* of Child Income Support. Some existing commentaries on this topic have pointed to the need for some form of integration of the various sources of Child Income Support. One version of this proposal was contained in the official document *Building on Reality 1985–1987* (Government Publications, 1985), which proposed the unification of FIS, Child Dependent Additions and Child Benefit into a significantly higher, taxable, monthly Child Benefit. In its analysis, the Commission on Social Welfare broadly endorsed this type of arrangement as ideal, but was conscious of the difficulty of removing FIS and CDAs from low-income families: this would require a very large, and therefore very costly, increase in Child Benefit to off-set the loss of CDAs and FIS for poor families. Essentially, the rationale for this proposal is that FIS is implicated in the poverty trap for employees, while CDAs are an important factor in the unemployment trap for families with children. Briefly, the CDAs have become so significant for social welfare recipients that the replacement ratios for families with children are relatively high. A reduction in the role of CDAs in the "income package" of poor families, and an increase in the role of Child Benefit, would both simplify the child income-support system and reduce any disincentives that might arise from the relatively high CDAs in the current system.

---

[4] Means testing of Child Benefit would be an alternative way of targeting. But there are administrative and social objections to such a course of action. No analysis of specific means-tests proposals has been undertaken.

If such a policy were pursued, would it have any relevance to lone mothers? A phasing-in of this kind of arrangement could have a number of outcomes depending critically on the details. Presumably, any pursuit of this policy which reduced CDAs would correspondingly increase Child Benefit (CB) and leave lone mothers and other social welfare recipients unaffected. However, an important indirect, but potentially significant, implication for lone mothers and other recipients is that CB is not means tested, whereas the main social welfare payments including CDAs are. Therefore, if the roles of CB and CDAs were altered, considerably more of the income of recipients would be "secure" — that is, not subject to deduction if earnings or other income increases. This would be potentially important for lone mothers whose concern — since they have children — is to maximise the degree of *certainty* about their income.

In the Budget of 1995, reflecting the recommendations of the Child Benefit Review Committee (Department of Social Welfare, 1995A), this strategy of enhancing Child Benefit and limiting the role of CDAs was initiated. CDAs were not increased, while Child Benefit was increased by £7 per month. This approach is to be welcomed, and if it is pursued in further Budgets it will have beneficial effects for lone mothers, and for families in general, by reducing the role of means-tested payments in social welfare incomes and expanding the role of Child Benefit, which is neutral with respect to families' employment status.

Two further, quite separate issues about Child Benefit also emerged in the study. It is clear from the women's experiences that the number of children and the ages of children are strongly related to patterns of deprivation. The current "tiered" rate of Child Benefit for families of different sizes should therefore continue. Also, the argument of the Commission on Social Welfare (Commission on Social Welfare, 1986; Chapter 13) in favour of an age gradation in Child Benefit is supported by the material in the study. Women with adolescent children find it distinctly more difficult to cope financially because of the budgetary costs of older children. However, there are diverging views on this issue, with the recent *The Cost of a Child* study supporting higher payments for older children (Carney et al., 1994), and the Child Benefit Review Committee deciding not to recommend age-related payments (Department of Social Welfare, 1995A).

9.5   Supplementary Welfare Allowances

A recent study of SWA revealed that lone-mother families have a high utilisation of SWA (Mills, 1991). This local study confirms this evidence.

Many of the women used the SWA system — as a "fill-in" payment, while awaiting a social welfare entitlement, or as a supplement to meet housing costs, or on an emergency basis to meet lump-sum needs such as rent arrears or ESB bills. A number of policy matters emerge from the study.

First, it is clear that the service whereby a basic SWA payment is paid while claimants wait for a social welfare payment is necessary at present. Many of the women spoke positively about its role as a "fall-back in emergencies". However, as argued above, it is not clear that this dual system is necessary or effective. The evidence of this study points up sharply the potential value of having a fully integrated, local service where the need to move from one payment to another is eliminated.

Second, the interviews were conducted just after the "cuts" in SWA lump-sum payments were rescinded.[5] In 1992, a limit had been placed on the amount/number of such payments that a family would receive. The women in the study were vivid in their accounts of the impact of this policy — either on themselves or on cases they knew well. As the material in Chapter 6 suggests, women simply went into debt, by allowing rent to build up or by borrowing from family, friends or elsewhere. With social welfare payment levels as they are, it appears that SWA lump sums are an indispensable part of the financial routine of poor lone-mother families. The policy of rescinding the "cut" is therefore to be strongly welcomed.

A wider argument can be made about the role of lump-sum payments. The Commission on Social Welfare acknowledged that long-term recipients of social welfare have a chronic inability to meet "capital" or "lump-sum" expenses — replacement of furniture, new clothes, equipment for a newly-born baby and so on. The solution they advanced was that regular, lump-sum payments be paid to all long-term social welfare recipients with dependants. Thus, families with children who had been receiving a social welfare payment as their only income source for a specified time period (say, 18 months) would begin to receive a quarterly lump-sum payment set at the levels of the dependant allowances being paid. Such an initiative would clearly benefit lone-mother recipients, most of whom would experience long-term reliance on social welfare. For all prospective beneficiaries, it would have the distinct advantage of regularising the payment of lump sums and obviating the recourse to SWA.

---

[5]   This "cut" was one of 12 restrictions in Social Welfare introduced in 1992 and widely referred to as the "Dirty Dozen" (see various issues of *Poverty Today*, 1992).

Third, the divergence among the women in the study in the type of service they claimed they received was striking. Some women were highly complimentary about the Community Welfare Officer (CWO) they had approached; others were scathing in their criticism. This highlights again the degree of variation in the way CWOs administer their discretionary powers, and it reveals the extent to which the service is a "personal" service, the quality of which is assessed by claimants on the basis of how "nice" or helpful the CWO is.

9.6   Child Care

This topic loomed large in the women's accounts of their lives, in both a general sense and a specific sense. At a general level, some women reported how demanding parenting alone was. More specifically, the absence of child-care arrangements, or the cost of available services to facilitate work outside the home, was often cited by the women as a serious problem.

A detailed analysis of what general, national policy should be pursued for child care is beyond the scope of this study, but some general principles of policy arising from the study can be made. First, it is important to realise that child-care developments and initiatives should not be confined to women working outside the home. The welfare of lone mothers, and presumably also of women in low-income two-parent parents, is significantly affected by the demands of parenting, whether women are attempting to work outside the home or are choosing to be full-time parents.

Second, it is clear that at national and local level, policy must simultaneously subsidise the *cost* of child care for those on low incomes and increase the *supply* of child-care services.

Third, if State resources are to be allocated to child care, it is clear that public policy must also have a role in defining standards and in regulating child care.

No specific measures relevant to the particular area in which this study was undertaken are suggested here: the significance of child care for the women in the study merely reflects a well-documented *national* policy need (see for example, NESC, 1991). The most recent and authoritative commentary and set of recommendations is contained in the *Report of the Second Commission on the Status of Women (1992)*. Its recommendations could, if implemented, have a considerable impact on the quantity, quality and variety of child-care services in Ireland generally — including the kind of area in which this study is based.

The Commission's recommendations (see pp. 464–67 of the Commission's report for a summary list) revolve around the establishment of a national unit in the Department of Health, with responsibility for provision of child care. Some specific recommendations are:

- Provision by the State of a Child-Care Development Budget of £20 million per annum

- Establishment of a favourable tax régime for capital and operating costs of new nurseries

- Development of local partnerships based on the model of the Local Area Employment Initiatives

- Establishment of national guidelines for day-care provision setting minimum standards on a range of criteria

- Ensuring the provision of training for child-care workers.

On the whole, these and other recommendations are vindicated in the context of this study. Two specific points should be noted, however. If the Commission's argument that "provision for children in need" should be a priority (p. 466) is accepted, as this study suggests it ought to be, the question of how this priority should be pursued is a matter for detailed deliberation. It could be argued that by subsiding *demand* — for instance, by excluding child-care costs from lone mothers' means assessment — an already available private market will be more accessible and affordable for low-income women. A somewhat different argument can also be made: that for women on low incomes the key issue is the *supply* of child-care services, and therefore policy should focus on a whole range of mechanisms to improve the availability of services, especially in "poor areas". Policy is currently uneasily straddling both approaches, and what the mix of these approaches should be in the future is not clear.

A second and related set of issues concerns the recent improvement in, and publicity about, the "child-care allowance" in the lone parents' means-test payments. The implication of women's comments in the interviews is that they might prefer a known and fixed amount per child in the allowance. Women might be more likely to contemplate a return to employment if they could be *certain* about the impact of child-care costs on their net income (if taking up employment) — this suggests a move away from the current arrangements, which are still discretionary. A more general question concerns the principle of such a disregard of child-care costs. If the precedent of such a disregard is now established in the social welfare system, is there not also a case for a more general recognition of child-care costs for *all* low-income (working) families, and, if so, what form should that take? No concrete proposal is made here, but it must be recognised that the current arrangements may be open to criticism on the grounds that they "discriminate" against certain categories.

9.7 Housing

The women in the study were distributed across the three main tenures — owner-occupation, local authority and private rented accommodation. Housing issues per se did not arise as a central policy feature in the study: few women mentioned it as a key area for policy improvement in their policy suggestions, nor did many women identify any aspect of housing — quality of, or access to, housing — as an element in the deprivation they experienced. This should not seem surprising as the women lived in ordinary, mainstream housing of a usual standard. Several points of concern emerge, however.

The cost of housing is clearly a serious issue for some of the families. Specifically, as was seen in the material in Chapters 5 and 6, some women found housing costs relative to their incomes to be a very significant problem. The SWA rent allowance system is, apparently, not being availed of by all who are entitled to it — the data on families' incomes below the SWA-minus-£5 threshold is evidence of this. Therefore, there may be considerable scope to improve the awareness and take up of the SWA rent allowance.

A further issue about the rent allowance is its structure. Its formula leaves families who receive the Rent Allowance with an income which is the appropriate SWA rate minus £5 after housing costs. The standard of living of some families in the study suggests that this formula results in an income, for some, that is simply inadequate. This general, potential deficiency is merely illustrated in this study: it clearly has a wider, national relevance and it is imperative therefore to review the operation of the rent allowance with a view to establishing an adequate, national housing benefit scheme. It is important also to note that there is no inconsistency between the absence of housing deprivation in a physical sense and the need for improved housing-related allowances. On the contrary, it is precisely *because* some women have adequate housing that they are trapped into a situation of high housing costs: separated women, for example, left in the family home with children, struggling to pay a mortgage that had previously been paid out of an earned income.

A different aspect of the cost of housing concerns the rent allowance as it impinges on the younger, unmarried women in the study. As has been shown, some of these returned to live with their parents, and continued to stay with parents, partly as a result of their constrained housing choices. Quite simply, the range and quality of housing — even that subsidised by rent allowances — is not adequate to meet the needs of some low-income lone mothers. As a result, some are living, not as independent families which is their essential preference, but as subsidiary families in a situation of some tension and, in some cases, sheer overcrowding. A general analysis of the housing system in Dublin is beyond the boundaries of this study. However, the findings converge with two themes in other recent commentaries on housing policy.

First, it is clear that the substantial reduction since 1987 in the role of local authority housing in meeting the housing needs of those on low incomes is having a significant impact on housing need — although this is difficult to quantify. Increasingly, lone mothers and other low-income persons rely on the rent allowance system to subsidise rents in what are often poor-quality private rented units. If this is the case, it clearly calls for a review of the costs and benefits to tenants and the State of this recent increased reliance on Rent Allowances.[6]

Second, it must also be recognised that a general return to State provision of standard "family" dwellings may not be an appropriate response to the housing needs of low-income lone mothers. On the contrary, the Lord Mayor's Commission on Housing (Dublin Corporation, 1993) pointed out that 34 per cent of Dublin Corporation's housing waiting list comprised lone-mother family units. The commission proposed the construction of separate, smaller accommodation units linked to Health Board services and social support. Whether this specific proposal is the appropriate one to adopt is a matter for some debate. What is undoubtedly clear is the need for a resumption of direct provision of local authority housing, and a clearer focus on the need for smaller units reflecting the housing requirements of lone-parent families.

An additional point to note concerns the operation of the housing waiting list. As reported by some of the respondents in the study, women who feel they need accommodation and who approach the housing authorities may be discouraged from applying. They may be told, for example, that they have not "enough points" or that their wait may be an extended one. In effect, the number of women who express a need for housing by inquiring about available housing is greater than the number who are formally registered on the housing

---

[6]   A review Group on the Role of Supplementary Welfare Allowance in Relation to Housing reported to the Minister for Social Welfare in December 1995 (Department of Social Welfare, 1995B).

"waiting list". The housing "waiting list" is best thought of therefore as a potentially significant *underestimate* of the need for housing among lone-mother families.

A final aspect of the operation of the housing system, which is relatively minor in the context of the housing system as a whole, concerns the administration of the differential rent-payment scheme. Some women reported difficulties in making arrangements to pay their rents. In some cases, the Corporation was refusing to accept arrears payments of particular amounts; in other cases, women who wanted to pay their rent on the day they received their social welfare payment were not permitted to do this and were required to wait until "rent day". This pattern of administrative inflexibility was unnecessary and rigid, and in the study was contributing to women's financial difficulties. It was harder for them to manage the finances and in some instances it reinforced their rent indebtedness. If this administrative régime applies on a widespread basis, it clearly suggests that the co-ordination of rent payments and weekly social welfare payments needs to be reviewed, and that a workable system of collecting and accepting rent arrears payments needs to be devised.

9.8   Family Maintenance Payments

The results in the study showing very low levels of family maintenance payments by husbands and fathers should not be viewed as surprising: they merely echo the findings of other evidence to hand for Ireland, the UK and other countries of the ineffectiveness of judicial systems of family maintenance (Ward, 1990). Before referring to the policy implications of this finding, one important cautionary note should be observed. Our sample contains only low-income women. A more representative sample which included women from middle- and higher-income groups might reveal other patterns. For example, middle-class couples, on separation, may be successful in reaching informal agreements, or in drafting legal separation agreements through solicitors, or in adhering to court-based maintenance arrangements. Likewise, young middle-class women may have greater success in obtaining maintenance from their child's father. Further, more representative, research is required to establish the true situation.

Two alternative lines of policy argument are proposed here. The first is based on the assumption (for purposes of argument) that the maintenance payments system is a general failure. If this were so, then it would clearly suggest that a wholesale departure from the principle of judicial maintenance should be considered. What specific arrangements might then be put in place is simply not clear, but the State would make a *preventive, guaranteed* payment and then pursue the errant father, without obliging the woman to trace and pursue her partner and attempt to obtain maintenance.

A second, alternative line of reasoning would be based on the argument that it is only very-low-income women who are bereft of maintenance. If this situation applied, then it would raise more specific questions about the link between social welfare and the legal family maintenance system. In particular, it would suggest that these systems should be co-ordinated to ensure that low-income partners have an incentive to pay maintenance. The current direction of policy, following the introduction of the Liable Relative principle in social welfare legislation and modifications to the means tests for social welfare, is to remove that incentive. Women are still legally obliged to attempt to obtain maintenance, but now the maintenance off-sets the State's welfare payment, removing the incentive for fathers/ partners to "top-up" the family's social welfare income.

There are difficult issues to be resolved here. On the one hand, the State may wish to enforce the father's obligations as a matter of principle. On the other, the State may also wish to give an incentive to fathers to pay so as to improve the income of lone mothers and their children. If the latter view were adopted, it would offer a strong argument for excluding from the relevant social welfare means tests any maintenance paid (in whole or in part) in respect of children, or some fixed amount or proportion of maintenance paid.

9.9   Issues for Future Research

This study, as has repeatedly been stressed, is not only small-scale but also local. Therefore, no statistical generalisations have been made about its findings. The study's limitations are a reminder of the need for research on many aspects of lone parenthood. In these final paragraphs an attempt is made to outline an agenda for future research which arises (in part) from this study.

Causes of Lone Parenthood

One set of issues that this study could not address is the underlying social change giving rise in Ireland to a growing number of lone-parent families. Two specific research exercises merit immediate attention. First, an analysis of trends in marital breakdown, with a view to identifying the broad social factors associated with marital breakdown. International research has focused on enhanced female labour

force activity, improved women's earnings, income maintenance provisions, and similar economic facilitators as key explanatory variables: the Labour Force Survey could be the prime data source for
Ireland in quantifying the long-run growth in marital breakdown.

Second, the distinct concentration of single lone mothers in low
socioeconomic backgrounds suggests that the factors giving rise to
this form of lone parenthood require separate analysis. Of particular importance here is the potential relevance of declining employment opportunities for young working-class men and women as factors shaping the context in which young women make decisions. Research on these socioeconomic factors is required, and, in particular,
an assessment is needed of the importance of these factors relative
to long-run changes in values and attitudes.

Consequences of Lone Parenthood

That poverty and deprivation are associated with lone motherhood is
clear from this and many other studies. A key question raised by this
study is the extent to which lone motherhood is correlated with poverty. Clearly, lone parenthood is hardly the *cause* of poverty for families: some lone parents may not be poor; *male* lone parents may be
less likely to be poor; some families are poor *before* they experience
lone parenthood. These complexities should highlight the fact that
although this study dealt with poor lone mothers, the source of poverty among lone mothers resides in the economic vulnerability of
women in general — low pay, poorer skills, lower earnings, and
gender inequality in society. This limited study could not hope to
address these wider questions. A large-scale national, representative
study is required to document the incomes, employment patterns,
health, housing conditions and so on of lone parents and of families in
general. Associated with this is the question of the impact of lone parenthood on the fortunes of children in such families. How family
structure may — or may not — affect different aspects of children's
welfare is also a central and urgent question for future research.

Inescapably, the methodology required to examine these questions
must be *longitudinal*. For example, the experience of lone motherhood
probably impels many women to re-enter work, and to obtain independent incomes. Similarly, the impact of lone motherhood on children's
educational performance can only be properly observed after a time lag.
Lone parenthood is a *process* and must be observed longitudinally. It is
also clear, a priori, and from this study, that research should *compare*
lone-parent families with other family types — such comparisons
alone will permit an analysis of the impact of lone motherhood per se

on women and children. Research in this area has tended to focus on lone *mothers*, but lone fathers too merit some research attention. Male lone parents might be *economically* less vulnerable than lone mothers, but it is distinctly possible that men may find the social role of lone father difficult and stressful. No research has yet been published on this topic in Ireland.

Policy Aspects of Lone Parenthood

Research into policy, and improvements in policy, need not await the completion of the broad research agenda outlined above. Policy analysis which does not require primary fieldwork could contribute to debate on, and developments in, a number of policy areas.

One strategic issue in social security/tax policy which has direct implications for lone parents is the emerging debate on "individualisation" of tax/benefit systems. The immediate issue is whether and how women who are "dependants" of men can procure entitlements to personal, individual tax/benefit treatment. Policy internationally is moving in this direction. If this strategy were embraced here, it might have the potential to neutralise the policy dilemma in relation to cohabitation. An institutional description and critique of other countries' arrangements is a priority research issue here. This priority is accentuated by the prospect of divorce being legalised and the future growth (which will occur in any case) in the numbers of lone-parent families.

A second institutional issue on which policy research should throw some light is the availability of alternative forms of family maintenance. Ireland's apparent difficulties with judicial maintenance are not unique in an international context. What is now urgently required is a *representative* assessment of the operation of the present arrangements. Associated with this, a study is also required of specifically what form of "non-judicial" or "guaranteed maintenance" (as the Nordic system is sometimes described) could be introduced in Ireland.

One striking feature of this and other studies is the extent to which young, single mothers manage to cope and the degree to which they feel positive about their situations. While admitting that this finding may not represent the situation of *all* young, single mothers the question arises as to what the rationale is, if any, of policy intervention focused on this group? Should the prime or exclusive policy concern be with their income needs, or should the policy focus be different? Since many unmarried mothers are young, is it their youth that should be the concern of policy? If so, is it hypothesised that their

youth impairs their *capacity as parents*, or that their early withdrawal from work/education training puts them at a long-term disadvantage? These essential issues of strategy and policy need to be urgently addressed. Some clarification of policy objectives and possibili-
ties could be achieved if a detailed review were undertaken of the
services currently in place, of the services developed in other countries, and of policy objectives that other countries attempt to achieve.

In particular, it should be noted in relation to young, unmarried
women that the benefits of specific interventions aimed at their education is being increasingly recognised. For example, Schofield's recent study in the UK of young working class mothers documented the
potential of school-based initiatives to offer these mothers specific
educational supports geared to their circumstances (Schofield, 1994).
The broadly positive orientation of the women in the study towards
work and training suggests that specific schemes should be developed
to facilitate young mothers to re-enter the mainstream school system
in their local areas.

These general suggestions do not comprise an exhaustive research
agenda. They identify key issues for the future which are of national
policy concern. Clearly, this agenda could be extended if the possibili-
ties for further small-scale, local research were identified. While some
further insight into national policy concerns could be gleaned from
additional local studies such as this, it is now necessary to put research in this area on to a stronger footing.

References

Abrahamson, H. (1984): *Issues in Adoption in Ireland*, Dublin: Economic and Social Research Institute, Broadsheet Series, No. 23.

Acock, A.C. and Keecolt, K.J. (1989): "Is it Family Structure or Socio-Economic Status? Family Structure During Adolescence and Adult Adjustment", *Social Forces*, 68: 553–71.

Amato, P.R. and Booth, A. (1991): "Consequences of Parental Divorce and Marital Unhappiness for Adult Well Being", *Social Forces*, 69: 895–914.

Blackwell, J. (1989A): *Family Income Supplement*, Dublin: Report to the Department of Social Welfare.

Blackwell, J. (1989B): *Women in the Labour Force*, Second Edition, Dublin: Employment Equality Agency.

Bradshaw, J. and Millar, J. (1991): *Lone Parent Families in the United Kingdom*, London: DHSS, Research Report Series, Paper No. 6.

Brannen, J. (1988): "Research Note: The Study of Sensitive Topics", *Sociological Review*, 36: 552–63.

Brown, J. (1989A): *In Search of a Policy: Social Security for Lone Parent Families*, London: National Council of One Parent Families.

Brown, J. (1989B): *Why Don't They Go Out to Work? Mothers on Benefit*, Social Security Advisory Committee, Research Paper No. 2. London: HMSO.

Callan, T., (1991): *Income Tax and Welfare Reforms, Microsumulation Modelling and Analysis*, Dublin: Economic and Social Research Institute, General Research Series, Paper No. 154.

Callan, T., Nolan, B., Whelan, B.J., Hannan, D.F. and Creighton, S. (1989): *Poverty, Income and Welfare in Ireland*, Dublin: The Economic and Social Research Institute, General Research Series, Paper No. 146.

Callan, T., Nolan, B., Whelan, C.T. (1993): "Resources, Deprivation and the Measurement of Poverty", *Journal of Social Policy*, 22(2): 141–72.

Carney, C., Fitzgerald, E., Kiely, G. and Quinn, P. (1994): *The Cost of a Child*, Dublin: Combat Poverty Agency.

Central Statistics Office (1985): *Census of Population 1981*, Vol. 3, Dublin: CSO.

Central Statistics Office (1989): *Census of Population 1986*, Vol. 3, Dublin: CSO.

Central Statistics Office (1994A): *Census '91*, Vol. 3, Dublin: Government Publications Office.

Cherlin, A.J., Fursternberg, F.F., Chase-Lansdale, P.L., Kiernan, K.,

Robins, P.K., Morrison, D.R. and Teitler, J.O. (1991): "Longitudinal Studies on Effects of Divorce on Children in Great Britain and the United States", *Science*, 252: 1386–9.

Children Come First (1991): "The Government's Proposals on the Maintenance of Children", White Paper: 2 Vols., London: HMSO.

Clulow, C. and Mattison, J. (1989): *Marriage Inside Out: Understanding Problems of Intimacy*, London: Penguin Books.

Combat Poverty Agency (1993): *Baseline Data Report, Coolock LDC*, Dublin, Combat Poverty Agency (unpublished).

Commission on Social Welfare (1986): *Report*, Dublin: Government Publications Office.

Commission on the Status of Women (1972): *Report*, Dublin: Government Publications Office.

Cousins, M. (1995): *The Irish Social Welfare System: Law and Social Policy*, Dublin: The Round Hall Press.

Darling, V. (1974): *Adoption in Ireland*, Dublin: CARE Discussion Paper No. 1.

Darling, V. (1984): *And Baby Makes Two*, Dublin: Federation of Services for Unmarried Parents and their Children.

Delphy, G. (1984): *Close to Home: A Materialist Analysis of Women's Oppression*, London: Hutchinson.

Department of Social Welfare (1991): *Report of the Review Group on the Treatment of Households in the Social Welfare Code*, Dublin: Government Publications.

Department of Social Welfare (1995A): *Report of the Child Benefit Review Committee*. Dublin: Government Publications.

Department of Social Welfare (1995B): *Report of the Review Group on the Role of Supplementary Welfare Allowance in Relation to Housing*, Dublin: Stationery Office.

Dilnot, A., and Duncan, A. (1991): "Lone Mothers, Family Credit and Paid Work", *Fiscal Studies*, 12(1): 1–21.

Dominian, J. (1968): *Marital Breakdown*, Harmondsworth: Penguin.

Donnison, D. (1988): "Defining and Measuring Poverty: A Reply to Stein Ringen", *Journal of Social Policy*, 17(3): 367–74.

Donohue, J., Fitzpatrick, A., Flanagan, N. and Scanlon, S. (1990): *Unmarried Mothers Delivered in the National Maternity Hospital, 1988*, Dublin: Department of Social Work and Social Administration, UCD.

Dublin Corporation (1993): *Lord Mayor's Commission on Housing*, Dublin (City Hall).

Duggan, C., Payne, D. and Ronayne, T. (1991): *Combating Long Term Unemployment in Coolock/Darndale: A Socio-economic Analysis of the Issues*, Dublin: Northside Partnership (unpublished).

Duncan, W. (1987): "Family Law and Social Policy" in Duncan, W. (ed.), *Law and Social Policy: Some Current Problems in Irish Law*, Dublin: Dublin University Law Journal.

Eekelaar, J. (1988): "England and Wales", in Kahn, A. and Kamerman, S. (eds.), *Child Support: From Debt Collection to Social Policy*, London: Sage Publications.

Elliot, B.J. and Richards, M.P.M. (1991): "Children and Divorce: Educational Performance and Behaviour Before and After Parental Separation", *International Journal of Law and the Family*, 5: 258–76.

Ermisch, J. (1990): "Demographic Aspects of the Growing Number of Lone Parent Families", in *Lone Parent Families: The Economic Challenge*, Paris: OECD.

Fahey, T. (1993): "Review Article", *Economic and Social Review*, 24(2): 199–210.

Farley, D. (1964): *Social Insurance and Social Assistance in Ireland*, Dublin: Institute of Public Administration.

Ferri, E. (1976) *Growing Up in a One Parent Family*, Windsor: National Foundation for Educational Research.

Ferri, E. (1993A): "An Overview of Research and Policy in the Lone Parent Family in Britain" in Hudson, J. and Galaway, B. (eds.), *Single Parent Families: Perspectives on Research and Policy*, Toronto: Thompson Educational Publishing.

Ferri, E. (1993B): "Socialisation Experience of Children in Lone Parent Families: Evidence from the British National Child Development Study" in Hudson, J. and Galaway, B. (eds.), *Single Parent Families: Perspectives on Research and Policy*, Toronto: Thompson Educational Publishing.

Ferri, E., and Robinson, H. (1976): *Coping Alone*. Windsor: National Foundation for Educational Research.

Finer Committee (1974): *Report of the Committee on One Parent Families*, Vol. 1, London: HMSO, Cmnd 5269.

Flanagan, N., and Richardson, V. (1992): *Unmarried Mothers: A Social Profile*, Dublin: Department of Social Policy and Social Work, UCD.

Gee, E.M. (1993): "Adult Outcomes Associated with Childhood Family Structure: An Appraisal of Research and an Examination of Canadian Data" in Hudson, J. and Galaway, B. (eds.), *Single Parent Families: Perspectives on Research and Policy*, Toronto: Thompson Educational Publishing.

Gilliand, P. (1989): "Evolution of Family Policy in the Light of Demographic Development in West European Countries", *International Social Security Review*, 4(4): 395–425.

Glendinning, C. and Millar, J. (eds.) (1987): *Women and Poverty in Britain*, Brighton: Wheatsheaf.

Government Publications (1985): *Building on Reality*, Dublin: Stationery Office.

Graham, H. (1984): *Women, Health and the Family*, Brighton: Wheatsheaf.

Graham, H. (1987): "Being Poor: Perceptions and Coping Strategies of Lone Mothers" in Brannen, J. and Wilson, G. (eds.), *Give and Take in Families: Studies in Resource Distribution*, London: Allen and Unwin.

Hart, N. (1976): *When Marriage Ends: A Study in Status Passage*, London: Tavistock.

Hudson, J. and Galaway, B. (eds.) (1993): *Single Parent Families: Perspectives on Research and Policy*, Toronto: Thompson Educational Publishing.

James, H. and Wilson, K. (1986): *Couples, Conflict and Change*, London: Tavistock.

Joint Oireachtas Committee on Marital Breakdown (1985): *Report*, Dublin: Government Publications Office.

Kahn, A., and Kamerman, S. (eds.) (1988): *Child Support: From Debt Collection to Social Policy*, London: Sage Publications.

Kamerman, S. and Kahn, A. (1989): "Single Parent, Female Headed Families in Western Europe: Social Change and Response", *International Social Security Review*, 4(1): 1–34.

Kiecolt, A.J. and Acock, A.C. (1988): "The Long Term Effects of Family Structure on Gender Role Attitudes", Journal of Marriage and the Family, 50: 709–17.

Kilkenny Social Services (1972): *The Unmarried Mother in the Irish Community*, Kilkenny: Kilkenny Social Services.

Kirke, D. (1979): "Unmarried Mothers: A Comparative Study". *Economic and Social Review*, 10(2): 157–67.

Land, H. (1983): "Who Still Cares for the Family?" in Lewis, J. (ed.), *Women's Welfare, Women's Rights*, London: Croom Helm.

Leethe, R. (1978): "One Parent Families: Numbers and Characteristics" in *Population Trends*, 13, Figure 1.

Lewis, J. (1989): "Lone Parents: Politics and Economics", *Journal of Social Policy*, 18(4): 595–600.

Lewis, J. (ed.) (1993): *Women and Social Policies in Europe*, London: Edward Elgar.

Lewis, J. and Piachaud, D. (1987): "Women and Poverty in the Twentieth Century", in Glendinning, C. and Millar, J., *op. cit.*

Mack, J., and Lansley, S. (1985): *Poor Britain*, London: Allen and Unwin.

Marsden, D. (1973): *Mothers Alone: Poverty and the Fatherless Family*, London: Penguin.

McCashin, A. (1988): "Family Income Support: Trends and Issues", in Healy, S. and Reynolds, B. (eds.), *Poverty and Family Income Policy*, Dublin: Conference of Major Religious Superiors.

McCashin, A. (1993): *Lone Parents in the Republic of Ireland: Enumeration, Description and Implications for Social Security*, Dublin: Economic and Social Research Institute, Broadsheet Series, No. 29.

McCashin, A. and Cooke, J. (1992): *Inequality, Litigation and Policy Resolution: Gender Dependence in Social Security and Personal Income Tax in the Republic of Ireland*, Conference Paper, York University.

McKay, S. and Marsh, A. (1994): *Lone Parents and Work*, London: Department of Social Security, Report No. 25.

McLanahan, S. (1985): "Family Structure and the Reproduction of Poverty", *American Journal of Sociology*, 90: 873–901.

McLoughlin, E., Millar, J. and Cooke, K. (1989): *Work and Welfare Benefits*, Aldershot: Avebury.

Millar, J. (1987): "Lone Mothers", in Glendinning, C. and Millar, J. *op. cit.*

Millar, J. (1991): "Lone Parent Families in the UK: Challenges for Social Security Policy", *International Social Security Review*, 6(4): 456–69.

Millar, J. and Glendinning, C. 1989. "Gender and Poverty", *Journal of Social Policy*, 18(3): 363–81.

Millar, J., Leeper, S. and Davies, C. (1992): *Lone Parents, Poverty and Public Policy in Ireland: A Comparative Study*, Dublin: Combat Poverty Agency.

Mills, F. (1991): *Scheme of Last Resort? A Review of the Supplementary Welfare Allowance*, Dublin: Combat Poverty Agency.

Moss, P., and Lav, G. (1985): "Mothers without Marriages", *New Society*, 9 August: 207.

Murray, C.A. (1984): *Losing Ground: American Social Policy 1950–1980*, New York: Basic Books.

NESC (1990): *A Strategy for the Nineties*, Dublin: National Economic and Social Council, Report No. 89.

NESC (1991): *Women's Participation in the Irish Labour Market*, Dublin: National Economic and Social Council, Report No. 91.

Nolan, B. (1990): "Low Pay and Poverty in Ireland", Dublin: The Economic and Social Research Institute, Seminar Paper, unpublished.

Nolan, B. and Callan, T. (1989): "Measuring Trends in Poverty over Time: Some Robust Results for Ireland, 1980–1987", *The Economic and Social Review*, 20(4): 309–28.

Nolan, B. and Farrell, B. (1990): *Child Poverty in Ireland*, Dublin: Combat Poverty Agency.

O'Connor, J., Aherne, R. and Walsh, E. (1986): *Social Assistance: The Experience and Perception of Applicants*, Dublin: Commission on Social Welfare, Background Paper No. 3.

O'Grady, T. (1991): *Married to the State: A Study of Unmarried Mother's Allowance Applicants*, Dublin: Department of Social Welfare (unpublished).

O'Hare, A., Dromey, M., O'Connor, A. Clarke, M. and Kirwan, G. (1987): *Mothers Alone? — A Study of Women who Gave Birth Outside Marriage*, Dublin: Federation of Services for Unmarried Parents and their Children.

O'Higgins, K. (1974): *Marital Desertion in Dublin*, Dublin: Economic and Social Research Institute, Broadsheet No. 9.

O'Higgins, K. and Boyle, K. (1988): *State Care: Some Children's Alternative*, Dublin: The Economic and Social Research Institute, Broadsheet Series, Paper No. 24.

O'Higgins, M. (1987): "Lone Parent Families — Numbers and Characteristics", Paris: OECD Conference on Lone Parents: *The Economic Challenge of Changing Family Structures*, Conference Paper, No. 3 (unpublished).

OECD (1985): *Role of the Public Sector*, Paris: OECD, Occasional Studies Series.

Phoenix, A. (1991): *Young Mothers?*, Cambridge: Polity Press.

Piachaud, D. (1991): "Peter Townsend and the Holy Grail", *New Society*, 10 September: 419–21.

Richardson, V. (1991): Paper to AGM of Federation of Services for Unmarried Parents and their Children, Dublin.

Richardson, V. and Winston, N. (1989): *Unmarried Mothers Delivered in the National Maternity Hospital, 1987*, Dublin: Department of Social Work and Social Administration, UCD.

Ringen, S. (1988): "Direct and Indirect Measures of Poverty", *Journal of Social Policy*, 17(3): 351–66.

Ruddle, H. and O'Connor, J. (1992): *Seeking Refuge from Violence: The ADAPT Experience*, Dublin: NCIR.

Ruddle, H., Lyons, A. and O'Connor, J. (1992): *Breaking the Silence: Violence in the Home*, Dublin: National College of Industrial Relations.

Schofield, G. (1994): *The Youngest Mothers*, Aldershot: Avebury.

Scott, H. (1984): *Working Your Way to the Bottom: The Feminisation of Poverty*, London: Pandora Press.

Second Commission on the Status of Women (1992): *Report*, Dublin: Government Publications Office

Seekamp, G. (1992): "Welfare Treats Parents Unequally", *Sunday Business Post*, 26 January: 138.

Townsend, P. (1979): *Poverty in the United Kingdom*, London: Allen Lane.

Walker, I. (1990): "The Effects of Income Support Measures on the Labour Market Behaviour of Lone Mothers", *Fiscal Studies*, 11(2): 55–75.

Walker, R. (ed.) (1988): *Applied Qualitative Research*, Aldershot: Gower.

Ward, P. (1990): *The Financial Consequences of Marital Breakdown*, Dublin: Combat Poverty Agency.

Weale, A., Bradshaw, J., Maynard, A. and Piachaud, D. (1984): *Lone Parents, Paid Work and Social Security*, London: Bedford Square Press.

Weitzman, L.J. (1988): "Child Support: Myth and Reality" in Kahn, A. and Kamerman, S., *Child Support: From Debt Collection to Social Policy*, London: Sage Publications.

White Paper (1992): *Marital Breakdown: A Review and Proposed Changes*, Dublin: Government Publications Office.

Wilson, J. and Neckerman, K.M. (1986): "Poverty and Family Structure: The Widening Gap between Evidence and Public Policy Issues" in Danzinger, S. and Weinberg, D. (eds.), *Fighting Poverty*, Cambridge, MA: Harvard University Press.

Wong, Y., Garfinkle, I. and McLanahan, S. (1993): "Single Mother Families in Eight Countries: Economic Status and Social Policy", *Social Service Review*, June: 177–97.